The Vio.

MW00583775

Published in English for the first time, this is a seminal work by an original and creative analytical thinker. Joyce MacDougall and Nathalie Zaltzman have provided an entirely new preface for this edition.

Piera Aulagnier's *The Violence of Interpretation* bridges the work of Winnicott and Lacan, putting forward a theory of psychosis based on children's early experiences. The author's analysis of the relationship between the mother's communications and the infant's psychic experience, and of the pre-verbal stage of development of unconscious fantasy starting from the 'pictogram', have fundamental implications for the psychoanalytic theory of development. She developed Lacan's ideas to enable the treatment of severe psychotic states.

Containing detailed discussion of clinical material, and written in the author's precise yet provocative style, *The Violence of Interpretation* is a welcome addition to the New Library of Psychoanalysis.

Piera Aulagnier was a French psychoanalyst in private practice, and a prominent member of the International Psychoanalytic Association. She died in 1991.

THE NEW LIBRARY OF PSYCHOANALYSIS

The New Library of Psychoanalysis was launched in 1987 in association with the Institute of Psycho-Analysis, London. Its purpose is to facilitate a greater and more widespread appreciation of what psychoanalysis is really about and to provide a forum for increasing mutual understanding between psychoanalysts and those working in other disciplines such as history, linguistics, literature, medicine, philosophy, psychology and the social sciences. It is intended that the titles selected for publication in the series should deepen and develop psycho-analytic thinking and technique, contribute to psychoanalysis from outside, or contribute to other disciplines from a psychoanalytical perspective.

The Institute, together with the British Psycho-Analytical Society, runs a low-fee psychoanalytic clinic, organises lectures and scientific events concerned with psychoanalysis and publishes the *International Journal of Psycho-Analysis*. It also runs the only UK training course in psychoanalysis which leads to membership of the International Psychoanalytical Association – the body which preserves internationally agreed standards of training, of professional entry, and of professional ethics and practice for psychoanalysis as initiated and developed by Sigmund Freud. Distinguished members of the Institute have included Michael Balint, Wilfred Bion, Ronald Fairbairn, Anna Freud, Ernest Jones, Melanie Klein, John Rickman and Donald Winnicott.

Volumes 1–11 in the series were prepared under the general editorship of David Tuckett. Volumes 12–39 appeared under the general editorship of Elizabeth Bott Spillius. Subsequent volumes are under the general editorship of Susan Budd. Ronald Britton, Eglé Laufer, Donald Campbell, Michael Parsons, Rosine Jozef Perelberg, David Taylor and Stephen Grosz have acted as associate editors for various periods.

ALSO IN THIS SERIES

THE NEW LIBRARY OF PSYCHOANALYSIS
41

General Editor: Susan Budd

The Violence of Interpretation

From Pictogram to Statement

Piera Aulagnier

Translated by Alan Sheridan

First published as *La violence de l'interprétation:
Du pictogramme à l'énoncé*, Presses Universitaires
de France, 1975

First published as *La violence de l'interprétation: Du pictogramme à l'énoncé*
in 1975 by Presses Universitaires de France, Paris

First published 2001
by Brunner-Routledge
27 Church Road, Hove, East Sussex BN3 2FA

Simultaneously published in the USA and Canada
by Taylor & Francis Inc
325 Chestnut Street, Philadelphia PA 19106

Brunner-Routledge is an imprint of the Taylor & Francis Group

© 2001 Piera Aulagnier

Translation © Alan Sheridan

Typeset in Bembo by Keystroke, Jacaranda Lodge, Wolverhampton
Printed and bound in Great Britain by TJ International Ltd, Padstow,
Cornwall

British Library Cataloguing in Publication Data
A catalogue record for this book is available from the British Library

Library of Congress Cataloging in Publication Data
A catalogue record for this book has been requested

ISBN 0–415–23675–4 (hbk)
ISBN 0–415–23676–2 (pbk)

For Corneille and Claude

Contents

Translator's note

In terms of psychoanalytic vocabulary, the author generally adopts what have become the accepted French translations of Freud's German: *ça* for *Es*, *investissement* for *Besetzung*, *acte manqué* for *Fehlleistung*, etc. In every case these are literal translations of Freud's 'everyday' German, and preferable by far to Strachey's pseudo-scientific, often preposterous Graeco-Latinisms (id, cathexis, parapraxis). The modern 'lay' reader, almost certainly lacking Strachey's classical education, may well be perplexed by such terms, but, for the English-speaking psychoana-lytic 'clerisy', they have become technical terms and to change them at this late stage would obscure rather than clarify. It does not, in any case, fall within the jurisdiction of a humble translator of the secondary Freudian literature to make such radical changes. I have therefore employed the usual Stracheyan vocabulary, while adopting one departure from it that has become commonplace, the use of 'drive' to render *pulsion*, Freud's *Trieb*, which, under 'instinct', Strachey conflated with Freud's *Instinkt*. In one important case, however, Piera Aulagnier departed from the usual French practice and rendered Freud's *Ich*, not as *le moi*, but as *le Je* (capitalised, which is not the practice in French). This term, clearly central to her thinking, has been translated here as 'the I' – and given neuter gender.

In the company of many French analysts of the past half century, Piera Aulagnier adopted, directly or through the work of Jacques Lacan, terms deriving from structural linguistics (sign, signifier, signified, referent, etc.). She also uses, almost unthinkingly, certainly without any particular axe to grind, terms that Lacan made much of. 'Metonymy' (a figure of speech by which the name of one thing is used instead of another related to it, as in 'He's taken to the bottle') is often used here, but without its explicit Lacanian contradistinction with metaphor. Similarly, *jouissance* is used without its Lacanian contradistinction with *plaisir*; indeed any such distinction seems to be absent here, except where the term is specifically used to specify *sexual* pleasure. The word has no satisfactory equivalent in English. Though 'enjoyment' covers some of its senses, as in the enjoyment of rights, for instance, it is altogether too 'light' a term to cover the use deriving from

Lacan, where it verges on 'delight', 'ecstasy' even, while having, buried within it, the verb *jouir*, which, among other things, means to ejaculate sexually, 'to come'. Where it seemed necessary, I have drawn the reader's attention to the French word, but Aulagnier generally uses the term in a way that can be rendered by 'pleasure' or 'sexual pleasure', which is what I have done here. Other Lacanisms found here include 'the Other' (*l'Autre*) and 'the Name-of-the-Father' (*le nom-du-père*). Readers seeking further elucidation might refer to my Translator's Notes to Lacan's *Écrits: A Selection* (Routledge, 1977) or *The Four Fundamental Concepts of Psycho-analysis* (Hogarth, 1977; Vintage paperback, 1998).

Aulagnier has also resorted to a number of neologisms of her own creation, usually involving hyphens and inverted commas. However, like Freud's, they derive from everyday speech and, while lacking in elegance, have the virtue of being self-explanatory. One of her terms, *porte-parole*, is (or used to be) rendered by 'spokesman'. This would be impossible here, not for reasons of 'political correctness' but because it refers to the mother. 'Spokeswoman' would have drawn attention to itself in the wrong way and, like 'spokesman', have failed to render the literal sense of the French word, which is important here. I therefore felt free to add a neologism of my own; namely, 'word-bearer'.

Foreword

This book is the first translated from its original language into another language under the auspices of the International Psychoanalytic Association (IPA). To bridge the linguistic and cultural gaps among the different language groups of psychoanalysts, the IPA is facilitating publication through underwriting and providing translation of a very significant contribution to psychoanalysis. This volume has not been previously available except in the original language and so is known only to those fluent in French. It is also evident that different psychoanalytic cultures have different 'psychoanalytic languages' with different theoretical frameworks and concepts, which have been altered as psychoanalysis has evolved.

The Violence of Interpretation is an unusual analytic work by a highly gifted, innovative, and ruggedly individual French author who was not a member of the IPA. Piera Aulagnier was deeply influenced by Freud's thinking on the importance of language, the development and differentiation of primary and secondary process, and the pathogenesis of psychosis. She conveys the French psychoanalytic cultural interest in linguistics and semiotics and some of the concepts of Lacan, but she is uniquely her own person in her research on cognition and language, their complex development, and their impairment in psychosis. Her profound investigation of psychotic communication leads her to both new inferences and new questions about thought and thought disorder.

In this age of the defined human genome and the discovery of specific gene activity and effects there are naïve expectations that the genetic, constitutional factors in psychosis, which Freud always recognised, will offer new and complete explanations of psychosis. The interpretation and reinterpretation of psychotic thought by Aulagnier attains fresh importance as it emphasises the complementary role of the caregiver. Language itself depends on hearing the spoken words of the mother tongue in an affectionate, affective mother–infant (caregiver–infant) dialogue. The infant has an impact on the mother, and the mother's unconscious fantasies, mediated through her behaviour in word and

xiv

act, have a powerful influence on the infant's psyche. Transcending associated psychic and physical trauma, the 'violent' impact of conscious and unconscious deleterious maternal fantasy and attitudes impairs development. Biogenetic factors are important in predisposition and vulnerability to psychosis, in resilience and recovery, but maternal and familial influences co-determine psychotic disorder.

Aulagnier's contribution is often convergent with North American and other studies of the familial background of psychosis. Many psychotic children have parents with thought disorders, contradictory attitudes and directives (double binds), misunderstandings, empathic impairment, and predominantly hostile ambivalence with domination, denigration, and devaluation of the child. As Aulagnier indicates this leads to a disordered sense of self and identity, efforts to conform to alien wishes and feelings, and highly disturbed thought and communication. Also researching the meaning of 'meaning', the hypothetical deformed mental representations and processes which eventuate are among the most intriguing and abstract propositions through which Piera Aulagnier interprets psychosis, as well as 'normal' thought.

Harold P. Blum, M.D.
Chairman, IPA Translation Committee

Preface to this edition

Piera Aulagnier is a psychoanalytic author and researcher of unusual quality. She embarked on the discipline of psychoanalytic thought in the manner in which a research worker might approach an exact science – aiming to discover and possess all existing analytic research on the subject of psychosis, with the intention of exploring the psychogenesis of mental illness as well as that of human passion, with the double aim of furthering the potentiality of psychoanalytic therapy in the field of psychosis as well as seeking to enrich our knowledge of the spirit of humankind.

She also approached her engagement in her personal psychoanalysis in the manner of a scientific positivist, and chose Jacques Lacan because she was inspired by his reputation as an innovative thinker, and in particular, because of his interest in psychotic states. She further claimed that she undertook the experience of a personal analysis in order to test the value of Freud's discoveries – but, as she later admitted laughingly to her friends, 'with no anticipation or preparedness for the subjective experience that I was destined to undergo'.

Some personal history

Born in 1923 to Italian parents, their only child, Piera Spairani spent the first years of her life in Egypt. She used to say that these years were shrouded in mystery since her mother, who was only seventeen years of age when Piera was born, was reluctant to discuss either the circumstances of her birth or give detailed information regarding her absent father. (This factor may have had some influence on Piera's later writings on secrecy and the right of analysands to maintain certain secrets during their analytic experience.)

She remembered being sent as a young child to Italy where she was then cared for by her maternal grandparents, to be joined by her mother some years later. It was also in Italy that she completed her medical studies but, in the early 1950s, she opted to come to France in order to pursue her interest in psychiatry and psychoanalysis. There she met André Aulagnier, a businessman from Burgundy who was to become her husband. They had one child, Claude, who today is a psychiatrist with a practice in the Yonne.

Some years after their marriage the couple made an amicable decision to divorce and Piera later married a philosopher-psychoanalyst of Greek origin, Cornelius Castoriadis. They had no children but together brought up Piera's son and Cornelius's daughter; this marriage also ended in separation. During this time Piera's widowed mother came to live with her and she continued to care for her mother with much devotion until her own untimely death from cancer in 1991.

With regard to Aulagnier's psychoanalytic career, as mentioned above, she chose Jaques Lacan as her first analyst and in consequence became a member of the Ecole Freudienne, of which he was the founder, but eventually decided to withdraw her affiliation in view of her serious disagreement with the manner in which this psychoanalytic school promulgated its requirements for the training of future psychoanalysts. She considered that these minimal requirements provided a highly inadequate background to those seeking to become accredited psychoanalysts. As a result she, along with two other prominent members of the Ecole Freudienne, publicly resigned since she judged the training programme to be 'incompatible with the rigorous guarantees that are necessary in order to become a practising psychoanalyst'.

The three dissidents then decided to found their own psychoanalytic school, which they named Le Quatrième Groupe. One year later Aulagnier became the chief editor of the new School's psychoanalytic review, *Topique*, a journal which has always received considerable praise, and continues to produce articles of quality and to be held in high esteem by the French psychoanalytic community.

We believe that the prime importance of Aulagnier's research into the genesis of psychotic thought lay in the exceptional interest and respect she consistently maintained towards the construction of all human thought processes. The Freudian concept of humankind as the subject of libidinal drives sees us as being equally determined by all that we are able – or unable – to think about. This perspective is evidenced in Aulagnier's conceptualisation of the vital conditions that underlie the potentiality, and indeed the necessity, for human beings to be able to think and thus give meaning to all that they have experienced from the very dawn of their psychic existence.

In her own words 'psychotic states offer us a macroscopic enlargement of one aspect of psychic phenomena that allows us to understand the conditions necessary for the achievement of non-psychotic functioning regarding the capacity to think and the activity of the "I"'.[1] For Aulagnier, what she referred to as 'le je' signified 'the speaking I', the person to whom we refer when we say, for example: 'I think this is wrong', 'I know the truth' or 'This is what I am feeling', and so on. It is analogous to the self in English psychoanalytic writing. In her fascination with the multiple psychic aspects of the way in which we use language she maintained the same intense interest and respect in her clinical work with young psychotic adults, and it was this devoted approach that led her to emphasise what she came to refer to as 'the prodigous work of re-interpretation'[2] that underlies psychotic thought processes.

Her years of research in working with psychotic patients led her to the following conclusions. When individuals have been exposed from earliest infancy and throughout childhood to an excess of bodily psychic pain on the one hand and, on the other, have been submitted to an excessive and deforming violence imposed by the maternal unconscious (as expressed through the mother's words and acts), such individuals are obliged to render thinkable some version of their personal history in order to maintain a potential investment of their lives, while at the same time attempting to make sense of the incoherences to which they have been subjected, stemming from the mother's own internal conflicts and distress. Aulagnier pointed out that when we listen to the highly elaborated psychic constructions of the psychotic I, these have a completely different point of departure from those of the neurotic sufferer; they are dealing with quite other urgent needs than those which contribute to the construction of the neurotic I, and what the psychotic sufferer conveys to us through language has therefore an entirely other aim. In *The Violence of Interpretation* Aulagnier undertook a profound exploration of the sources of these singular productions, thereby giving us new insights into the organisation of psychotic, schizophrenic and paranoiac thought processes.

She frequently stated that the act of thinking has the same importance for the I that dreaming has for the psyche. In other words, Aulagnier claims in her metapsychological elaboration of thinking (as governed by the agency called I) that the activity of thinking is equivalent to the profound significance given by Freud to dreams and the dynamic importance of the unconscious, prior to the fantasy organisations of desire. Aulagnier lays more emphasis on the role of pre-fantasy sources of a corporeal-affective nature, as witnessed by the content and functions she attributes to this speaking I and its identificatory project.

From 1962 right up until her death in 1990, Piera Aulagnier's weekly seminars at the celebrated Sainte-Anne Psychiatric Hospital enabled generations of psychiatrists and psychoanalysts of all schools of thought throughout France to gain insight into the intelligibility of many previously unexplored aspects of psychotic phenomena as well as giving them an innovative theory of their origins. The reader will not be surprised that, at first reading, *The Violence of Interpretation* resembles a metapsychological treatise, since it is the fruit of the author's creativity during her many years of lecturing and of clinical practice.

Although no introduction can do justice to the richness and complexity of Aulagnier's creative conceptualisations, we shall nevertheless attempt to give an overall picture by introducing certain of her key concepts, namely:

1 the *primal process*;
2 the theory of the *pictogram*;
3 the role of the mother as the *word-bearer*, not only of language but also in her
   vital function as interpreter of her infant's needs (with the concomitant risk
   of the mother making an excessive use of her power);
4 the concept of the speaking *I*;
5 the construction of *primary delusional thinking*.

The primal process

Proceeding from the assumption that the act of mental representation is one
of the main tasks of the psychic apparatus, and that this activity originates in the
encounter between the psychic space of the infant and all that lies beyond
the psyche, the author emphasises that there will be an inevitable clash between
what the infant perceives and environmental stimulation, since the latter is a
source that is heterogeneous to the infant psyche. However, this inaugural clash
has immense importance because it stimulates the infant to represent psychically
what he or she is experiencing.

In an original and creative survey of the processes underlying psychic
representation as formulated by Freud, Aulagnier identifies three simultaneous
metabolic processes or systems, all of which are essential in order to transform
the effects of the encounter between the infant and the external world into
a representational mode, and that this mode is significantly different for each
of the three systems. (In seeking a new term that refers to a psychic process that
precedes what Freud designated as the 'primary and secondary processes',
Aulagnier coined the phrase 'processus originaire' translated here as 'primal
process'.)

According to Aulagnier, each of these three mental processes has its specific
form of psychic representation: the primal process is represented by a pictogram;
the primary process by an unconscious fantasy; and the secondary process by the
self-representation of the subject's I. This last process includes the transformation
of the primal scene into a representation that gives meaning to the subject's
personal history and sense of identity. For it is the acquisition of a sense of time
coupled with a sense of one's life-history that allows primal experiences to be
transmuted into a sense of identity – and it is these very transmutations that are
disturbed in the construction of psychotic thought processes.

The pictogram

In Aulagnier's view the pictogram is a mental representation created by the infant
psyche from its bodily experience of the earliest sensations of pleasure – following

the model of the inaugural encounter between the mouth and the breast. Thus the pictogram, composed of a continuous corporeal encounter, although devoid of any word-representation is destined to become the prototype of all future encounters between any erogenous zone and its part object. The pictographic representation is specifically marked by a total ignorance of the duality of which it is composed.

Aulagnier's long clinical experience with young psychotic adults led her to the view that that which is represented is received by the psyche as a representation of itself: the infant's representational faculty experiences the psychic representation as the result of its own autonomous activity. In other words the primal process is experienced as self-engendered along with its figurative mode, the pictogram, which encompasses both the experience and the infant who is experiencing it. When the encounter is associated with pleasure the representation, in Aulagnier's terminology, is the 'pictogram of conjunction', representing the conjunction of the erogenous zone and its complementary object (based on the prototype of the mouth–breast conjunction), the whole being experienced as self-engendered and self-devouring. When feelings of displeasure or pain do not permit this pictogram, the experience is then treated with total rejection: rejection of the erogenous zone and its complementary part object, as well as the psychic activity which believes it has engendered the experience. Thus not only is the subject totally excluded from the psyche, but so is the representation and the experience itself. This creates what Aulagnier names the 'pictogram of rejection'.

She further demonstrates that one common theoretical postulate underlies all three systems of representation: the primal process and its pictograms, the primary process and its fantasies, and the secondary process with its verbal announcements. Her assumptions are as follows:

1 Every being creates itself according to the most primitive system of self-representation; the primal process functions therefore in accordance with this primitive logic.
2 Every being exists because of the omnipotent will of the 'Other'; this postulate is characteristic of the primary process.
3 Every being has an understandable origin whose terms may be revealed through the parental and social discourse; this comprises the postulate according to which the secondary process functions.

When, for whatever reason, the primary and secondary psychic processes fail to function normally, the individual automatically regresses to the level of the primal process, which then infiltrates the mind and subsequently becomes the source of psychotic thought processes. Aulagnier's conception of the primary process and its fantasy basis is essentially faithful to the Freudian model and – in contradistinction to her conception of the primal process – involves two people as well as the recognition of two psychic spaces, whereas there is no awareness of this duality in the primal process. However, Aulagnier adds that the fantasised representations are invariably attributed totally to the all-powerful wish of the Other. When displeasure results it is presumed to be a response to the Other's desire. It follows from this postulate that the experience of displeasure, paradoxically, becomes a source of satisfaction in that it is felt to conform to what the powerful Other wants the subject to feel. It may sometimes happen, however, that this vision of what this Other expects is infiltrated by the postulate of self-creation that characterises the primal process, and in that case we then witness neurotic constructions that are infiltrated by psychotic elements.

The word-bearer

Although the primal process is experienced as self-created, Aulagnier emphasises that the pictographic representation as well as the elements that compose it are nevertheless created from material stemming from the activity of the maternal psyche. She further points out that psychoanalytic research has clearly demonstrated that the necessity for the existence and presence of an Other is not limited merely to assuring the supply of vital needs. In this sense her work is reminiscent of Winnicott's concept of the mother–child unit in which he states that an infant's basic need is not simply to be fed, but to be fed by an Other who loves to feed him.

In the same vein, the adequate functioning of both the primal and the primary processes depends upon material constructed by the secondary processes that are active in the mother's psyche. In order for the perceptions and sensory experiences of the infant as well as its feelings of pleasure and pain to become psychically representable, therefore, it is essential that these different experiences be invested libidinally by the maternal psyche (a conception that is akin to Bion's concept of maternal 'reverie').

Thus the function of the mother as the word-bearer includes both a literal and a metaphorical dimension: it is through contact with the mother's body, voice and self that the infant comes to exist as a being, and to be contained by this speaking Other who, little by little, comments on, prepares and contains the nexus of experiences that the infant comes to know. The word-bearing function also includes the mother's role as the representative of an external order by which she conveys the rules and obligations that emanate from the outer world. In this fashion the word-bearer, as Aulagnier phrases it, enables the construction of a sense of reality to take place which will be modulated by her own psychic activity, in this way providing a representative space for her infant's earliest experiences. In other words, the maternal psyche lays the foundation for a human reality-sense which the baby can subsequently invest with meaning in place of an otherwise sense-less experience. This initial 'violence', set in motion by the mother's psychic functioning, is the primordial and indispensable requirement for the three processes of psychic metabolisation to take place. From this perspective, the primal, primary, and secondary processes are all dependent upon and remodelled through the mother's transmissions and communications to her infant, this being the sole reality that will, in turn, enable the baby's psyche to function. It is this reality, with its disorganising potential, that the future psychotic must either strive to exclude from the psyche (giving rise to a 'psychotic potential') or else must deny by constructing a new interpretation (giving rise to a 'system of delusional thinking').

Excessive violence in the mother's interpretation of her baby's needs arises fundamentally from her refusal to accept that her nursling does not depend uniquely on her, that she is not the sole provider of the objects of psychic necessity and of the infant's need for love.

The concept of the speaking 'I'

Returning to her proposition that thinking represents for the I what dreaming represents for psychic activity as a whole, Aulagnier underlines that the agency called I can only create a permanent self-construction when this is founded on a 'prehistory', followed thereafter by a 'basic history' which, in turn, can only be constructed in accordance with what the word-bearing mother has been able to communicate – or to cloak in silence. It is the task of the I to assure its permanence by means of an 'identificatory project' whose aim is to render meaningful the word process of which the infant is unaware, as well as the beginnings of the repressed childhood story, along with its present and its future. The primal process, as well as this 'prehistory', cannot be preserved through repression in the form of verbal configurations and therefore remains for ever unknowable. With regard to the beginnings of the basic or personal childhood history, these can only be interpreted as fantasies according to what was originally invested with meaning by the word-bearer. When this occurs the I must manage to create a coherent version of the original foundation of its existence, thereby giving meaning to human desire along with its concomitant pleasurable and painful aspects.

Aulagnier summarises these notions as follows: 'As we have seen, regarding the question of one's origins, the I alone must attempt to put into words a response that is able to be invested by the child concerning the cause of the existence of the I itself.' Only in this way will children be able to create a 'scenario of their conception of the world'. However, regarding the question of the origins of the I, should the maternal transmissions have been restricted to a rationalisation which thinly veils the fact that the mother has no satisfactory response (simply because for her the I of her infant is not truly another I that she must strive to understand and 'interpret'), in such an event the child's I will be treated as a mere inversion of the mother's incestuous relationship to her own mother – little more than the echo of a closed maternal system.

Primary delusional thinking

The aim of the system of primary delusional thinking is an attempt to find a solution that appears to make sense of what otherwise is experienced as senseless by the childlike I: in other words, there is a total incompatibility between the version imposed by the word-bearer and what the child has actually experienced. The system of delusional thinking seeks therefore to create an interpretation that makes sense to the I in its desperate attempt to resolve the contradiction between what the mother declares is true and the child's genuine affective and bodily experiences, the latter having been treated as unknown, ignored, or forbidden to recall.

On every occasion in which a reality experience finds no verbal expression and confirmation, any psychic representation of the relation of the I to the outer world becomes problematic. When children become aware for the first time of such a conjunction, this gives rise either to mute astonishment or, more often, to a plunge into wordless terror. The 'reality' that is then experienced short circuits any possibility of a redeeming fantasy. This is the central concept in Aulagnier's clinical theory of the construction and fundamental aim of psychotic thought processes. In short, it is because every attempted wish-fulfilling fantasy on the child's part fails lamentably to deal with its painful experiences that the child is thrown back to primal process thinking – that of the pictogram of rejection which the primary processes will now attempt to relibidinise in order to make the experience liveable for the child's I.

Thus by the construction of a system of primary delusional thinking the I protects itself against the danger of being crushed, condemned to annihilation, or thrown back upon the modes of representation employed by the primal process: in sum, the menace to the self is either the fusional danger of engulfment (contained within the 'pictogram of linking') or the condemnation to psychic death (that results from the 'pictogram of rejection').

We might summarise Aulagnier's theoretical position as stating that the specific factor underlying psychosis is not linked to an unconscious fantasy but arises from the consequences of an insoluble discordance between what the small child experiences somatically and psychically and the meaning imposed by the mother's discourse. The system of delusional thinking that develops is therefore an attempt to make sense of the excessive violence to which the child's thinking has been continually exposed.

In this way the primary delusional construction aims at creating a personal history which the child is able to invest with meaning regarding its origins, its relation to others, and the sources of pleasure and pain, all of which are

constructed in order to preserve the mother as an object of libidinal investment in spite of the fact that she is the source of suffering, and of an implicit
prohibition to think about these affective experiences – and yet it is impossible
to reject her. Thus those individuals who are destined to find a psychotic solution
to their profound pain and anguish create an intelligible basis to account for
their existence and hope to invest this singular system with libidinal meaning.

The mother's fundamental position frequently appears to be that of a non-
desire for this child or a wish that, should it survive, it will not truly exist as a
separate and psychically alive being. In this way the primary delusional construction furnishes the child's I with its ultimate reason for living.

Aulagnier goes on to emphasise that, within the psychoanalytic relationship,
an inherent difficulty for both partners arises from the ambiguous attitude of
the analyst towards the analysand's delusional thinking, for the psychoanalyst also
must strive to make sense of the psychotic discourse, while at the same time
being unable to accept the causal foundation for it that is proffered by the
analysand.

Let us close this introduction to Piera Aulagnier's ground-breaking work by
quoting her words in 1963 at that point in time when she began her momentous
research: 'When listening to a psychotic discourse I discover with continual
astonishment the extent to which it discloses a measure of ultimate truth that
appears to be inaccessible to ordinary humans, perhaps because it is incompatible
with the illusions we all maintain in order to invest life with meaning.'

Joyce McDougall
Nathalie Zaltzman

Preface

Why this re-examination of the meta-psychological model?

The answer is directly linked to my original aim in writing this book; namely, to find a way of analysing the psychotic's relationship to discourse that would bring psychoanalytic practice closer to achieving the ambition of its project. As I proceeded, I realised, often to my own surprise, that certain questions that I thought had been resolved had become once again obscure, certain concepts that I believed to be no longer problematic had lost their apparent clarity. Unsurprisingly, psychosis forced me to rethink the conceptual models with which I approached the psyche. As a result, what was originally intended to be an introduction explaining the concepts used in my book came to occupy a large part of it – and the achievement of my original aim had to be postponed.

But this 'postponed' aim was and remains close enough to my thinking for it to be regarded as the backcloth on to which all my propositions have been woven. To forget this would make my chosen perspective, the possible value of my hypotheses, and the model proposed scarcely comprehensible. It is obvious that the aim of research affects the way in which it is carried out, the method adopted, the kind of questions asked. Although I have not been able at this stage in my work to carry my thinking on psychosis as far as I would have wished, nevertheless, taken as a whole, the book does represent an examination of psychosis or, rather, a way of examining the psyche that may enable us to confront the question of psychosis in a different way.

My long-standing debt to psychotic discourse is far from settled. It is thanks to that discourse, so often listened to, so often not understood, that I have finally lost any illusions as to the existence of a model whose application would no longer encounter 'anomalies': for this salutary reminder I can only offer in exchange the hope that my approach will make it possible for us to listen more sensitively, more attentively to its message. Confronted by this discourse, I have often felt that I was receiving it as *the wild interpretation made to the analyst of the non-evidence of the evident*. This experience, which is not always easy to bear, is the only one that gives the analyst the right to speak of an adventure, that of the psychotic, which, very often, he has not experienced subjectively. Indeed on one nodal point the psychotic and I find ourselves once again in a relationship of strict reciprocity: the absence of shared presuppositions makes my discourse as debatable, questionable, and deprived of all power of certainty as his may be when I listen to it. Two discourses meet and each is revealed to the other as the locus in which there arises an answer for which no third party can any longer ensure that it is well founded, the locus in which any statement may be radically requisitioned, in which no evidence is any longer called upon to maintain this status for the other psyche. The encounter with the psychotic has some chance of being positive for him or anything more than pure violence exerted in the name of 'supposed knowledge', well sheltered in the head of one of the interlocutors, only if the latter is ready to recognise that both discourses in their reference to the evident are in a strict relationship of analogy. Psychosis questions this shared heritage of certainty, a precious deposit that has been sedimented in an early phase of our psychical life and which we suddenly realise is the necessary condition for our questions to make sense to our own ears and not to project us into the vertigo of the void. Confronted by psychosis, I have discovered, not simply that Freud's model left some of these questions unanswered, but, a fact more decisive for my research, that *the application of this model to the response that this discourse aroused in me left part of my own experience excluded.* Rightly or wrongly, I do not think as a psychotic, so the 'anomalies' encountered when analysing my response could no longer be justified by a type of resistance, defence or fixation specific to psychosis: it had to be recognised that, as soon as one privileges one particular form of interrogation, the model presented anomalies, whatever the functioning of the psyche to which it applies. My 'theoretical calm' was shattered: there opened up the split that had hitherto comforted it and which may be summed up by this formula:

- the presence of a theoretical model *that enables us to understand* psychotic discourse;
- its possible ineffectiveness being attributed to *the refusal to hear* when confronted by that same discourse.

It would be wrong to smile at what might seem, expressed in this way, naive. If it is naive, it is a naivety that is shared by both parties, which may come as a surprise to those who by nature are not naive. I proposed the term 'split': I believe that it is precisely a sort of split that operates here, the analyst adhering at one and the same time to the following two contradictory propositions:

- in the field of Freudian experience there can be no knowledge of a psychical phenomenon that may not in principle – which does not mean that it necessarily can – be applied in action brought to bear on the phenomenon;

- there exists a knowledge of the psychotic phenomenon which cannot be acted upon in the field of Freudian experience.

The question now arises as to the risk presented by this split: what are we not seeing? Before we go any further, I should like to make it quite clear that I am not claiming that any neurotic symptom may disappear once the subject accepts analytical experience. Firstly, because, whatever affirmation they relate to, the adverbs 'always' and 'never' ought, with a few rare exceptions, to be banished from our discipline and, secondly, because such a claim would amount to imputing magical powers to experimentation, to claiming absolute knowledge possessed once and for all. On the other hand, however, it may be said that in the register of neurosis the model is able, in a good number of cases, to account for the failure or for the subject's rejection of it. Moreover experience seems to confirm that analyst and analysand, confronted by the irreducibility of a type of resistance, may understand what is involved. Even if this understanding remains insufficient to overcome it, it is rare for the experience to be concluded while leaving intact the initial status quo. The Freudian model may claim, quite rightly, to cover the field of knowledge of neurotic phenomena; the fact that it experiences failures when applied *is not an anomaly, but a possibility that the same theory and the same model account for.*

It is a different matter with psychosis, it is true, and it can hardly be denied that here the order of magnitude is reversed: for one 'successful' analysis how many have been abandoned on the way? How many have confronted the analyst with the ineffectiveness of his efforts? It is not enough, I believe, to explain the failure by resorting to the concept of transference. This 'impossibility' ought first to confront us with the need to redefine the concept, which would make it possible to understand more clearly why the transference as demonstrated in the neurotic relation requires not only the libidinal cathexis of an image projected on to the analyst, which the psychotic is a past master in doing, but that a demand addressed to the knowledge of the Other, a demand that finds its source in an inaugural subject-discourse encounter, is transferred to the experimental situation. The psychotic will also operate this 'transference' and, paradoxically, it is there that the fundamental cause of the failure in the analytical project lies. Indeed he will transfer to the analytical situation what he continues to repeat in his relation to the discourse of the Other, and therefore to the analyst's discourse. This relation, whether it is seen as the consequence of a lack of progress or as regression – it hardly matters here – does not confront the analyst with any transparency to the unconscious, with any simple repetition of what would be the normal functioning of an initial phase of psychical activity: this is a myth as false as it is persistent. These psychical elaborations that we are asked to listen to are highly elaborated, but they have a different starting point from that of the neurotic;[1] they correspond to different requirements and have a different aim. The I–discourse relation, or subject–knowledge relation in the sense I am giving to this term, has an identical foundation in every subject as long as one remains outside the field of psychosis: it allows a definition that I would defend as true, but this implies that *it becomes true only at a certain level of psychical elaboration and on condition that during this stage the subject is able to avoid certain pitfalls.* This 'level' is the one from which the I of the analyst, thinking and functioning, functions: there is therefore a before that forces us to try to resolve the paradox that consists of thinking, on the basis of our relation to knowledge, that which would be thinkable only by modifying that relation. This is a necessary step if one wishes to try to reconstruct the model of a pre-existing stage in which the I-discourse relation was by definition unthinkable, thanks to the constitution of the I agency and the acquisition by the psyche of the ability to handle language.

Two solutions are now possible:

1 Change nothing in the model that accounts for this relation; do not question what came before and analyse what is at work in those to which the model cannot be applied without modifications, thanks to the presentation of a series of differences. The psychotic's relation to discourse will now be defined by a series of *deductions* in relation to the model that is supposed to define what ought to be the subject–knowledge relation. Now, if this definition by deduction may just possibly explain part of the psychotic problematic, it says nothing about the *addition* evident in psychotic creation. It may account for certain phenomena of 'regression', but says nothing about the prodigious work of reinterpretation carried out by psychosis. Furthermore, this being the case one forgets the essential anomaly that, in my opinion, the application of the model encounters: leaving part of the phenomena that psychotic discourse arouses in the psyche of one who does not think in this way, the analyst.

2 The other solution is the one that I have chosen: to acknowledge that what the model ignores of my own response requires that one sets about reconstructing the various theoretical constructions that account for the constitution of the I and of the function of discourse, that one manages to catch a glimpse of what that unthinkable 'before' was that we have all shared. So we must learn to depend on what our thinking experiences when one forces it to confront the discourse that no longer leaves anything in doubt, which opposes the certainty of delusion to the logic of our reason, and suggests that there was a time long ago when it too encountered a discourse that seemed to have exclusive possession of the truth, a discourse at the service of a violence radical enough to give access to that shared heritage that is language.

My theoretical construction does not claim to be a new model of the psyche: its ambition is to give back access to part of what remained outside, which does not make it any less risky. Not only is it in no way definitive, which would be incompatible with my own conception of knowledge such as it is, but it deliberately privileges, aware of the inconveniences entailed by any privilege, that which, in the psychical process, maintains a particular relation with the problematic of knowledge; that is to say, that which specifically concerns the relation of the I to the register of meaning.

My conception of this relation was strongly shaken by what, it gradually occurred to me, was the specific factor of our subjective experience when faced with psychotic discourse:

Independently of the manifest meaning of its statements, I subjected myself to this discourse as a 'speech-thing-action' – it will become clearer later what this rather obscure trinomial signifies – which, irrupting into my psychical space, led me, often after the event, to 'rethink' an outdated response, usually reduced to silence.

Hence my hypothesis concerning this mode of representation, which will be defined by the concept of 'primal': testimony to the perennial activity of representation that uses a pictogram that ignores word-presentation and has as its exclusive material the image of the physical thing. It was psychotic discourse that led me to postulate a form of psychical activity foreclosed from the knowable, always and for every subject, and yet always at work, a 'representative background' that persists parallel to two other types of psychical production: the one proper to the primary process and the one proper to the secondary process.

Although the primal defines a form of activity common to every subject, it must be stressed that the effectiveness of the concept may be understood only if one is willing to test it in analytical practice in the register of psychosis. The same goes for the place that I gave the body and the sense organisation, which provide the semantic models that the original process repeats in its representations.

Although the part directly devoted to psychosis has been reduced, nevertheless this work has little chance of interesting the reader for whom the enigma that it poses is not of particular and constant interest. I might add that such a lack of interest is in my opinion incompatible with our function. If I wish to stress what was the essential motivation of my effort, it is not to console myself for having partly abandoned it, but because, while not being perceptible on every page, the presence of the same question that spurred me on would appear less clearly given the little space devoted in this work to what might be called an intuition of the ineffable, and what I owe to the clinical experience that has shaped and induced my formulations. Without wishing to offer the reader a summary or guide, and I am the first to acknowledge that this work is far from possessing the clarity and order that I would have wished, it seemed to me to be useful to indicate at the outset the postulates on which my theoretical construction will be based. These postulates refer to my conception of the body, of the sense organs-functions, of information and of the metabolisation that the psyche imposes on them. They do not define a question; what they do is offer a 'preliminary option' that makes possible, if the reader provisionally accepts its hypothesis, a reading of this book that may justify and provoke his interest.

1 *The body.* Side by side with the biological body of science and the analytical definitions of the erogenous body, another image met my gaze: that of a set of sense functions, themselves the vehicle of continuous information that cannot fail, not only because this information is a condition for somatic survival but also because it is the necessary condition for a psychical activity that requires that both the informed and the informant be libidinally cathected. I shall show how sense activity and the erogenisation of the zones, the seats of their organ, are identical. This makes possible another conception of the part-object and a better understanding of mutilation anxiety as the equivalent of castration anxiety in the psychotic.

The psyche–body relation originates in the borrowing that the first makes from the model of activity proper to the second: this model will be metabolised into a quite different material, one that will remain the unchanged scaffolding of an primal scenario that is repeated indefinitely.

This repetition of an unchanging representation defines the functioning and production of what I call the primal.

Psychosis is characterised by the force of attraction exerted by the primal, an attraction to which it opposes that 'addition' represented by the creation of a 'delusional' interpretation that makes 'sayable' the effects of that violence.

2 *The situation of encounter.* The peculiarity of the living being is its situation of continuous encounter with the physico-psychical milieu. This encounter will be the source of three productions whose loci of inscription and the processes producing them mark out three 'function-spaces':

- the primal and pictographic production;
- the primary and scenic representation (fantasy);
- the secondary and ideational representation; that is, 'sense-making' as the work of the I.

From the first moment of existence the subject finds himself confronted with a series of encounters one of the characteristics of which will be always to anticipate its possibilities of response and foresight. This *state of encounter* lies at the source of three types of production, metabolising according to their own postulate[2] the information that results from it. Every act, every experience, gives rise conjointly to a pictogram, to a *representation* and to 'sense-making'.[3] The subject can have no direct knowledge of the pictogram; it is in the power of the analyst to glimpse certain of its effects and to try to construct out of it a model knowable by the I; on the other hand, the work of representation proper to the primary, as in fantasy production, has the power to infiltrate the field of the secondary, even though the secondary remains governed by a work of 'sense-making' that one owes to the agency known as I.

The analysis of this agency will be centred around the following three postulates:

1 the requirement of interpretation as the force organising the field of discourse;
2 the function of part-object begun by holding both the voice-object and 'thinking' as last part-function and last stake of a mother–child relation that precedes the dissolution of the Oedipus complex;
3 the impossibility of analysing the function of the I without taking into account the sociocultural field in which the subject bathes.

The 'narcissistic contract' will denote that which is at the foundation of any possible subject–society, individual–whole, singular discourse–cultural referent relation.

In the section introducing the psychotic problematic all these hypotheses will make it possible to show how and why it is to the activity of the I that one owes this 'addition' that I shall call *primary delusional thinking*.

I shall conclude this preface by stressing that a long road separates us from any conclusion: reality is shifting; the history of the relation of analysis to theory is, like any history, a dynamic process whose broad outlines inherited from the past may be traced, in which a few aspects of the present may be glimpsed, but very little of its future predicted.

As for the psychotic problematic, I remain convinced that we are a long way from the time when reason will be able to claim that it can provide an exhaustive analysis of it. Will it be able to do so one day, or must we believe that madness will keep buried a kernel 'outside reason', that it shows us our limitations and that this opaque kernel guarantees that we belong to the field of the 'reasonable'? Psychoanalytic theory has provided valuable data in this domain; the radical strangeness of the madman has given place to the disturbing strangeness of a familiar in turn too close and too distant: the difference is important and testifies to progress made. But here more than elsewhere we must be on the lookout for the anomalies encountered by our model, which one tends to misconstrue: whether one denies the existence of madness in order to reduce it – and this certainly amounts to a reduction – to a mode of being like any other, or, on the contrary, whether one denounces its presence, but this time by reducing it to the effect of some exclusive defect (diabolical, sociological, organic or genetic, depending on the fashions of the day), it makes little fundamental difference.

Certainty and knowledge differ from one another to the extent that their respective statements may be found to be questionable: the first rejects this test, the second accepts it, if only in spite of itself. It remains to be hoped that the questioning of, by and concerning psychoanalysis may continue.

PART ONE

From pictogram to statement

1

The activity of representation, its objects and its aim

Originally the mere existence of a presentation was a guarantee of the reality of what was presented.

Freud, 'Negation', S.E., XIX, p. 237

1 General considerations

This book sets out to test a model of the psychical apparatus that privileges the analysis of one of its specific tasks: the activity of representation.

This model does not escape the inconvenience that occurs whenever one gives precedence to one aspect of psychical activity; namely, leaving to one side other equally important aspects. One may regret the price to be paid, but accept it, admitting that, with few exceptions, one of whom was Freud, most of us find it difficult to avoid it. I now have to show what may be expected from the approach chosen and what contribution may be made by the theoretical approach and its application in the clinical field.

I shall devote this first chapter to general considerations concerning psychical activity in order to show the factors that, in every system, despite the specificity of their mode of operation, obey laws that are common to psychical functioning as a whole.

By the activity of representation, I mean the psychical *equivalent* of the work of metabolisation proper to organic activity. The latter may be defined as the function by which an element heterogeneous to the cellular structure is rejected or, on the other hand, transformed into a raw material that becomes homogeneous with it. This definition may be applied at every point to the work carried out by the psyche, except that, in this case, the 'element' absorbed and metabolised is not a physical body but an element of information.

3

Although I see the activity of representation as the task common to the psychical processes, it may be said that its aim is to metabolise into an element homogeneous with the structure of each system an element of a heterogeneous nature. The term 'element' thus defined covers two sets of objects: those whose presence is necessary to the functioning of the system and those whose presence is imposed on the latter, which finds it impossible to ignore its action, when manifested in its field.

Before continuing and conjecturing as to the analysis that will be offered of it, certain terms must be clearly defined. My model defends the hypothesis according to which psychical activity is constituted by three modes of functioning, taken together, or by three processes of metabolisation: the primal process, the primary process and the secondary process. The representations resulting from their activity will be respectively the pictographic representation or pictogram, the fantasy representation or fantasy, the ideational representation or statement. The agencies resulting from the reflection of these activities on each other will be called the representative, the fantasiser or presenter, the statement-maker or I. Lastly, the hypothetical locus presumed to be the seat of these activities and to contain the productions deriving from them, I shall call the primal space, the primary space and the secondary space. As for the terms 'conscious' and 'unconscious', I shall give them back the meaning that they have in part of Freud's work: that of a 'quality',[1] by which a psychical production may take place that the I may be conscious of or, on the other hand, from which it is excluded. The three processes that I postulate are not present in psychical activity from the outset; they follow one another in succession and their activation is provoked by the need felt by the psyche to become aware of a property of the object outside it, a property that the previous process had to ignore. This temporal succession is not measurable. Everything leads one to believe that the gap between the activation of the primal process and that of the primary process is extremely short; similarly, I shall show that the activation of the secondary process occurs very early on. The implementation of a new process never entails the silencing of the earlier one: in different spaces, with non-homologous relations between them, the activity proper to them takes place. The information that the existence of something outside the psyche imposes on that activity will continue to be metabolised in three representations homogeneous to the structure of each process. Among the heterogeneous elements that each system will be able to metabolise, the same place must be given to those that derive from outside the psychical space and to those that are endogenous to the psyche, but heterogeneous in relation to one of the three systems. The psychical 'objects' produced by the original are as heterogeneous to the structure of the secondary, as is the structure of the objects of the physical world that the I encounters and of which it will only know the representation that it makes of it. There is a homology between the treatment imposed by the three processes on the objects belonging to physical reality and the one that they impose on objects belonging to psychical reality: of the two, only one representation, which has metabolised the object deriving from those spaces into an object whose structure has become identical with that of the representative, can exist for each system .

The sense that I am giving to the term 'structure' depends on that given to the object to which I apply it: representation. Every representation confronts a double shaping: the shaping of the relation imposed on the elements that make up the object represented – here again the metaphor of the cellular work of metabolisation describes my conception perfectly – and the shaping of the relation between the representative and the represented. The latter is the corollary of the former: indeed, for each system, it is a question of representing the object in such a way that its 'molecular structure' becomes identical with that of the representative. This structural identity is ensured by the unchangeability of the relational schema proper to each system, the first result of which is that every representation is indissociably representation of the object and representation of the agency that represents it; and every representation in which the agency recognises itself is representation of its mode of perceiving the object.

If one displaces what I have just said into the sphere of the secondary process and of the I that is its agency, one may make an analogy between the activity of representation and cognitive activity. The aim of the work of the I is to forge an image of the reality of the surrounding world – and of the existence of which it is informed – that is coherent with its own structure. To know the world is equivalent for the I to representing it to itself in such a way that the relation linking the elements that occupy its stage is intelligible to it: by intelligible is meant here that the I may insert them into a relational schema that conforms to its own. In the section devoted to it, I shall show why, in my opinion, the I is simply the I's knowledge of the I: if for the moment we accept this definition, it follows that the relational structure that the I imposes on the elements of reality is a carbon copy of the relation that the logic of discourse imposes on the statements that constitute *it*. This relation that the I has begun by appropriating to itself is the necessary precondition for the schema of its own structure to become accessible to it. That is why in my text on the concept of reality, I say that reality, for the subject, is never anything more than the set of definitions that cultural discourse gives of it. The representation of the world, the work of the I, is therefore a representation of the relation present between the elements that occupy its space and, at the same time, of the relation between the I and these same elements. As long as one remains in the register of the I, it is easy to show that this setting up of the relation does not entail the acquisition of any knowledge of the object in itself – that is, the illusion of the I – but the ability to establish between the elements an order of causality that makes the existence of the world and the relation present between these elements intelligible to the I. The activity of representation for the I therefore becomes synonymous with an activity of interpretation: the way in which the object is represented by its naming unveils the interpretation that the I gives itself of what is the cause of the object's existence and function. That is why I shall say that the peculiarity of the structure of the I is to impose on the elements present in its representations – whether a representation of itself or of the world – the relational schema that conforms to the order of causality imposed by the logic of discourse.

This detour concerning the agency of the I was intended to throw light on what I define as the structural, relational or causal postulate specific to each system: a postulate that takes account of the law according to which the psyche functions and from which no system escapes.

This postulate, once one tries to make sayable that which by nature does not belong to this register, may be expressed by three formulations according to the process under consideration:

- Every existent is self-procreated by the activity of the system that represents it; this is the postulate of self-procreation according to which the primal process functions.
- Every existent is an effect of the omnipotence of the Other's desire; this is the postulate proper to the functioning of the primary.
- Every existent has an intelligible cause of which discourse[2] might provide knowledge; this is the postulate according to which the secondary functions.

In contrast to the difference of formulations is their immutability for a given system; it follows that the law proper to the activity of representation as a whole also denotes its aim: to impose on to the elements on which each system rests for its representations a relational schema that confirms each time the structural postulate proper to the system's activity. Let me add that the elements that would not be suitable to undergo this metabolisation cannot have a representative in the psychical space; they therefore have no existence for the psyche. One proof of this is provided by the Freudian approach: although the id or the unconscious, as Freud defines them, existed before his discovery, nevertheless it would be correct to say that before Freud they had no objective existence for the I and that they could acquire this status only when that same I was able to forge ideational representations making those psychical 'objects' that were essentially heterogeneous conform to its structure.

Whether we are dealing with the primal, the primary or the secondary, one may therefore give the same definition of the aim proper to the activity of representation: to metabolise heterogeneous raw material in such a way that it may become part of a representation that, in the final analysis, is only the representation of the postulate itself. One can go no further as long as one remains in the register of a general law.

We are now going to consider the relation between the postulate and what I have called the element of the psyche that informs the psyche of a property of the object, which will enable us to reflect on the present relation between the activity of representation and the libidinal economy, here again taking account only of what is generalisable to the whole set of systems. To speak of information presents a risk that must be pointed out at once: that of forgetting that no information can exist for the psyche that can be separated from what I shall call 'libidinal information'. I understand that every act of representation is coextensive with an act of cathexis, and every act of cathexis is motivated by the psyche's tendency to preserve or rediscover an experience of pleasure. As soon as one introduces this term, more perhaps than any other, one is confronted by what is irreducible in Freud's warning 'it is evident that everything new that we have inferred must nevertheless be translated back into the language of our perceptions, from which it is simply impossible to free ourselves'.[3] Whether one likes it or not, the term 'pleasure' always suggests an experience of the I on the basis of which theory presupposes that the same experience would be present whenever an agency, other than that of the I, succeeds in realising the aim of its activity. If we apply this definition to the activity of representation, one might therefore, in an initial approximation, conclude from it that pleasure defines the quality of the affect present in a psychical system whenever it has been able to achieve its aim. Now, the activity of representation cannot but attain its aim, but it may only go so far · as a representation that confirms the postulate proper to the system to which one owes it. Must it be said, then, that any act of representation entails an experience of pleasure? In one sense I shall answer in the affirmative, adding that if such were not the case the first condition necessary for there to be life there, that is to say the cathexis of the activity of representation, would be missing. It is there, one might say, that is to be found the *minimum pleasure* necessary for an activity of representation and psychical representatives of the world, including the psychical world itself, to exist.

The minimum pleasure indispensable for there to be life: such a definition proves the omnipotence of pleasure in the psychical economy; it must not evade the problem posed by instinctual duality, the experience of unpleasure and the paradox represented for the logic of the I of having to postulate the presence of an unpleasure that might nevertheless be an object of desire:[4] the I can only reject the contradiction present in a statement that claims that pleasure may result from an experience of unpleasure. Theory will resolve this contradiction by postulating the presence of two contradictory aims that split desire itself. This duality is present from the outset in the energy at work in psychical space and is responsible for what I define as the desire of a non-desire: *the desire not to have to desire*, such is the other aim proper to any desire. As a result, psychical activity, from the beginning, will forge two contradictory representations of the relation between the representative and the represented, each conforming to the realisation of one aim of the desire:

- a first representation in which the realisation of the desire will entail a state of reunification between the representative and the object represented and it will be this union that will be presented as the cause of the pleasure experienced;

- a second representation in which the aim of the desire will be the disappearance of any object capable of arousing it, which means that any representation of the object is presented as a cause of the representative's unpleasure.

This duality inherent in the aims of desire itself may be illustrated with the help of two concepts that discourse calls love and hate. The first (love or Eros) will define the movement that leads the psyche to be united with the object, the second the movement that leads it to reject and destroy it. I would say, then, that pleasure and unpleasure refer, in this text, to the two representations of affect that may exist in the psychical space: the first denotes the affect present whenever representation gives shape to a relation of pleasure between the elements of the represented and by this fact represents a relation of pleasure between the representative and representation. Unpleasure will denote the state present whenever representation gives shape to a relation of rejection between these same elements, and therefore the same relation between the representative and representation. These aphoristic definitions will be taken up again and discussed when I come to analyse the effect that this has on the functioning of each system. This detour concerning pleasure was intended to help me explain the relation that I postulate as being present between the activation of a system and what I have called an element informing the system with a quality proper to the object. In my opinion, there exists a relation between the successive modes of psychical activity and the evolution of the perceptual system: this relation is a consequence of the condition proper to all life. To live is to experience in a continuous way what results from the *situation of encounter*: by this I mean that the psyche is plunged from the outset into a space that is heterogeneous to it, whose effects it undergoes in just as continuous and immediate a way. It may even be argued that it is by the representation of these effects that the psyche is able to forge an initial representation of itself and that this is the primal fact that sets psychical activity in motion. The analysis of what I mean by state of encounter will enable me to explain the meaning given to the two concepts present in my title: violence and interpretation.

2 The state of encounter and the concept of violence

Psyche and world meet and are born with one another and by one another; and they are the result of a state of encounter that is coextensive with the state of living being. The inevitable violence that theoretical discourse imposes on the psyche as object of its scrutiny stems from the need to dissociate the effects of this encounter, which it can analyse only successively and at best in a backwards-and-forwards movement between the spaces from which they emerge. To denounce this 'remodelling' of being and the object demanded by theory does not abolish it: the exhaustive agreement between analytical discourse and the psyche as object is an illusion that must be abandoned.

To say that the initial encounter brings psyche and world face to face does not take account of the reality of the situation experienced by psychical activity at its origin. If by the term 'world' I denote the totality of space outside the psyche, I would say that, during the first stage, the psyche meets this space in the form of two very special fragments – namely, one's own bodily space and the psychical space of those around one, in particular the mother's psychical space. The first representation that the psyche forges of itself as representing activity will be carried out by relating together the effects that result from this double encounter with the body and the productions of the maternal psyche. If we go no further than this stage, I would say that the only quality, proper to these two spaces, of which the primal process wishes to be and can be informed, concerns the pleasure/unpleasure quality of the affect present at the time of this encounter. When I come to analyse the pictogram we shall see what the consequences of this are.

The activation of the primary process and of the secondary process will result from the fact that psychical activity has to recognise two other special characteristics of the object whose presence is necessary to its pleasure: the characteristic of extra-territoriality, which amounts to recognising the existence of a space separate from one's own, and this information may be metabolised only by the activity of the primary process, and the ability to signify, or carry meaning, possessed by this same object, which involves recognising that the relation present between the elements that occupy external space is defined by the relation present between the meanings that discourse gives of these same elements. This information, which cannot be metabolised by the primary process, will require the activation of the secondary process by which a 'sense-making' of the world will be able to take place that will respect a relational schema identical with the schema that constitutes the structure of the representative, which, in this case, is none other than the I.

The encounter takes place, therefore, between the psychical activity and the elements that it can metabolise and which inform it of the 'qualities' of the object that is the affective *cause*. For the primal, one notes that this quality is reduced to the representability that certain objects are shown to possess. From what I have said, it is obvious that the term 'representability', whatever the system under consideration, denotes the ability of certain objects to appear in the relational schema proper to the postulate of the system: the specificity of the schema proper to the system will decide which objects the psyche may have knowledge of. This definition throws light on the interaction between what might metaphorically be called the power of objects and the limited autonomy of the activity of representation. What is within the power of the psyche – and here we should speak not so much of power itself as of the conditions inherent in its functioning – concerns the reshaping that each imposes on any living being when inserting it into a pre-established relational schema. But, on the other hand, for psychical activity to be possible, it must be able to appropriate to itself, or incorporate, if one prefers this term, exogenous raw material. Now this material is not amorphous matter: it concerns information emitted by the support objects of cathexis, whose existence and therefore the irreducibility of certain of their properties psychical activity will have to recognise. This is why the experience of the encounter and, I would add, of any encounter confronts psychical activity with an excess of information that it will ignore until that excess forces it to recognise that what falls outside the representation proper to the system returns to the psyche in the form of a denial concerning its representation of its relation to the world. An example of this denial is provided by the experience that the infant's psyche may have at the moment when it is hallucinating the presence of the breast, and is therefore forging for itself a representation of the mouth–breast junction and may, suddenly, experience a state of privation. But what is true for this initial phase of psychical activity remains true for all its experiences. I shall end this chapter with some general considerations concerning the state of encounter.

If I had to choose a single characteristic to define man's *fatum* I would choose the effect of anticipation, by which I mean that his destiny is to confront it with an experience, a discourse, a reality that usually anticipate his possibilities of response and always anticipate what he may know and foresee of the reasons, the meaning, the consequences of the experiences with which he is continually confronted. The further back one goes in his history, the more this anticipation assumes all the characteristics of excess: excess of meaning, excess of excitation, excess of frustration, but, equally, excess of gratification or excess of protection: what is demanded of him always exceeds the limits of his response, just as he will always be presented with something short of his expectations, which are unlimited and timeless. One might add that one of the most constant and most frustrating features of the demand addressed to him is the projection on to his horizon of the expectation of a response that he cannot give, with the consequent risk that any response is then perceived as capable only of disappointing the demand to which one gives it, and that any demand on his part is received as proof of a frustration that it wishes to impose. The mother's words and deeds always anticipate what the infant may know of them, if, as I wrote in a text quite a long time ago,[5] the offer precedes demand, if the breast is given before the mouth knows that it is up to it to respond, this gap is even more evident and more total in the register of meaning. The mother's flow of words is the bearer and creator of meaning, but that meaning only anticipates the infant's capacity to understand it and to act on it. The mother offers herself as a 'speaking I' or an 'I speak' who places the infant in the situation of receiver of a discourse, whereas it is beyond his capacity to appropriate the meaning of the statement and what is heard can only be metabolised into a homogeneous material with a pictographic structure. But although it is true that any encounter confronts the subject with an experience that anticipates his possibilities of response at the time it occurs, this anticipation will find its most absolute form at that initial moment when the infant's psychical activity is confronted with the psychical productions of the maternal psyche and must forge a representation of itself from the effects of this encounter, whose frequency is a vital necessity. When I speak of the mother's psychical productions I mean specifically the statements by which the mother speaks of the child and speaks to the child. It is therefore the mother's discourse that is the agent responsible for the effect of anticipation imposed on the infant, from whom a response is expected that it is not in his power to give; it is also this discourse that illustrates in an exemplary way what I mean by the concept of primary violence.

As long as we remain within our cultural system, the mother has the privilege of being for the infant the speaker and privileged mediator of an ambient discourse whose injunctions and prohibitions she transmits to him, in a form pre-digested and pre-shaped by his own psyche, by which she indicates to him the limits of the possible and the allowable. This is why, in this text, she will be called the 'word-bearer' (*porte-parole*), a term that denotes what is at the basis of her relation to the child. Through the discourse that she maintains to and on the infant, she forges for herself an ideational representation of that infant, beginning by identifying 'the being' of the infant forever foreclosed from her knowledge. The order governing the statements of the mother's voice has nothing random about it and is merely evidence of the subjection of the I who speaks to three preconditions: the kinship system, the linguistic structure, the effects imposed upon discourse by the affects at work on 'the other stage' (*l'autre scène*). This trinomial is the cause of the first radical and necessary act of violence that the infant's psyche undergoes at the time of its encounter with the mother's voice. This violence is the consequence and living testimony, on the living being, of the specific character of that encounter: the difference between the structures according to which the two spaces organise their representation of the world. The phenomenon of violence, as I understand it here, refers in the first instance to the difference separating one psychical space, that of the mother, in which the action of repression has already taken place, and the psychical organisation proper to the infant. The mother, by right at least, is a subject in whom repression and the setting up of the agency called I have already operated; the discourse that she addresses to the infant bears that double mark responsible for the violence that it will operate. In turn, this violence reinforces in the infant who undergoes it a pre-existing division that has its source in the primal bipolarity that splits the two contradictory aims proper to desire. But the semantic overload that weighs on the concept of violence requires me to define my understanding of the term: I propose to separate a *primary violence*, which denotes what is imposed from the outside on the psychical field, at the cost of an initial violation of a space and of an activity that obeys laws heterogeneous to the I and to discourse, and a *secondary violence* that makes its way in the wake of its predecessor, of which it represents an excess, usually harmful and never necessary to the functioning of the I, despite its proliferation and diffusion.

In the first instance I am dealing with a *necessary action* of which another's I is the agent, the tribute that psychical activity pays to gain access to a mode of organisation that will be set up at the expense of pleasure and to the benefit of the future constitution of the agency called I. In the second instance, on the other hand, violence[6] works against the I, whether it is a question of conflict between 'I's or of conflict between an I and the *diktat* of a social discourse that has no other aim than to oppose any change in the models that it has set up. It is in this conflict area that is posed the problem of power, of the additional justification that it always demands of knowledge and of what may follow on the plane of identification: I shall come back to these matters during the analysis of the I. But it is important to stress that, although this secondary violence is as widespread as it is persuasive, to the point of managing to be misunderstood by those who are its victims, it succeeds in abusively appropriating the qualifications of necessary and natural, the very same that after the event the subject recognises as proper to the primary violence from which his I emerged.

So it is of this secondary violence that I shall speak when I define the category of the necessary or of necessity in our work: the set of conditions – factors or situations – that are indispensable if psychical and physical life is to attain and preserve a threshold of autonomy below which it can only survive at the cost of a state of absolute dependence. In the domain of psychical life, it is evident, for example, that a subject suffering from paraplegia can only live if another individual agrees to provide for his physiological needs: one result, among others, of this is that any autonomy in the area of feeding will be lost and an absolute dependence established between the subject's need and another subject agreeing to obtain food, give it to him, decide on the quantity and quality appropriate to the patient's state. In the physical domain, it is easy enough to find examples. But what about the psychical domain? And, to begin with, what do we mean by psychical life? If we mean any form of psychical activity, it requires only two conditions: the survival of the body and, to this end, the persistence of a libidinal cathexis resistant to a final victory of the death drive. As long as these two conditions are given, the presence of psychical life is guaranteed, whatever its mode of functioning and its productions may be. That is why I do not speak of psychical life in general, but rather of the form that it acquires beyond a certain threshold – a threshold that is not there from the outset. Once this threshold is reached, it will be possible to acquire and strengthen a certain autonomy in the activity of thinking and behaviour; the achievement of this will coincide with the decline of the Oedipus complex and with the repression, outside the space of the I, of a series of statements that will form the secondary repressed. That is why I say that in the register of the I there exists a threshold below which the I finds it impossible to acquire, in the register of meaning, that degree of autonomy that is indispensable if he is to appropriate an activity of thinking that allows between subjects a relationship based on a linguistic heritage and a knowledge of meaning, in which one recognises that one has equal rights, without which will always be imposed the will and the words of a third party, subject or institution, which will become sole judge of the subject's rights, needs, demands and, implicitly, desire. This is an expropriation of a right to exist that may be manifested overtly in psychotic experience, but which may also be present without assuming, for observers, the form of a manifest psychosis. In this case, the expropriation experienced by the I will be just as serious and it will have the illusion of functioning normally only in so far as outside itself there *really* exists another reality that will serve as prosthesis and anchorage. The state of passion, whatever the object of the passion may be, provides an example: the disappearance or privation of the object entails the disappearance or privation of the I's normality; the same phenomenon may appear in certain forms of ideological dependence.

To return now to the concept of violence, I would say that I called *primary violence, the psychical action by which one imposes on another's psyche a choice, a thought or an action that is motivated by the desire of the person who imposes it, but which is based on an object that responds for the other to the category of the necessary.*

By linking the register of the desire of the one to the register of the other's need, the aim of violence is assured of victory: by using desire on the object of a need, primary violence achieves its aim, which is to make of the fulfilment of the desire of him who exerts it what will become the object *demanded* by him who undergoes it. There now appears the intrication that primary violence establishes between these three fundamental registers: the necessary, desire, demand. This is an intrication that makes it impossible for primary violence to be unmasked for what it is, as long as it assumes the appearance of the demanded and the expected. It should be added that usually it allows *the two partners in question* to misconstrue its constituent characteristics. The primary violence exerted by the effect of anticipation of the mother's discourse is essentially manifested by this offer of meaning that has the result of making it emit a response that it formulates in the infant's place. I find in this pre-response the paradigmatic illustration of the definition given of the concept of primary violence, especially as the mother's behaviour will respond to what the analyst will define as 'normal', by which is meant behaviour that encourages to the maximum a functioning of the I close to the model proposed by psychoanalytic theory.

What I have just said about the mother's action and discourse has imperceptibly brought us from the state of encounter, conceived as an experience coextensive with life itself, to the moment at which this experience has its origin, to an inaugural encounter between two psychical spaces. I have said that what specifies them is the radical gap between the infant, representing to himself his state of need or satisfaction, and the mother, who responds to the effects of these representations, interpreting them according to an anticipated meaning, which will become intelligible to the infant only gradually and which will require the activation of two other processes of metabolisation.

The anticipatory effect of the mother's response is present from the outset; the anticipatory effect of her speech and of the meaning that it transmits, and which the child will have to appropriate, will only take place later. Before any analysis of what is at play in the two opposing spaces, it should be remembered that to separate the factors proper to the representative from those belonging to the maker of the statement (the mother) is a need to explain and that in reality there is a constant interaction. Otherwise there is a risk of sliding either to the side of a biologisation of psychical development, or, on the other hand, of opting for a theory of the signifying chain that ignores the role of the body and of the somatic models that it provides. The only necessary condition for the psyche to become active is that to the work of the infant's psyche is added the prosthetic function of the mother's psyche, a prosthesis that, for me, is comparable to that of the breast, in so far as it is an extension of one's own body, because it is an object whose juncture with the mouth is a vital necessity, but also because it is an object that gives erogenous pleasure, which is a *vital necessity* for its psychical functioning.

By making the first mouth–breast encounter – while being perfectly aware that it does not coincide with the newborn's entry into this world, since it comes after a first cry, of which its accompanying representation remains enigmatic – the starting point of my theoretical construction, I posit at its source the primal experience of a triple discovery: for the infant's psyche, that of an experience of pleasure; for the body, that of an experience of satisfaction; and for the mother . . . here nothing universal can be postulated, one can only suggest that the first experience of suckling will be for her both the discovery of a physical experience – a sensation of pleasure, of pain or of an apparent sensorial neutrality in the breast – and the first realisation, after pregnancy, of a gift necessary to the infant's life. What she now feels about this encounter will depend on her pleasure in having had the child, her fears concerning it, her displeasure at being a mother, how she conceives her role, etc.

But in any case where the breast is offered two remarks should be made:

1   However ambivalent it may be, the act is evidence of a desire for life on the part of the other and, at the very least, of a prohibition concerning the risk of his possible death.
2   In most cases, the offer of the breast will be marked, in its form and in its temporality, by the cultural forms affecting the act of suckling. Suckling, therefore, depends on:
    •   the mother's desire *vis-à-vis* the infant;
    •   that which is manifested of this desire in the feeling that the mother's I has for the newborn child;[7]

14

- that which cultural discourse proposes as a good model of the mother's role.

This list would be enough to demonstrate the complexity, the over-determination and the heterogeneity of the forces at work that, from the first encounter, the primal process will have the function of representing: at the moment when the mouth meets the breast it meets and swallows a first mouthful of the world. Affect, meaning, culture are co-present and responsible for the taste of those first molecules of milk that the infant takes into himself: the food element is always duplicated by the swallowing of a psychical food, which the mother will interpret as the swallowing of an offer of meaning. One looks on spellbound at the metamorphosis that the primal activity will undergo.

With this my general considerations on the representation and state of encounter come to an end. They bring new confirmation of what I have already stressed twice, concerning the arbitrary nature of any separation between these two psychical states – that of the infant and that of the mother – in which the same object, the same experience of encounter will be inscribed by using two forms of writing and two heterogeneous relational schemata. At each stage one sees analytical reflection come up against the same stumbling-block: having to separate the inseparable. It is a methodological requirement imposed by dis-course, but one must constantly recall its presence and warn of the cost entailed when we arbitrarily cut the umbilical cord that links the two confronting psyches and turn away from the infant and that first work of the psyche: pictographic representation.

2

The primal process and the pictogram

1 The postulate of self-procreation

I have said that the distinctive characteristic of each process of metabolisation, activated by the encounter between psychical space and the space outside the psyche, is defined by the specificity of the relational model imposed on the elements of the represented, a model that is a copy of the structural schema of the representative itself. In the phase that I am analysing, all the productions of the psychical activity will conform to the postulate of self-procreation. In my analysis, I distinguish between what concerns the pleasure–unpleasure economy proper to that postulate and what concerns the particular characteristic of the represented that it produces: the pictogram.

I have said that the primal encounter is played out, in theory, at the very moment of birth, but that we may shift the moment forward, situating it at the first, inaugural experience of pleasure: *the encounter between mouth and breast.* When I speak of the primal moment, or of the primal encounter, I am referring to that starting point. That shift forward will be compensated for, by a movement in the opposite direction, when I come to speak of the I, the agency that the discourse of the Other anticipates in a much more obvious way.

If we remain on the side of the infant, we may isolate a series of factors responsible for the organisation of psychical activity in the phase under consideration:

1   The presence of a body whose property is to preserve its state of energetic equilibrium by self-regulation. Any break in this state will be manifested in an unknowable experience, an x that, in the deferred action of language, is called pain. Any appearance of this experience triggers off, when possible, a reaction aimed at eliminating its cause. This reaction, which derives from the homeostasis of the system, eludes all knowledge on the part of the psyche. The psyche is nevertheless informed of a possible state of pain in the body, to which it reacts by the only action it is capable of: the hallucination of a modification in the encounter situation, resulting in a denial of its *state of lack*; it will be seen that this

lack has a very particular relationship with what is, in theory, its physiological equivalent, the state of need.

There appears at once the major scandal of psychical functioning: its first 'natural' response is to misunderstand need, to misunderstand the body and to 'know' only 'the state' that the psyche wishes to return to. The behaviour of appeal appears only when faced with the failure of the pictogram's omnipotence. This scandal exposes the original presence of a rejection of living in favour of the search for a state of quiescence, of *non-desire*, which remains the aim, unknown, but always at work, of desire. It should be recognised that the primal presence of Thanatos is more scandalous for the I then that of Eros, the already-there of hate more disturbing that the always-there of love.

2   A power of excitability to which one owes 'the psychical representative of the stimuli originating from within the organism and reaching the mind, as a measure of the demand made upon the mind for work in consequence of its connection with the body'.[1] Freud's definition of the drive is applicable at every point to the one that I am proposing for the pictographic activity. The work demanded of the psychical apparatus will consist of metabolising an element of information coming from a space that is heterogeneous to it, into a material homogeneous with its structure, in order to allow the psyche to represent to itself what *it* wishes to rediscover of its own experience.

3   An affect bound up with this representation, representation of an affect and affect of representation being indistinguishable for and in the register of the primal.

4   From the outset the double presence of a link and a heterogeneity between the x of physical experience and the psychical affect, manifesting itself in, and through, its pictographic representation. Indeed the affect is coextensive with representation, while representation may or may not conform to the reality of the physical experience. If we imagine a representation of the mouth–breast unity accompanying the experience of suckling we have a similarity between affect and physical experience. If, on the contrary, we envisage the hallucinatory representation of our mouth–breast union that temporarily imposes a psychical silence on the real state of need, we shall have an objective contradiction between affect and physical experience, but a contradiction totally ignored by the psyche and existing at best only for the observer.

5   The constant demand of the psyche: nothing can appear in its field that has not first been metabolised into a pictographic representation. The pictographic representability of the phenomenon is a necessary condition for its psychical existence: this law is as universal and irreducible as that which decides on the conditions of audibility or visibility of an object. Sound waves and light waves go far beyond the spectrum proper to the sensitivity of the human organs: but outside this spectrum they do not exist for the human being. Similarly the primal can 'know' only those phenomena that correspond to the conditions of representability; others have no existence for it.

17

The conditions of representability that must be possessed by objects if they are to provide material that may be used by the primal can only be reconstructed at a later stage, when one encounters only a few offshoots. This reconstruction seems to me to be likely in that the conditions of representability must correspond to the particular properties that I shall now describe.

2 The conditions necessary for the representability of the encounter

The activity of the primal process is coextensive with an experience responsible for the activation of one or several functions of the body resulting from the excitation of corresponding sensory surfaces.

This activity and this excitation require an encounter between a sense organ and an external object possessing the ability to stimulate it. It is this sensory model that the primal process takes up in the form that it assumes. The pictographic representation of this encounter has the peculiarity of ignoring the duality that makes it up. The represented is given to the psyche as a presentation of itself: the representing agent sees in the representation the result of his autonomous work, sees in it the production of his own image. Representation, therefore, is a 'presenting' of the psyche for the psyche, a self-encounter between a primal activity and an equally primal 'product' that is offered as presentation of the act of representing for the agent of the representation. This *'over-meaning'* and this *over-determination* of the represented are its essential characteristics.

The first condition of the representability of the encounter refers us, therefore, to the body and, more specifically, to the sensory activity proper to it. This first condition will be analysed in greater detail when I discuss the *borrowing* made by the psyche from the sensory model, which will enable me to explain the particular texture of the pictogram. Before doing so, I shall consider in what conditions the representation of the encounter may be a source of pleasure and in what conditions it will be a source of unpleasure. At this point, we meet a second general law of psychical activity: its aim is never gratuitous, the expenditure of work that it involves must possess a bonus of pleasure, without which the non-cathexis of the activity of representation would put an end to the vital activity itself. This is a danger from which the psyche is generally protected by the presence of what I have called 'minimum pleasure', a consequence of any linkage, corresponding to the postulate, between the elements of information that gain access into the psychical space and the state of quiescence that results from it for the activity of representation, providing the represented is offered as a support that magnetises and fixes for its own use the energy possessed by this process. It is obvious that if this 'minimum pleasure' were alone in question, it would have no other aim but the permanence of an initial representation, which would become the support, first and last, of the totality of psychical energy. This would be an impossible aim to achieve, but one that, in my opinion, is evidence of the complicity present from the outset between the pleasure principle and the death drive. For that complicity not to have total victory over Eros, this minimum pleasure must be combined with the quest and expectation of a 'pleasure bonus', the psychical equivalent of a 'pleasure organ', a bonus that, as soon as it is experienced, becomes the aim of psychical activity. Although it is true that, in the represented of the pictogram, there can be no difference between the representation that accompanies suckling and the representation of that experience in the absence of the breast, I postulate nevertheless a very early perception on the part of the psyche of a bonus of pleasure experienced when an experience of real satisfaction is accompanied by its representation, on condition that this satisfaction can bring pleasure and is not reduced to satisfying need.[2] We shall see to what conditions it must correspond for this to be possible, but I shall say at the outset that the essential condition is that this experience may be represented as bringing pleasure to the two entities of what I shall define as 'the complementary object–zone'. The bonus of pleasure, as the aim of the activity of representation, is therefore linked to the possibility of a representation and of an experience that may respectively depict and make present the conjunction of two pleasures: that of the representative and that of the object that it represents and which it encounters in the course of the experience (the satisfaction of need).

As to the conditions relative to the affect of unpleasure, I would say that this affect is present whenever the state of fixation becomes impossible and that psychical activity must recreate a representation. We may have recourse to the energy metaphor and say that the work necessary to the setting up of a new representation leads to a state of tension, which is responsible for what I shall call 'minimum unpleasure', symmetrical with what I have called minimum pleasure.

More important and more essential in understanding psychical functioning is the relation between the affect of unpleasure and the representation that is inextricably linked to it. This relation will force us to confront the question posed by the death drive, using the concept that I proposed when speaking of a radical hate, which is as primal as its opposite.

The representation of the affect of unpleasure could not be understood without postulating the primal presence of the contradiction proper to the two aims of desire: the desire to cathect the object by metabolising it in the representation of part of one's own body, a desire to incorporate it and, as a result, a desire to cathect the 'incorporator' himself and a desire for self-annihilation, which makes the representation of the representing agency the self-presentation of the agency producing unpleasure. Whenever the persistence of need forces psychical activity to be informed of it and to represent, in and by the pictogram, what would be a cause of unpleasure, a representation that clearly respects the postulate of the primal, but which proves its submission to the aims of Thanatos, will win the day: in this case the agency that sees itself in the represented contemplates itself as a source of its own pain; it then tries to annul and destroy that image of itself. Unpleasure has as its corollary and synonym a desire for self-destruction, the first manifestation of a death drive that sees in the activity of representation, in so far as it is an original form of psychical life, the tendency that is contrary to its own desire to return to the state prior to any representation. This hypothesis has the advantage of explaining what separates the two concepts called by Freud the Nirvana principle and the death drive. If the first may be seen as the manifestation of a pleasure principle that tends to quiescence and to the unchanging persistence of a first representation, offering the psyche proof of its omnipotent self-creation of the state of pleasure and as evidence of its power to create the object in accordance with its aim and make it forever present, the second must be seen as an equally archaic and insistent tendency. It is as if 'the need to represent' as corollary of 'the need to desire' disturbed an earlier sleep, an unintelligible state prior to our thinking in which everything was silence. What we are seeing here is a manifestation of the radical hate, present from the outset, for an activity of representation whose activation presupposes, because of 'its link with the body', the perception of a state of need whose function it is to annul. Whenever psychical activity is accompanied by an excitation informing it of a state of need, its aim will be to metabolise it and to represent it by its negation, hence its ambivalence regarding its own production. The state of pleasure that it induces conceals the perception of an experience that one avoids at all costs: one's love of representation is the opposite, but also the corollary, of the hate that one has for need in so far as it is evidence of the existence of an autonomous physical space. Any upsurge of the desire to represent has its source in the desire to debar any upsurge of need and of anything associated with it: at this point desire itself runs the risk, paradoxically, of finding itself desiring a state that would make it useless and without object. The desire not to have to desire is an inherent aim of desire itself. *The desire of non-desire*: this formula, which I have often used, expresses my conception of the death drive.[3] Because it is an integral part of the aims of desire, hate for any object manifesting the presence of desire may win out, whenever the represented is no longer able to ignore need and therefore whenever it may be accompanied by an experience of unpleasure. In this case the psyche will contemplate in the result of its own work the demonstration and proof of the existence of *its elsewhere, the space of the body*, which it can only hate and wish to destroy, whenever it has to be subjected to a power over which it has no control. It is the strange destiny of the body, fraught with consequences, to be at one and the same time the substratum necessary to psychical life, the provider of somatic models from which representation borrows, but which, because it obeys laws heterogeneous to those of the psyche, and which will nevertheless have to impose their demands and obtain real satisfaction, begins by appearing to the psychical agency as the irreducible proof of the presence of an elsewhere, and therefore the privileged object of a desire for destruction. On the other hand, it is true that, if life continues, the body as that set of organs and sensory functions by which the psyche discovers its power — to see, to hear, to taste, to touch —

becomes the source and locus of an erogenous pleasure that makes it possible for certain of its fragments to be immediately cathected by the narcissistic libido at the service of Eros.

We shall see how this self-discovery of the power of its sensory functions will be presented in the pictogram by the model of a 'taking-into-oneself', a self-produced object.

What I have said so far offers a first schema of the elements organising the original situation of the mouth–breast encounter when one privileges what is at work solely on the side of the infant.

We have encountered in turn:

- an experience of the body, what I have called the unknowable x, which accompanies an activity of representation giving rise to the pictogram;
- an affect that is inextricably linked to it, and which may be an affect of pleasure or of unpleasure;
- the original presence of a radical ambivalence of desire when confronted by its own production, which may, equally well, be the support of its tendency to become fixed there and the support of its wish to destroy it, because it is proof of the existence of an elsewhere that eludes its power, but also of an elsewhere that forces it to continue its work of representation, thus forbidding it to preserve the state of fixation;
- lastly, the ambivalence of any cathexis concerning the body. As the provider of a model that the pictogram takes over, it will appear, in turn, as a set of erogenised zones and, as such, as a space cathected by the narcissistic libido and as that abhorred elsewhere, whenever it denounces the limits of the psyche's power and denies the legend of hallucination over the non-existence of an outside-the-psyche.

After this initial setting up of the factors organising the activity and economy of the primal process, I shall consider, from a different point of view, the psyche–body relation, explaining what I mean by borrowing from the model of the body.

3 The borrowing made from the sensory model by the activity of the primal

I set out from the hypothesis that the life of the organism is based upon a continuous oscillation between two elementary forms of activity that I call:

- 'the taking-into-self',
- 'the rejecting-outside-self'.

21

These two activities are accompanied by a work of metabolisation of the 'taken in', which transforms it into a raw material of one's own body, the residues of this operation being expelled from the body.

Breathing and eating are a simple, clear example. This double mechanism may, *mutatis mutandis*, be extrapolated to all the sensory systems whose function entails analogically the 'taking-into-self' of information, a source of excitation and a source of pleasure, and the attempt at 'rejecting-outside-self' that same information when it becomes a source of unpleasure. One initial difference merits attention: it is possible to vomit the mother's milk; it is impossible, at this stage of existence, to block up one's nose or cover one's ears. Furthermore, all sensory information has the power to exceed the threshold of tolerance and to be transformed into excitation, a source of pain.[4] The term 'information', which I introduced at the beginning, is intended to give precedence to the role of the sensory functions. When I speak of information I do not intend to confine myself to a new form of organicism inspired by cibernetics; on the contrary, I hope to place in the foreground a set of functions whose task it is to inform psyche and world of their mutual interdependence in a very particular and very 'psychical' register – if I may be permitted to say so, that of pleasure and its relation to discourse. Seen, heard, tasted, touched will come together, as soon as there is access to language, under the aegis of a statement that will decide on the *affective* message that informed and informing voice expect and receive one from the other. The instrumentation of the message on the sensitive object will ensure that it will be that which is stated by the message that will decide on the relation of sensory experience and sensitive object to pleasure and unpleasure, to the lawful and the forbidden. It should be added that recent experiments of sensory disafferentiation seem to prove that, during the waking period, parallel with such objects of need as food, air, an adequate intake of calories, a continuous supply of sensory information is also necessary: without it the psyche seems to have difficulty functioning without having to hallucinate the information that is lacking.

In psychoanalytic terms, the 'taking-into-self' and the 'rejecting-outside-self' may be expressed at the outset by another binomial: the cathexis or decathexis of that of which one is informed and of the object of excitation responsible for this information. It is important to stress that the pictographic representation of the concepts of 'taking in' and 'rejecting' remains at this phase the only possible representation of any sensory experience: seen, heard, tasted will be either well perceived by the psyche as a source of pleasure of its own production, and therefore especially forming part of what is 'taken' inside itself, or as a source of pain to be rejected and this rejection *implies* that the psyche cuts off from itself what, in its own representation, brings into play the organ and the zone, the source and seat of excitation.

Speaking of this double model of the taking-into-self and rejecting-outside-self we come to the description of representation that the psyche gives itself of *its* experience of pleasure or unpleasure. The terms 'sensory' or 'physical' model and 'borrowing' refer to the raw materials present in the pictographic representation, by which the psyche informs itself of an affective state that concerns it alone. It would be pointless in this register to lay down an order of precedence between the affect and its representation or between the experienced and the information that the psyche has of it; similarly, it would be pointless to make representation the source of an affect that its upsurge would trigger off, or to see the affect as a pre-existing state that the activity of representation would bring to the fore. We must postulate the coalescence of a representation of the affect that is inseparable from the affect of the representation that accompanies it. They are no more separable than is the look from what is seen: to see is the encounter of a sense organ with a phenomenon endowed with visibility; no temporal hierarchisation is possible. If I were speaking of the I, it would be readily acknowledged that it would be incongruous to wish to decide whether a feeling of joy, frustration or envy does or does not precede its naming by the I: there is no feeling separable from the possibility of expressing it in a statement. The expression, whether internal or communicated, explicit or implicit, of the feeling is correlative with the state that it manifests and which would simply not exist *for the I* without this possibility of naming it. If we agree to call feeling the affects present and manifesting themselves in the sphere of the I, their formulation thus becoming the equivalent of the representation for the affect, the inseparability of the two terms of this second binomial will be clearer.

There now arises the question of the relation between the term 'borrowing' that I suggested and that of anaclisis, or 'leaning on', used by Freud: their proximity is obvious, though they do differ on one point. Anaclisis, in the sense given it by Freud, is closer to a 'ruse of the psyche',[5] which would take advantage of the way opened up by the perception of need, or the state of satisfaction, to allow the drive to inform it of its vital needs, and so, as Freud writes, 'they make far higher demands on the nervous system and calls it to undertake involved and interconnected activities by which the external world is so changed as to afford satisfaction to the internal source of stimulation'.[6]

The heterogeneity between need and drive, posited at the outset by Freud, is a nodal concept of psychoanalytic theory; this heterogeneity, however, does not mean that one cannot find between these two entities a relation that is no longer one of support, but one of an affective and persistent dependence in the register of the represented. We shall find traces of this persistence in the scenic representations created by the primary, in which the preponderant place given to the image of the body will become apparent. My hypothesis concerning the primal, as creation repeating itself indefinitely throughout existence, implies an enigmatic interaction between what I call the 'representative background' against which every subject functions and an organic activity, whose effects we can perceive, in the psychical field, only at special, privileged moments, or, and here, too, in a disguised form, in psychotic experience. Having defined the term 'borrowing', we can now turn to the analysis of the represented: that is to say, what we suppose that a hypothetical, impossible look would see if it could observe the pictographic representation. To speak of a hypothetical, impossible look is enough to recall that we only reconstruct what seems probable to us, on the basis of knowledge that the analyst may have of the experiences of subjects who have long since gone beyond the moment when only the primal process occupied the stage.

4 Pictogram and specularisation

In the section devoted to the I, I shall analyse the concept of the mirror stage, as defined by Jacques Lacan. But well before that stage, indeed at the very origin of psychical activity, one notes the presence and potential of a *phenomenon of specularisation*: any creation of the psychical activity is presented to the psyche as a reflection, a presentation of itself, a force producing that image of thing in which it is reflected; and a reflection that it contemplates as its own creation, an 'image' that is for the psyche both presentation of the producing agent and the producing activity. If one accepts that in this phase the world – the outside-the-psyche – has no existence other than in the pictographic representation that the primal makes of it, it follows that the psyche encounters the world as a fragment of specular surface, in which it mirrors its own reflection. At first all it knows of the outside-self is what may be given as image-of-self, and the self in turn presents itself to itself as, and by, this activity and this power, which have produced this fragment of the outside-self that is its specularisation.[7] It is a term that is very close, in the sense that I am giving it, to that of complementarity: if, in the problematic in question here, one considers only what belongs to the activity of representation, it will be noted that representative and representation of the world are complementary to one another, each being the other's condition of existence. This work of continuous reflection is the very pulsation of psychical life, its mode and form of being, a demand as imperious as the demand to be able to breathe for the survival of the organism.

This specular complementarity between psychical space and the space of the world finds its model of representation in the borrowing made by the psyche from sense experience. It is on the '*sensory vector*' that the instinctual 'leans'; the perception of need itself opens up access to the psyche thanks to a representation that brings to the fore the absence of a sensitive object, a source of pleasure for the corresponding organ. If I have chosen the initial experience of an experience of pleasure as the starting point of my construction it is because of the function that I give sensory activity, the original source of a *pleasure* (of taste, hearing, seeing, feeling, touching) which is the *condition and cause* of the cathexis of a phys-ical activity that the psyche discovers in its power – an experience of a pleasure that it obtains, which is *the necessary prerequisite for the cathexis of the activity of representation and of the image that results from it*. I should stress here the synchronic

24

intrication of these different moments that are added together to form an overall, inextricable experience:

- the sense perception of a noise, a taste, a touch, a smell, something seen, a *source of pleasure*, temporarily coinciding with the experience of satisfying alimentary need and the effective excitation of the oral zone, but also with the satisfaction derived by the sense organisation from waiting, enigmatic as the presence of this elementary need for information by the senses and this pleasure resulting from their activation still are for me;
- the discovery of a power 'to see, to hear, to feel, to touch, to taste', which will be metabolised by the psyche in the representation of its power to produce for itself the object and the state of pleasure;
- the representation of this 'sensory-object zone as cause of excitation' by an image that presents them as a single, inextricable entity; it is this entity that I call 'the image of the corporal thing' or, a formulation that I prefer, '*the image of the complementary object–zone*'. This image is the pictogram, in so far as it is the formation of a relational schema, in which the representative is reflected as a totality identical with the world. What psychical activity contemplates and cathects in the pictogram is this reflection of itself, which ensures that, between psychical space and the space outside-the-psyche, there exists a relation of reciprocal identity and specularisation.

When discussing the voice, I shall return in a more detailed way to the concept of erogenous zone, but I must now stress that from the outset the experience of pleasure, any pleasure derived from any of the zones, is necessarily an overall pleasure of the whole set of zones. The experience of suckling is accompanied by a series of perceptions affecting the various sensory organs: pleasure, from its first appearance, will paradoxically anticipate this experience of an inexpressible totality of the experience that, long after the event, will be called pleasure (*jouissance*). We shall see, with the activation of the primary, that this reflection is found in the first phase of this activity: the first recognition of an outside-self derives from a first relation of identity in which the recognition of an 'otherness' is both recognised and denied – recognised in the way that a double whom I know is not me may be recognised, denied because for the reality of difference is substituted the illusion of sameness between what appears in an elsewhere recognised as such and the form in which the psyche conceives of itself and represents itself.

On the basis of these observations one may define as follows what specifies pictographic representation: the shaping of a perception by which are presented, in the primal and for the primal, the affects of which it is in turn the seat, an initial activity of the psyche for which any representation is always self-referential and remains for ever inexpressible, unable to respond to any of the laws to which the expressible must obey, however elementary it may be. This self-world specularisation demonstrates the ambiguity of the meaning frequently given to the concept of primary narcissism. If the representative *is* the world, and conversely, this 'mad' reflection of the world by the representative makes it present itself to itself as a reflection of the 'all' or as a reflection of the 'nothing': Eros and Thanatos give their names to two self-presentations that subsume the person's totality. Side by side with a narcissistic presentation of a self-world, we must now posit the (narcissistic?) presentation of a self-nothingness: of course one may call narcissistic the reduction of the world to a 'nothingness', which refers, in fact, to a state of the psyche, but in this case the idea of an original, paradisiacal stage in which the psyche perceived in the world only a full totality, offering itself as proof of its omnipotence over pleasure, collapses.

5 Pictogram and erogenous pleasure

The synchronic totality of the excitation of the zones is of fundamental importance: a precondition necessary to the integration of the body as future unity, but also the cause of a fragmentation of that 'unity', which is at the source of an anxiety of fragmentation – one can readily imagine what disintegration of the image of the body it involves. This synchrony of the erogenous pleasures is moreover coextensive with the first experience of suckling, which brings together a mouth and a breast and is accompanied by the first act of swallowing food, which, in the register of the body, makes its state of need disappear. If the concept of orality, or of an oral stage, holds such a place in analytical theory it is because it refers to this initial experience of pleasure that brings together:

- the satisfaction of need;
- the swallowing of an object taken into oneself;
- the encounter by the sensory organisation of objects, as source of excitation and cause of pleasure.

The breast must be regarded, at this stage, as a fragment of the world that has the peculiarity of being at once audible, visible, tactile, olfactory, feeding and therefore of being the dispenser of the totality of pleasures. By its presence, this fragment triggers off the activity of the sensory system and of that part of the muscular system necessary to the act of sucking: from now on the psyche will establish an identity between what is really the effect of muscular activity, by which an external element is swallowed and therefore a need satisfied, and what results from the sensory excitation that, in turn, one might say, 'swallows' the pleasure that it experiences during its excitation. This is why the mouth will become a pictographic and metonymic representative of the activities of all the zones, the representative that *creates for itself by swallowing* the totality of the attributes of an object – the breast – that will in turn be represented as the overall

26

and single source of sensory pleasures. Primordial zone and object exist only through one another; their inextricability is a correlative of their representation and of its postulate, just as in the experience of hearing the activity of the sensory organ and the sound wave, the source of excitation, are inextricable. This 'complementary zone–object' is the primordial representation by which the psyche represents any experience of encounter between it and the world. It is the protorepresentation of what will be found at the source of the fantasy activity of the primary, that is the primal fantasy of a primal scene. What the primal activity perceives of the ambient (psychical) milieu in which it bathes, what it intuits as to the affects for which are responsible the shades that surround it, will be presented for it and will be represented by it by the only form at its disposal: the image of an external space that, being able to be only the reflection of itself, becomes the equivalent of a space in which there exists between objects the same relation of complementarity and reciprocal interpenetration.

The pictographic presentation, which the primary will transform into a primal scene, metabolises the parental couple in the representation of two parts that can exist only in a single inextricable form: taking-into-self or rejection of one by the other, without precedence being given to either.

So far I have spoken of the complementary object–zone as coextensive with the experience of pleasure. But unpleasure and physical pain are also present. I have already examined my hypothesis concerning the representation that accompanies the affect of unpleasure: what I have just said about the pictogram makes it easier to understand my view. The zone–object complementarity and its corollary – that is, the illusion that every zone produces for itself the object that corresponds to it – means that the unpleasure resulting from the absence of the object or of its inadequacy, by excess or by shortcoming, will present itself as the absence, excess or shortcoming of the zone itself. At this stage 'the bad object' is inseparable from a 'bad zone', the 'bad breast' from the 'bad mouth' and, more generally, the bad, as totalisation of the objects, from the bad as totalisation of the zones and therefore as totalisation of the representative. But, since their inextricability remains complete in the pictographic register, there will follow the setting up of an impossible tearing apart, a violent, mutual separation, that is perpetuated between zone and object: a mouth trying to snatch the breast, the breast trying to snatch itself away from the mouth. The pictogram will represent a similar 'object–zone' unity as locus of a double desire for destruction, as locus in which a deadly and endless conflict will take place. The 'rejecting-outside-self' finds its first illustration in the representation of a mutual rejection between zone and object and, by this fact, *a mutual rejection between the representing agency and the represented*, a consequence of the specular refraction proper to this stage. The result will be that the rejection of the object, its withdrawal of affect, will involve a similar rejection of and withdrawal of affect from the complementary zone. The wish to destroy the object will always be accompanied, in the primal, by the wish to annihilate an erogenous, sensory zone, as well as the activity of which that zone is the seat: at this stage, the object seen may be rejected only by abandoning the visual zone and the activity proper to it. In this mutilation of a zone-function as source of pleasure, we find the archaic prototype of the castration that the primary will have to reshape. In the primal, any organ of pleasure may become what is cut off in order to undo the unpleasure for which it suddenly seems to be responsible. In the course of psychical evolution, the castration fantasy will give its final, definitive form to an anxiety that the subject can only experience later: the anxiety that seizes him when he sees rising up at his frontiers that destructive force that is ever ready to annihilate whatever presents it with an experience of unpleasure.[8] It is here, in my opinion, that the following passage by Freud takes on its full importance:

> The ego hates, abhors and pursues with intent to destroy all objects which are a source of unpleasurable feeling for it, without taking into account whether they mean a frustration of sexual satisfaction or of the satisfaction of self-preservative needs. Indeed, it may be asserted that the true prototypes of the relation of hate are derived not from sexual life, but from the ego's struggle to preserve and maintain itself.
>
> So we see that love and hate, which present themselves to us as complete opposites in their content, do not after all stand in any simple relation to each other. They did not arise from the cleavage of any originally common entity, but sprang from different sources, and had each its own development before the influence of the pleasure–unpleasure relation made them into opposites.[9]

According to my conception, hate is neither prior to nor posterior to love: the two terms denote the affect and the aim proper to two initial representations, once discourse wishes to account for them. The first has its source in the all-encompassing, unifying and centrifugal aim of Eros, which, by zone–object inextricability, gives form to the image of a world in which every object tends towards and meets its complement, is united with it in a perfect totality. The second takes root in the region of Thanatos; its aim will remain the annihilation of desire and of its quest; its tendency will be to hate radically anything that, presenting itself as complement necessary to satisfaction, demonstrates the dependence of the zone on the object, and recalls that the psyche might find itself in a state of lack, and be forced to desire that which is not there, to present itself to itself as lacking power over pleasure, as a capacity for pain and waiting. It is this presentation of itself that is at the initial source of hate. The setting up of separation and rejection between zone and object is *also* the representation of the relation of hate between Thanatos and Eros, as soon as Eros fails to catch Thanatos in the trap of a fixation between libido and object, a fixation that brings the illusion of a return to silence and to an eternal status quo.

These two initial representations of the two affective experiences, of which the psyche is in turn the seat, are the infrastructure responsible for what will be *re-produced* on the stage of the primal throughout life: this re-production of a represented, always identical to itself, is one of the distinctive features of the primal. It is responsible for what I have called the 'representative background' that accompanies the experience of the I.

6 The re-production of the same

The term 'primal' defines therefore a form of activity and a mode of production that are alone present at an initial stage of life. The relation between energy at work and its production tends to the maintenance of a static state. This aim may be achieved in two ways:

1 By the fixation of energy to a support (the represented) that it cathects; in this case there is attraction between representing activity and the image represented whose presence and return the psyche will desire. This predilection for representation, this desire of presence is what I call Eros. We see how the sexual will be able to follow on from the erogenous, from which it will remain inseparable.
2 By the attempt to destroy all reason for quest and for waiting thanks to a return to an initial silence, to a state before desire in which one was unaware of being 'condemned to desire'. Hence the hate that accompanies the first experience of non-pleasure, which reveals the existence of an elsewhere and psychical dependence upon it. This regressive tendency towards an impossible 'state before' is what I call Thanatos. It is not death, as discourse conceives it, that is desired, but that 'state before' that is *inconceivable* for discourse: before life, before desire, before a pleasure always paid for as soon as unpleasure is, or would be, possible, and also before the 'having to represent', which is synonymous with the 'having to exist'.

There is, therefore, a contradiction between the two ways offered to psychical energy to attain its goal. The conflict is present from the outset since whenever the state of desire surges up – what was previously experienced as a state of lack,[10] however temporary – there would have been, at one and the same time, a quest for the object expected and a rejection of all activity of quest, a desire for presence and a hate of encounter, which is indirect proof of the existence of need and of lack. Henceforth Eros can win out only if the expectation of pleasure is not prolonged, its ruse being to offer Thanatos *by the way of the object* the illusion that it has reached its goal: the silencing of desire, a state of quietude, rest from the activity of representation.

In the economic register, the primal remains in the power of this blind force, which tends to preserve a state of quiescence and which, left to itself, could only oscillate between perpetual fixation on the first support encountered and impossible annihilation of itself. From this point of view it might be said that death is the last snare that man encounters on his way, that in wishing to die he 'madly' hopes to attain a state prior to desire, forgetting that this prior state entails the annulment of any possibility of enjoying it. We see the tenacity of a hate whose object is 'in truth' desire, a hate that manages to turn death into a trick, by which Eros will be able to believe that he has finally found an object that measures up to his expectations, whereas what is in fact expected 'elsewhere' is the definitive annihilation of all desire and of all reason for having to desire.

I have argued that nothing may appear on the psychical stage except in and by this representation: hence the importance accorded to what is represented on the stage, to the borrowing made from the sensory model and from the concept of the pictogram that results from it. The pictogram is simply the first representation that psychical activity gives itself of itself by its shaping of the complementary object–zone and by the relational schema that it imposes on these two entities. Pleasure and unpleasure will depend on the relations respectively set up between object and zone. The state of mutual attraction, of magnetisation of one by the other, will be the coextensive representation of any experience of pleasure: the state of rejection, of aggression of one by the other, coextensive with any experience of unpleasure.

Whatever the diversity of the infant's experiences of pleasure or unpleasure, whichever zone and object are concerned and whatever their cause (endogenous or exogenous), the experience itself, the experience in itself, one might say, will be metabolised either into a representation in which the act of taking into self, of merging inextricably with its complement, is correlative with the state of pleasure, or into a representation in which the act of rejecting, of tearing apart is correlative with the state of unpleasure. In other words, the psyche contemplates in representation its own form of activity (taking or rejecting); in the first case, it cathects that productive force and the product that results from it; in the second, it sees in the representation of its activity and of its product the hated cause of its pain. This relational schema, the first metabolisation of the psyche–world relation *and* of the psyche's relation to its psychical productions, remains, in my opinion, always at work: man's actions, the succession of his experiences, will be expressed on the stage of the primal by that 'representative flux' in which the psyche's relation to what it produces, and to what it experiences, is expressed and manifested by a pictogram in which the relation of the representative to the represented expresses, either their coalescence, their mutual cathexis, or their hate, their rejection, their attempt to destroy one another. This representation remains derivative of the borrowing made from the image of a thing and of a function of the body. It is by this same representation that the primal process will metabolise the psychical productions that derive as much from the primary as from the secondary, whenever these productions are concerned with the representation of an *affect* and the attempt to give it meaning. Joy and pain, as feelings of the I, will be metamorphosed by that process into corporal hieroglyphics. Any representation of an erogenous zone, and of its function, becomes a metonym of the totality of the body's space and activity and, therefore, of psychical space and activity. Any production of this space will be metabolised by the primal and represented as an effect of its power to produce the object of pleasure, or as the effect of its power to produce the object to be destroyed. It is the image of the reunification of the two entities forming the complementary object, the source of continuous pleasure, or the image of an object in which the two entities that make it up tear each other apart, which represent in turn, on the stage of the primal, what is at work in the other two spaces that belong to the same psyche. It is an immutable repetition of representation that can use only these signs. The pleasure or unpleasure experienced by the I and the relation of the I to 'thinking', conceived as its production and by which it becomes aware of its experience and reshapes it by naming it, will be represented on the stage of the primal by a pictogram illustrating in a way conforming with its postulate the relation of thinker to what is thought and, therefore, of the I to the idea produced. The radical heterogeneity separating the ideational representation of the I from the pictographic representation of that same I entails a gap between the intensity of the affects coextensive with the pictographic representation of the I-thinking relation and the feelings present between the I and the representations that conform with its postulate. If, in the second case, there is the possibility of a gradation, a relativisation, of the coexistence of various feelings, the primal is always under the power of the law of the 'all or all' of love or hate. This involves the risk of a sudden and destructuring irruption into this space of the I, however well defended it may be (and it is), of an uncontrollable affect that will be able to throw the subject into the void either of fusion or of murder (of himself or of the Other). It is this possibility that justifies the importance that I give to my hypothesis in understanding certain clinical phenomena proper to psychosis[11] and to which I shall return in the section devoted to it.

Nevertheless, it might be stressed that a specific feature of psychosis is to make possible the re-presentation between the primal space and the space outside-self of a state of specularisation. Even in psychosis, this possibility appears only at certain dramatic points, which the observer calls acting out. As such, the pictogram has no place in fantasy presentation, which involves the presence of a third pole represented by an observer outside the stage; still less has it any place in the register of the sayable.

On the other hand, the stage of reality may lend itself to its projection whenever the I might perceive, on the stage of the real, an image of itself close to its own pictographic representation. In this case the I, far from finding identifying markers outside that consolidate its power to foreclose any production of the primal, looks on amazed at an image of itself that it cannot recognise but which resonates with the pictographic representation of the I, in and by the primal. Two identical reflections reflect one another; in whatever direction the I turns it comes up against the same unknowable, because unsayable, rising up at the two frontiers of its psychical space. The I-primal and I-world relation can no longer be differentiated. As a result the perceiver will be put out of action, there will be a temporary cancellation of any gap separating observer and observed, a fading of the I and of these residues, which represent it in psychosis. What we shall witness, then, is not an 'it speaks', but an 'it reacts' or an 'it acts': onto the space of the real will be projected the radical hate or the desire for fusion that mark the pictogram. That one's own body or the body of the other becomes the space to be destroyed or with which to merge shows that they have rediscovered a primary state of undifferentiation. The pictogram is clearly not specific to psychosis; it nevertheless makes it possible to understand why psychosis retains the possibility of acting out an unthought that is also, for other subjects, an unthinkable.

Before ending this chapter on the primal with a review of the characteristics that I have proposed for it, and in order to justify the importance that I give to the representation that this process gives itself of the I and of its productions, I shall make a parenthesis in order to give an initial glimpse of what I mean by the activity of thinking and by ideational representation, two synonymous formulations, in my view, of the I itself. An analysis of these will be found in Chapter 4.

7 Concerning the activity of thinking

From a certain point, which marks the passage from the state of infant to that of the child, the psyche will acquire at one and the same time the first rudiments of language and a new 'function': as a result, a third psychical locus will be set up in which every human being will have to acquire the status of 'thinkable', which is necessary if he is to acquire the attribute of sayable. This sayable-thought may be defined by the term intelligible: in this way is set up a 'function of intellection' whose product will be the *ideational flux* that will accompany all activity, from the most elementary to the most elaborate, of which the I can be the agent. Any source of excitation, any information, may have access to the *register of the I* only if it can give rise to the representation of an 'idea'. It should be added that all activity of the I, implicit or explicit, will now be expressed by this 'thinking flux'. What we have here is a veritable 'simultaneous translation' into 'idea' of any kind of experience of which the I is conscious. This translation represents a latent, usually silent background, but one that the I is usually able to make present by an active reflection on its own activity.

The sayable, then, is the quality proper to the I's productions. If we now turn from the I to that intermediary phase between the primal and the secondary constituted by the *primary*, I would say that the 'thinkable' has its place there, that ideational representations may be seen at work there, that word-presentation and thing-presentation have, after an initial phase, come together, but also that the links between those thoughts–ideas give birth to 'language', whose logic is different from the one that, in stages, the constitutive discourse of the I will impose.

32

The upsurge of the 'function of intellection', as a new form of activity, will, during an initial phase, be joined to the pre-existing part-functions. This function is presented to the psyche as a new erogenous 'function-zone', whose 'idea' would be the object that conforms to it and to the source of its pleasure; this is a necessary condition for there to be cathexis by the primary process of that 'thinking zone' and its form of activity. As I shall show more explicitly in the case of the pleasure of hearing, in so far as it is a prerequisite of any desire to hear, a 'pleasure in thinking' must precede a 'wish to think'. It may be said that the activity of thinking, the condition of the I's existence, is constituted as the equivalent of a function and of a 'part' pleasure, which will be imposed on the cathexis of the primary thanks to the erogenisation that this pleasure induces.

If we go back to the stage of the I, once the setting up of the limits defending its own *topos* has been completed, one notes that any experience, any act entails the co-presence of an 'idea' that makes it thinkable and therefore nameable. That of which the I may have an ideational representation cannot have any existence for it, which does not mean that the I cannot undergo its effects. That is why all activity of the I entails an ideational production, a *self-informing*, a sort of commentary on the part of the experience that is at work and the very aim of the activity of thinking, the function of the secondary. What takes place in this register is accompanied by what I call *feelings of the I*, or *the affect in its conscious form*. But it is a characteristic of the psychical system never to abandon its successive modes of representation: the participation of the primary in the activity of the I no longer needs to be demonstrated.

My hypothesis concerning the pictogram postulates its co-presence, in a locus foreclosed to the I, where the I cannot hear it, during any thinking, any experience, any production claimed by the I as *its* work and *its* property.

As a result, any act of cathexis operated by the I and therefore the whole set of relations present between the I and an object – whether another I or one of the 'property-objects' that the I possesses or covets – will give rise to a threefold inscription in the psychical space:

- In the register of the I we will find the inscription of the statement of a feeling, the statement by which the I acquires and gives knowledge of its relation to the 'object-emblems' cathected by it, which also have the function of markers.
- In the register of the primary the I's wishes and feelings are expressed by a fantasy that will represent the already-there of a reunification brought about or a dispossession undergone.
- In the register of the primary we will have a pictogram in which – and this is its specificity – the I itself is presented as a complementary zone, the cathected object – idea or image – that takes the place of the complementary object.

This pictogram is the representation that the primal makes of the feelings linking the I to its objects. This hypothesis implies that the idea, whether the statement of the feeling, the source of pleasure or pain, will be represented by the object inextricably linked to that complementary zone that represents for the primal the activity of the I: their relation will be presented by the representation of an act of swallowing, of mutual attraction or, on the other hand, of an act of rejection, repulsion, hate. I owe this hypothesis to what I heard in psychotic discourse: beyond the manifest meaning what long struck me, especially in schizophrenic discourse, is the relation of the speaker to the very act of speaking and the response that it arouses in the person who receives 'the spoken object'. There is a sort of strange reification of the discursive flux, or of its retention, which makes one think irresistibly of a mouth that pours out a flow of food that invades the Other, to feed it and to stifle it, of a mouth that retains a mouthful of food-excrement that is poisoning it. The subject's relation to what 'is thought' seems to be close to what had been an archaic relation to the swallowed or the vomited. 'The activity of thinking' becomes once again, in part, the equivalent of the activity of a 'part-function-zone', which may, like any part-zone, be perceived in turn as a source of permitted pleasure, as a zone in which the other may mutilate you, or as a zone whose activity is forbidden by the verdict of the Other's desire.

8 The concept of the primal: conclusions

From the outset I have stressed that to analyse psychical activity by hypostasising a psychical space isolated from its milieu and without any links to it was a fiction impossible to avoid, but one whose sole advantage is that it privileges the analysis of the characteristics proper to 'the primal in itself'. The activity of the primal is specified by its metabolisation of all experiences, the source of affect, in a pictogram, whose structure I have defined. The only condition necessary to this metabolisation is that the phenomenon responsible for experience responds to the characteristics of representability.

This makes it possible to posit an initial separation between two types of human beings, whether the source is the body or the world:

- The first comprises that which the subject will never have any knowledge of, the term 'subject' including here all the agencies present in the psychical space.
- The second comprises two subsets: the subset of the representable and the subset of the intelligible.

What belongs to the first type has no other form of existence for man than that which he owes to mythical or scientific knowledge, which declares that the visible is far from including the human being, that what we can know of the world is partial and, what is more, in the domain of science, that one cannot *subjectively* know anything or perceive anything of part of the fundamental activities of our organism: genetics offers us a series of fascinating formulae about it that give such strange, unrepresentable, and in a sense, too, unthinkable ideas of the human body, as the formulas in physics concerning light waves in relation to the perception that the subject has of light.

Conversely, the second register comprises those aspects of the living being that gain access to psychical space:

- representable phenomena (the productions of the primal);
- imaginable and thinkable phenomena (the productions of the primary and secondary).

The relation between the two is different: indeed, although every thinkable has a representative in the space of the representable, the primal representations, on the other hand, remain foreclosed from the space of the primary–secondary.

We shall now return to the register of the representable and recall the hypothesis with which we began; the sensory information that one owes to the properties of stimulation possessed by a series of objects, of which, initially, the mother's body is the privileged dispenser, results in the activation of the sense organs. On the level of at least one of the senses, taste, this activity corresponds temporarily to the experience of the satisfaction of need and the ingestion of food. I believe that what results from this initial encounter does not depend on the fortuitous juxtaposition of the pleasure of taste and the satisfaction of alimentary need, but that there exists in the register of the sensibility an 'expectation' of the object that possesses an ability to excite and a 'need' of information that explains that the activation of the various sense zones has the property of being accompanied by what I call erogenous pleasure. There is therefore *an equivalence between the zone's excitability and erogeneity*: it follows that it is the activity deriving from their excitation at the time of encounter with the objects (seen, heard, tasted) that is cathected by the libido and becomes a source of pleasure for the psyche. This cathexis of sensory activity is the very condition of existence of a psychical life, since it is *the condition for the cathexis of the activity of representation*. Indeed, all sense information is such only in so far as it is a representation in psychical space: 'excitation, erogenisation, representation' form an inextricable trinomial; they denote the three qualities that an object must *necessarily* possess if it is to have the status of living being for the psyche.

That the cathexis of the activity of representation is the very condition of the living being seems to me to be self-evident, and it is only in this way that the body's functions can be erogenised and what results from this can become for the psyche that object of pleasure whose presence it hallucinates. The identity of perception entails the identity of the affect that accompanies the hallucinated representation of experience. The hallucination of the breast 'leans' on a movement of sucking by the lips that reproduces the activity proper to the oral zone when swallowing milk, the thumb coming in turn to reproduce, at the tactile

35

level, the excitation associated with the breast. It is here that what I proposed concerning the totalisation proper to erogenous pleasure takes on its full importance. From a 'real' activation of the movements of the oral zone, and the pleasure that results from it, what representation reproduces is *the hallucination of the presence of all the attributes*, the source of excitation, with which the breast has been endowed. The visibility, audibility, tactility of the absent object will be hallucinated: the activity of all the erogenous zones and the presence of the objects conforming to them are therefore hallucinated. The pictogram is the representation that the psyche gives itself of itself as representing activity; it re-presents itself as a source producing the erogenous pleasure of the body parts; it contemplates its own image and its own power in its production, whether in that seen, that heard, that perceived that presents itself as self-produced by its activity. If by *affect* one denotes the pleasure or unpleasure resulting from the psyche's experience at the time of its encounter with the world, including that fragment of the world represented by its own bodily space, it follows, as I have already suggested, that the quality of the affect will depend on the positive or negative relation that links in the pictogram representative and represented. *Condemned to represent* what is experienced by it – and this experience that is imposed upon it also comprises the experience of need and pain – being able in terms of its own structure to represent the experience to itself only as its own creation, the affect is that which in the representation is manifested by the attraction or repulsion linking representative and represented. The two inextricable elements that constitute the complementary zone–object linked by the pictogram take the place of the representing agent and its production; their relation, of attraction or rejection, is that by which representation represents the affect experienced by the representative. The image of the bodily thing, as created by the pictogram, is therefore that by which the primal represents to itself that which is representable for it of its encounter with the world: of that infinite space there appears on its stage only that which may be a reflection of bodily space, of its mode of functioning and of the representative's structural schema. A major consequence derives from this for our understanding of psychical functioning: *the representation by the primal of that which results from the activity of the I obeys the same law, is subjected to the same metabolisation.*

It is when confronted by the risk to the I incurred in its pictographic representation by the primal process that this same I will appeal to the particular type of defence that is called delusion: we shall return to this later. Meanwhile, I shall sum up this chapter, listing the theoretical implications that derive from it:

1   The space and activity of the primal are for me different from the unconscious and the primary processes. This activity has the property of metabolising any affective experience present in the psyche into a pictogram that is, inextricably, a representation of the affect and an affect of the representation.

2   This representation can have as 'represented' only what I have defined by the term 'complementary zone–object'.

3   This shaping is a representation of the affect linking object and zone, but this affect is also a representation of the relation between the representative and the experiences imposed on it by existence outside-self (one's own body and the world).

4   The affect, *qua* experience of the primal, is represented by an *action* of the body and more specifically by the action of mutual attraction or rejection of zone and object, an action that reflects the relation of attraction or rejection between representative and represented.

5   This swallowing or this attraction and rejection are the pictographic illustration of these two fundamental feelings that discourse calls love and hate: it follows that any positive movement from the representative to the world is illustrated by a desire to swallow, any negative movement by rejection and a desire for annihilation.

6   The shaping of the pictogram is based on the model of sensory functioning: that is why all experience of pleasure reproduces the sense organ/perceived phenomenon coalescence, any experience of unpleasure entails the desire for self-mutilation of the organ and the destruction of the corresponding objects of excitation.

7   The result of this borrowing from the functions of the body is that only that deriving from the world which may be given as specular reflection of bodily space can be represented in the primal. The self/world specularisation is in fact a psyche/body specularisation, the body denoting here the locus of that series of experiences dependent on the subject/living-being encounter, experiences that the psyche represents to itself as *effects of its power to produce objects that are a source of excitation*, and to produce that which causes pleasure or unpleasure.

8   This metabolisation operated by the activity of representation lasts through-out life. Intellectual activity and the 'idea' that it produces are accompanied on the stage of the primal by the same representation: the I presents itself for and is represented by the primal, as a 'thinking function' that takes its place beside the other part-functions, 'the idea' as object conforming to it and produced by it. In other words, space and the productions of the psyche that are *not* the primal are represented for the primal as equivalents of a complementary zone–object whose activity may be a source of pleasure or unpleasure.

9   This is what I call the 'representative background' that is foreclosed to the power of the I's knowledge. But the effects on the I will be manifested, outside the field of psycho-pathology, by those indefinable feelings that language expresses in metaphors whose profound meaning has been blunted by use: 'to feel good in one's skin', 'to be in good form', 'to feel ill at ease', 'to carry the world on one's shoulders', 'to fall to pieces', and many others.

10   In the field of psychosis this representative background may sometimes occupy the foreground: not that the pictogram, as such, invades the stage of the conscious, but the work of the secondary process, which in its own way continues its struggle and tries to defend itself against this incursion, will see its task reversed. What we have is no longer a making sense of the world and of the feelings that one claims correspond to encounters as they arise, but *a desperate attempt to make sense of and to be able to describe in words experiences that have their source in a representation in which the world is no longer anything more than the reflection of a body swallowing itself, mutilating itself, rejecting itself.*

11   Outside the register of psychosis there are moments of the fading of the I, which will be accused of lucidity or blindness according to the philosophy of the person describing it, in which vacillates that construction, the work of the I, that makes sense of the world and makes it conform to a principle of intelligibility. The I discovers that, between the world and the idea that makes it knowable, correspondence is undecidable. Whenever the idea of the world runs the risk of vacillating, in an unforeseen and uncontrollable way, the psychical functioning runs the risk of no longer being able to encounter any other image of the world than one close to the primal. If the gaze anticathected the external scene and turned exclusively towards the primal scene, it could not but look on, amazed, at those images of the bodily thing, that force producing an image of the world that has become a reflection of a bodily space, torn apart by affects that are, completely and at all times, love or hate, an action of fusion or an action of destruction.

12   Those moments are seldom absent from the experience of the psychotic's I: they are manifested by what discourse calls acting out, amazement, certain catastrophic forms of anxiety. One often forgets that these terms, which one likes to think are pathognomic of psychosis, sometimes occur in our own lives. What is different, for the non-psychotic, is the possibility that the I retains of retaking possession of one's space and mode of functioning, of forgetting those moments of tribulation or of controlling them, *but only in their deferred action*, treating them as 'foreign bodies', 'passing symptoms', whose cause one will impute to this or that external event.

13   In the end, the primal is for me that pictographic 'reservoir' in which remain active, and for ever fixed, those representations that, in the final analysis, are those by which is represented and for ever made present the relentless conflict between Eros and Thanatos, the struggle between desire for fusion and desire for annihilation, love and hate, the activity of representation as desire for pleasure and as hate of having to desire. The pictogram is a representation in which action, linking the two complementary entities, shows in turn which, Eros or Thanatos, has temporarily gained the upper hand. As long as subjective experience is sheltered from pain and lack, between representative and represented, psyche and body, psyche and world, a relation of fusion, of mutual attraction, will be able to be maintained: whenever body and world

prove to be a cause of pain, one will witness a relation of hate, a return of the desire to destroy whatever the represented testifies to, to rediscover a 'before' in which nothing would upset the silence of desire and the silence of the world.

We must now analyse the effects of the primal structure, as I have defined it, replacing them in the 'real' situation of their appearance and functioning: that encounter in which the 'secondary' responds to the primal, governing the mother's behaviour, an encounter whose first effect will be the activation of the primary process. If it may be said that the pictographic representation is proof of the total metabolisation operated by the psyche on the image of the world to which the 'I' of others gives credence, there appears beside it the equally radical violence that subjects the psyche to the discourse of the Other and the demands of that representative that is able to respond to the infant's needs only by claiming 'to know' something of which it has, in fact, no knowledge. In the name of this 'knowledge' the affects of representation and the demands that derive from them will be able to find no response that is not accompanied by an abuse of power committed by the respondent, an abuse as absolute as it is necessary. From now on the 'knowledge-object' is at the source of the problematic of identity and becomes that 'good' whose appropriation will be imposed on the infant. The way in which this appropriation will take place will decide the place and function that the agency called I will occupy in the psyche.

The fantasy representation of the primary process: thing-presentation and word-presentation

I THING-PRESENTATION AND BODY FANTASISATION

My conception of the primary process and its fantasy representation of the psyche–world relation remains more or less faithful to the one that we owe to Freud. That is why I shall confine myself to analysing the factors that radically differentiate its psychical productions from those proper to the primal, stressing more particularly three concepts that the activation of this process forces us to consider: thing-presentation, primary masochism, word-presentation.

The ability of the primary to use word-presentations in its representations is not there from the outset; it appears only in a second stage and gives rise to those cross-bred productions that are the work of what I shall define by the term *primary–secondary*: an analysis of these will be given in the second part of this chapter.

The activation of the primary is a consequence of the recognition by the psyche of the presence of another body, and therefore of another space, separate from its own. This recognition is not compatible with the postulate of self-procreation proper to the primal, a self-procreation in which there can be no place for the representation of any separation between procreator and procreated. It is the recognition of the separation between two body spaces and therefore of two psychical spaces, a recognition imposed by the experience of absence and return, that will have to be represented by the representation of a relation linking the separated. This representation is, at one and the same time, a recognition of separation and its negation: the peculiarity of fantasy production is a representation in which there is certainly a representation of *two* spaces, but these two spaces remain subject to the omnipotence of the desire for a single one.

In other words, if the psyche is forced to recognise that the breast is an object separate from one's own body, and that therefore it is not an object whose possession is guaranteed, it can but refuse, with some justification, to see a separation that it would have no power to abolish as the effect of its own desire. Furthermore, if this were the case it would have to conclude that a desire might be powerless, a conclusion that is unacceptable for the primary. The response to this double need to safeguard the postulate of the omnipotence of desire and to appropriate the first information about the separation of the psychical and bodily spaces, is the setting up of a representation of the Other, as agent and guarantor of the omnipotence of desire, and the representation of one's own bodily space as separated, as a consequence of this desire: the pleasure or unpleasure of which this 'space' may be the experience will be presented in turn as the effect of the desire of the Other for a reunification of the two separated spaces or, on the other hand, as the effect of its desire for rejection. What we have here is the infrastructure of the relational schema that will be found in any fantasy representation and, moreover, in any representation of the fantasiser himself. Before dealing with the structure of the fantasy I would like to elucidate the sense given here to the term 'thing-presentation' in the primary process.

I subsume under this term the raw material present in the representations made by the primary of the fantasiser and of the Other, in a phase that precedes the entry onto the stage of word-presentation. Whatever the 'thing' may be that the primary will metabolise in the image that it makes of it, there will always result a relation between the elements present in the fantasy, which will be a copy of the representation that the primary makes of the relation linking the erogenous parts and functions of one's own body and, at the same time, of the relation linking those same parts and functions to the body of the Other. It might be said that in this phase of the activity of the primary there is a coincidence between the image representing the space of the world, together with the elements that occupy it, and the image representing the space of the body, together with the parts that make *it* up. It is a coincidence that must not be confused with what I have called the specularisation proper to the primal: indeed, if the relation existing between the elements of the world is supposed to coincide with the relational schema on which the image of the body is constructed, then, on the other hand, what we might, metaphorically, call the image 'of the body of the world' is recognised as possessing the power of a desire opposed to that of the 'inhabitant' of the body image. But whatever 'thing' the primary represents to itself by the image, this image will also be that by which an erogenous part of the body is presented; whatever the relation linking the images one with another, it will also be a representation of the relation linking the erogenous parts of the body. As a result, in any act of fantasising, there will always be present, explicitly or as a background, the fantasy representation of one's own bodily space, perceived as a set of erogenous zones. The pleasure or unpleasure that they experience and which they have the power to offer or to impose will be supposed to depend on the presence or

41

absence of the body of another possessing the same power. If every fantasy is the fulfilment of a desire, one might add that any act of fantasy is aimed at obtaining an erogenous pleasure and that, by this fact, every fantasy refers us, in the final analysis, to the successive representations that the primary makes of what may be the cause of sexual pleasure.

1 Fantasy representation and the unconscious

According to my view, the pictogram is to fantasy what the primal is to the unconscious: fantasy and unconscious result from the combined work of the postulate that constitutes the primal and a first judgement, imposed by the reality principle, on the presence of an external and separate space. This first participation of the reality principle in the work of the psyche is responsible for the heterogeneity between pictographic production and fantasy production. The 'primal scene', which is the kernel of any fantasy organisation and evidence of what I call the pictographic engram, may be situated between these two entities and these two modes of activity as a sort of borderline production.

The primary constructs the primal scene by borrowing a scenario from the primal and reshaping it in such a way that, between the experience of the subject observing the scene and what appears in it, a first relation of cause to effect may be inscribed in it. The recognition of the mother's body as an autonomous entity will induce the psyche to admit the existence, on the external stage, of a couple that is no longer represented as the equivalent of a complementary object. There is a separation of the elements that the pictogram presented as inextricable. The link between the mother and this third party, present in the space most familiar to the infant, is no longer one of fusion but an act that may come to unite what is by nature separate, or reject any possible unification. The infant perceives this 'act' as a manifestation of love or hate. But because for him, in this phase, any love is represented by a joining with one body part and all hate by its rejection, there exists, preceding any possible understanding of coitus, either the model of a body part penetrating another body and becoming one with it or the model of a body rejecting a part whose destruction it wishes. This is a model by which any response made by the infant to the questions of desire, of its own origin, of the present relation between its body space and the space of the Other is now acted out 'naturally'. It is this model that I call the pictographic engram, by which I mean that the borrowing made by the primal from the somatic model of taking-into-self and rejecting-outside-self will provide the primal with raw material that it will metabolise in order to make it capable of representing the relation between it and the mother's body, between the father and the mother, between him and the parental couple. These successive representations will always send back to him the image of a penetration that is proof of a possible desired reunification, or that of an object violently expelled from a body that rejects it. This double model therefore is a prefiguration of the sexual act conceived either as an act of desire and love or as an act of rejection. As an act of love it enables the cathexis of two supports, whose encounter testifies to the existence of a 'loving' world that is united and unifying: the subject contemplates in this 'outside' the 'before' that gave him origin. One can understand the risk represented for the psychical structuring by the impossibility of representing this scene to oneself as an act of love and being able to represent it only as the fulfilment of a desire for mutual rejection. We shall see what results this can have in psychosis.

If a single scene represents at one and the same time the origin of the subject, desire and pleasure, it is because being presented as the cause of love or hate, but in either case as *cause* of the affect experienced, it places the fantasiser in the position of someone to whom one offers a pleasure of seeing, hearing, being, or of someone who is rejected by the seen, the heard, the existing – a rejection that will make it impossible for him to experience anything during the contemplation of the scene of pleasure. The first perception of a 'separate' world requires the recognition that affects exist that scour the external world, that the affect of the world is not always identical with the affect of the fantasy, but the representation of this world presupposes the metabolisation of a model that, again, leans on a bodily model. This metabolisation will nevertheless give to the fantasy a status that does not conform to the postulate of the primal.

2 The postulate of the primary and the economic principle that results from it

The postulate of the primary has two essential consequences:

- to give a scenic interpretation of a world in which any event and any being find their cause in the intention projected on to the desire of the Other;
- to make of displeasure, the experience of which is inevitable, that which proves the fulfilment of the Other's desire: unpleasure, which may, henceforth, become a source of pleasure, since when experiencing it one is assured of following the Other's desire. This interpretation projected on to the Other's desire lies at the origin of primary masochism. Whatever price the psyche may pay for this interpretation, it is this interpretation that allows the psyche to metabolise a wish for self-destruction, which can culminate only in the annihilation of the fantasiser, in a wish for unpleasure that demands, in order to be fulfilled, that the fantasiser may spare himself in order to experience it.

By scenic interpretation, we must now understand the representation of the breast's supposed intention. Once the existence of this primordial object is recognised, its presence or absence will no longer be able to be conceived as the effect of chance, a concept radically alien to the psyche, and which is always either pure theoretical concept or a secondary rationalisation. Presence and absence will be interpreted, by and in the fantasy, as a consequence of the breast's intention, before the intention of the mother's desire, to offer pleasure or to impose unpleasure, is substituted for it. This interpretation, like everything pertaining to the primary, whatever its degree of elaboration, demands that the subject experiencing it may find its cause in the intentionality of a desire posited at first as the Other's desire with regard to the subject. The aim that corresponds to the psyche's desire will always and solely remain the state of pleasure: it is a desire for pleasure. If the pleasure is lacking it cannot be for the psyche anything other than the effect of a desire, and the psyche cannot imagine this desire as anything other than that of an Other whose object would be its unpleasure. The image of the fantasiser and of the world specifying the primary will mean that what is represented is always a relation between these two desires or, rather, between the two complementary positions of any desire: everything that testifies to the existence of the outside-self will be interpreted as a manifestation of the Other's desire, the experience of the fantasiser as an effect of the response that this desire expects or imposes.

The organisation of the fantasy construction is such that the fantasiser is unaware that he is the presenter of this scene, that its *constructum* is the result of a projection onto the Other of a desire that concerns him. This misconstruction, which is also the recognition of the existence of the representative of the Other, is responsible for a specific characteristic constitutive of fantasy organisation: the demand, for the fantasiser, to posit in the scenario that he contemplates *two* objects and, outside the scene, a third represented by the *observer* contemplating it. If all fantasising is always at one and the same time representation of the relation between the space of one's own body and the space of the body of the representative of the Other, we understand why, in the scenario, two objects must be the metonymic representatives of those two spaces. The need to posit outside the scene an observer who is supposed to experience pleasure, or unpleasure, is the consequence of the postulate according to which the primary functions, a postulate that requires that the relation of cause to effect must always be posited between the experience of pleasure, or unpleasure, and the omnipotence of the Other's desire. By affirming that the activation of the primary entails a recognition of the presence of a breast separate from one's own body, I have left in the shade that which immediately follows: the recognition of a 'breast's-elsewhere', cathected by the first representative of the Other on the stage of the real, an elsewhere by which are prefigured to the psyche the existence of the father and the acknowledgement of the parental couple. Before this 'elsewhere' is occupied by the attributes that prove the paternal presence, it is that by which the psyche presents to itself the existence of an enigmatic object or locus that would allow the Other to fulfil a wish that no longer appeals to the subject observing the scene. There will now be set up the threefold infrastructure of all fantasy organisation: an observer experiencing an affect of pleasure or unpleasure whose cause is imputed to the relation set up between the representative of the Other and that elsewhere.[1] This infrastructure will make possible the phenomena of return, substitution, change of aim, that define the instinctual game. One might add that the form of fantasised relation between the two objects of the scene that the observer contemplates will depend on the prevalence that this or that part-drive will assume and will be revealed by the form that the action linking the two objects will take. But as long as one remains in the unconscious fantasy, the image of the object will always be the presentation of a bodily thing; that is to say, an erogenous part of a body.

I shall return to my analysis of the fantasy representation conceived as representation of the relation of the fantasiser to desire and to pleasure when I deal with psychosis.

Before seeing what is entailed for the activity of the primary by the appearance on the scene of word-presentation, I shall show how, from the first phase of its activity, the primary sets in place the prototypes of the secondary, without which the psyche could not have access to what will become the third representation of its relation to the world. These prototypes concern reality, the I, castration and the Oedipus complex.

3 The prototypes of the secondary

By the reality of the Other must be understood, in the first instance, the reality of the difference between the mother's and infant's desire.[2] This is the first obstacle encountered by the pleasure principle and an obstacle much more difficult to overcome than any other will be. That this desire of the Other concerns him is an observation that the primary cannot abandon: although the psyche manages to erogenise even the state of need, although it can transform the 'nothing' into what the anorexic feeds on, it could not, on the other hand, exist in a world in which desire and nothing coincided. To have access to the primal, every phenomenon must be representable by a pictogram; for this to take place a function-zone, the seat of perception, must be erogenisable. At this point one notes that it is as a source of pleasure that the object may have access to psychical space. The field of the primary obeys the same law: the turning of experience into fantasy must be accompanied by its cathexis; fantasy is never indulged in gratuitously. By this activity one seeks the representation of a state of pleasure the first experience of which was at the source, except that the fantasy reshaped a fragment of the world recognised as belonging to the *external world*, but made to conform to the purposes of desire. The primary activity sets out from the observation that there are fragments of the world that are knowable because they are occupied by cathected objects, but in order for these objects, like the space that they occupy, to be cathected, the cause of their existence and order must be illustrated in terms of desire. The existence of the desire of the Other is for the psyche what the concept of God is for theology: a nodal point and postulate on the basis of which the entire system may be set up; whether it belongs to fantasy or to metaphysics is unimportant. The certainty of the existence and power of that desire is a logical necessity for fantasy activity, the only way by which it can posit the existence of an Other and, later, of others and, in doing so, of the existence of a reality. On this basis may be elaborated a reciprocity between two desires enabling the psyche to recognise itself in turn as a source of desiring activity and no longer as a passive effect of response. From now on, and this is the other side of the realisation of the difference of the desire of the Other, the psyche will be confronted by those categories on which the human order is founded, namely, prohibition, guilt, envy, the desire for mastery. The dialectic-isation of desire demands that the desire of the one – to transgress, to possess, to destroy, to make reparation – encounters as ally or enemy another desire, and not a 'psychical reality' that as such can have no psychical status *in any of the three processes*. If the baby's bottle were not offered or refused by a hand, there would probably never be such a thing as anorexia – or the possibility of being human.

The identifying prototype

The term 'identification' applied to the primary process seems to me to be a source of confusion; it ought to be used only in the register of the I, the agency constituted by language and the system of interpreting the world that it imposes. If we are to say, with Freud, that incorporation is its prototype, then we should add that this prototype has the same kinship with the I as the one that may exist between two classes of vertebrae. Although one finds a similar neurophysiological structure, the differences proper to each of them will lead to quite different modes of being and existence. The primary comprises all the prototypes on which the function of language leans to operate that work of metabolisation that will make them conform to the laws of the secondary process and to those of 'making sense' under the aegis of discourse.

As the precursor of the I, the identifying prototype denotes the represen-tation of the fantasiser in so far as it results from the reflection of the activity of the primary on itself, a reflection to the source of what I call *the subject of the unconscious*. It is around that reflexive position that all the representations present in this field will gravitate. The subject of the unconscious is that self-presentation in and by which the fantasiser recognises himself as response and effect of the interpretation that the primary activity makes of the desire of the Other. This amounts to saying that the precursor and representative of the I, in this phase of psychical activity, is constituted as an image of the response given to the desire projected on to the mother; it is *the representation of a relation*. It is not therefore with an object or an attribute of intentionality that the subject of the unconscious identifies, but with a response; that is why it always refers back to the representation of the *relation* and, in the first instance, to the fantasised relation between the mother's desire and the child's pleasure. The representation of this relation entails the psychical action that is defined by the term 'introjection' – an introjection that presupposes, on the part of the psyche, the perception on the external stage of the presence of a 'sign' interpreted as proof of the presence of the Other and as a manifestation of its desire to give or to refuse pleasure. This interpretation is at once *projection* onto a fragment of the external of a desiring Other and acknowledgement of receipt or *introjection* onto the psychical stage of a manifestation concerning the desire imputed to one and to which one responds. It is the relation between these two desires that is projected–introjected, for if the subject of the unconscious rises up in the very place where the trace of the response is written, it is still from that same place that its response to the response will leave for the Other.

This first symmetrical dialecticisation that the psyche makes of the 'pleasure of the subject/desire of the Other' relation explains why any representation of desire involves the introjection of the response that the Other is supposed to give: a response by which its projection onto the Other of the relation between fantasiser and the occupants of external space returns to the psyche.

I shall illustrate these formulations, which may seem obscure, by an example. This will allow me to sketch out the projection–introjection mechanism on which any instinctual dialectic is based.

1   Let us imagine that a state of non-satisfaction is the result of a certain way of offering the breast, or again that this state, endopsychical in origin, cannot be appeased by the offer of the breast. The act of offering will then be perceived and interpreted as a 'sign' of the desire of the breast and therefore of the external space, of *not-offering-pleasure*. A *desire for non-pleasure* is projected on to the breast.

2   The unpleasure experienced will now be represented as the response induced by this desire for unpleasure on the part of the Other: the experience will be interpreted by the primary as an effect of the act of aggression that it fantasises to be the intention of the Other.

3   It is therefore as an aggressed object that the subject sees himself in the representation that he represents (what I have called the fantasiser's representation as response to the desire of the Other).

4   From that position, he will now experience for the aggressing object a similar desire for aggression (his response to the response).

5   But, in doing so, he will be able to fantasise as a response to his desire for aggression only his own experience; the aggression of the Other reflects back to him his own response to aggression, that is a new aggression.

6   As result, the scenario represented comprises *all the positions* that aggressor and aggressed may occupy in a dialectic governed by an aggressive impulse.

If we now imagine the opposite starting point − that is, the perception of a sign interpreted as an intention of offering pleasure − we will have the same consequences, which may be summed up as follows:

1 The act of offering will be interpreted as a sign of the breast's desire 'to give pleasure'.
2 The resulting pleasure will be represented as the cause of that desire: the affect experienced will be represented as the effect of the desire of the Other.
3 The fantasiser now contemplates in his presentation the effect of that desire-for-pleasure that turns him into him whose pleasure is desired.
4 From that place, he sees sent back to the Other a similar desire to be the source of his pleasure.
5 In doing so, what he represents as a response will be the resumption of his own response: to be a source of pleasure.

These considerations enable us to understand better who and what function are represented by the prototype of the I: not any unity, but a succession of *scenarios*, in which *are represented the relations* that the psyche experiences in its encounter with the objects that it cathects, relations by which it represents situations, the source of its pleasure or unpleasure, *to itself*. It is to the organisation of these relational representations that we owe the setting up in the secondary of the first model on which the Oedipal problematic in the strict sense will be structured. It should be added that even though, already in this phase of the activity of the primary, one encounters the precursor of the I, it will nevertheless be the appearance of word-presentation that will endow it with the attributes that will allow its successor to respond to the demands of the functioning of the secondary and to make its own this identifying project, which defines in a specific way the structure of the I.

The prototype of the Oedipus complex

I said that all fantasisation involves a scene with three elements: the observer of a scenario in which two objects are present. The looking–seen relations and the relation between the two objects of the scenario are complementary to one another. From the time the child posits the mother's desire as different from his own he will have to represent for this desire an object that is no longer exclusively himself. As long as he is able to believe that he is the exclusive object of maternal desire and as long as he remains certain that she desires him as sole object of her pleasure, she continues to desire exactly what he desires. He will have to abandon that identity as soon as he gleans the possibility of the mother's desire for an 'elsewhere' that dislodges him from his position as her exclusive object of pleasure. From now on the triangulation of the fantasy shows that a place is given to him in that 'elsewhere' occupied by an x denoting the enigmatic object of the mother's desire. However confusing this first realisation is for the child, it poses, before him, a scene in which the fantasised instinctual action between the two objects means that, whereas one of the objects will continue to be the representative of the desire imputed to the mother, the other object (the object *x*) will become the representative of a paternal attribute. By paternal attribute must be understood, in the first instance, any bodily object that may have a relation with the mother's erogenised body, an object that is no longer fantasised as an appendage of that same body, but as an object that comes from 'elsewhere', complementing that body, aggressing it, giving it something or taking away a piece of it.

To this scenic representation will be added its 'Oedipal' quality, which is played out, in fact, on the external stage, and which the infantile psyche is beginning to perceive. Near the mother there is usually that other subject, to whom she is linked by a privileged relation, whatever it may be, who is usually responsible for the breakdown in mother–child communication, who has something to say, and often to shout, about the tears by which the child conveys his refusal to remain alone, who may give him, though much less frequently, a *bodily pleasure*, caressing him, whispering in his ears a series of sounds whose tone transforms into the equivalent of a cradle song, which no longer comes solely from the mother's voice.

Thus the pleasure of the child's body learns to discover the *breastless other*, one who may nevertheless turn out to be a source of pleasure for all his erogenous function-zones, to become a presence that is desired, even if it is often an inconvenient presence.[3] The father's appearance on the psychical stage obeys the universal condition governing this access for any object: to be the source of an experience of pleasure that makes it an object of cathexis for the psyche. The object responsible for unpleasure always refers back to a first experience of pleasure that he has dispensed and which he later refuses or prohibits. But we must also take account of the relations that link these two occupiers of the external stage and, above all, of the consequences of their own repression of the Oedipus complex. It will now be noted that the precursor of the Oedipus complex in the primary is simply that which, from the parental Oedipus complex, gains access to that same activity. The mother's 'wish for a child' was, in the distant past, first of all 'a desire to have a child with her own mother' and, if everything takes place 'normally', her childhood will have been marked by a 'wish for a child by the father', then by a 'wish for a child' whose imaginary father, while no longer her own, remained nevertheless that future man who would possess his qualities and be his legal successor. As for the father, his 'wish for a child' is first formulated as 'giving a child to and receiving a child from his mother' before the term 'wife' has taken its place. The couple's child, therefore, is actually the successor of a 'child' the desire for which has its origin in the transmission of an 'always having been there' in the structuring configuration of Oedipal desire, a structure that testifies to the historicisation of desire in the human order. From the time when the primary activity sets up a system by which the child's psychical space can communicate with the mother's psychical space, the observer contemplates a scene in which any affective event bears the mark of the Oedipus complex: I should add that this mark will be manifested by *that which is to be kept in the repressed*. The behaviour of the mother and father is the consequence of that element of Oedipal desire that can no longer be expressed, must not be manifested and, by this fact, is *expressed and manifested* through those feelings called tenderness, attachment, search for the well-being of the child. It should be stressed that the lawful forms of love, like the prohibitions that the child encounters, are the direct consequences of the parental Oedipus complex; they represent what the parents allow themselves, in the register of feelings, in order to preserve its repression, while offering free expression to the narcissism, love or aggression towards the child that may and must find expression in a form permitted and valued by the culture. If the 'real' child is the historicised successor of 'the child' of a primal desire,[4] the feelings that one has for him, just as really, are the historical successors of the 'affects' as they were experienced in their time. The primary process, confronted by the work of others' secondary processes and, in the first instance, by their discourse, will undergo a series of modifications that ensure that the prototypes of the secondary take shape in its own space, whereas its aim requires that it resist the action of the secondary. Before this decisive turning point, in which word-presentation will erupt into the primary, one encounters a last prototype concerning castration.

The prototype of castration

The first form that will be assumed by what survives, in any subject, as that castration anxiety, whose shadow can never be entirely eradicated, at whatever psychical stage, will be a fear of mutilation. It will be the task of the secondary to arrange matters in such a way that this anxiety no longer features, except at special, but always possible, moments, as the fear of bodily mutilation, but is transformed into a fear of being deprived of some 'good' – the beloved, the fulfilment of the identifying project, the child, health, beauty, sexual pleasure – whose absence acts as an obstacle to pleasure. In other words, after the Oedipus complex, the fear may always arise that one may suddenly lose the object of pleasure, but this fear – like the renunciation of pleasure, which one may regard as preferable to encountering an expected trauma against which one would be defenceless – is no longer experienced as a deadly mutilation, or as a fragmentation of one's own body. It may be said that, by renouncing pleasure, the neurotic allows himself to live as a unified body; what he sacrifices is his sex as *instrument* and locus of pleasure, in order to preserve an unfragmented body image. He thus protects a unified form of the image of his body space, a *necessary condition* if he is to preserve, of his own psychical space, the image of a surface from which no fragment has been torn away and captured by another's psyche.

As long as one remains in the primary, the psyche pays a heavy price for its dependence on a representation that uses the images of the bodily thing to represent its relation to erogenous pleasure and to the desire of the Other. This price has the consequence that, as long as the affect experienced by the psyche can be represented only by the representation of images of erogenous zones, whether of the mother's body or one's own, and therefore by a relation that links representatives of bodily space, any event occurring in the world will be identified by the observer as an accident happening either to his own body or to that of the Other. Whether it is the mother's body or his own does not matter, since observing the aggression to the mother's body or, on the other hand, its plenitude, places the observer in the position of a mutilated or unified body, a consequence of the desire imputed to the actors of the scenario. On the subject of the primal, I have said that the representative can annihilate what is seen, a source of unpleasure, only by depriving himself of the function of the gaze and its organ. In the primary activity the psyche cannot act out or undergo any event without representing it as a cause of desire and, therefore, as an *action* aimed at the pleasure of his own body space.

The psyche, then, will be confronted by two types of experience:

1 Those that have an integrating effect on the different part-zones. Any experience of pleasure, in whichever object–zone the representation takes place, is such only thanks to the totalising irradiation of the pleasure experienced. Metaphorically one might say that the observer also *sees* a sound, a taste, a touch, a smell. There cannot be at the same time the pleasure of seeing and the unpleasure of taste or hearing: if there is pleasure, it cannot be accompanied by a lack of pleasure experienced as such in another zone. That is why each erogenous zone is *a metonymic representation of all the zones*, its activity a metonymy of the overall function of the body's ability-to-perceive and therefore *a metaphor of the power of the psyche*, which will represent the fantasiser and the world as two totalities that are ignorant of lack.

2 On the other hand, and for the same reasons, any experience of unpleasure will be fragmenting. In this instance, function–zone and object will represent what the observer encounters as rejecting–rejected. The 'seen' is transformed into the object of an 'activity of seeing', which is no longer proof of a power that the psyche recognises as its own, but proof of *the requirement-of-having-to-see* imposed by an observer that is not the psyche. The activity of observing persists, but is transformed into a function of the power of the Other; and the observer finds that he is like a blind man on to whom has been grafted an 'eye', whose functioning remains linked to the optical nerve of an alien brain and to what that brain decides to see or not to see.[5]

That is why unpleasure will involve the fantasy of being mutilated of the *autonomy* of a function of one's own body, a mutilation that affects what in the world might be a source of the pleasure of seeing. This mutilation *amputates* the subject's own psychical space of its power over a function that comes under the control of an 'alien body', proving to the psyche the Other's desire to expropriate and capture it.

Using the same term, 'mutilation', for what occurs in the primal and in the primary may lead to confusion. Now, there is an essential difference between these two phenomena: as long as one remains in the primal the psyche can reject the perceived – seen, heard, touched – only by mutilating itself of the function-zone that is the seat of perception.

In the functioning of the primary the rejection of the perceived is accompanied by the amputation, not of the function-zone, but of its *autonomy*. The activity of 'seeing' persists, but one is dispossessed of any form of choice that the observer might exercise on his activity. As long as the mode of functioning remains such, the prohibition affecting the object that is the source of pleasure will be accompanied by the prohibition of the activity associated with it: that is why what is *actually* being played out on the maternal stage will decide whether or not the tendency to integrate the body image will prevail over the tendency to mutilate. We should stress what is specific and dramatic in the fantasy activity as long as thing-presentation is the only possible representation. By this fact is excluded any access to protosymbolisation, which is necessary if we are to distinguish between the totality of a function and the *moment* when that function is in operation, between the activity of observing, or any other erogenous zone, as *a continuous activity*, and *a particular, actual experience*, and if we are to maintain the continuity of the cathexis as something more than a succession of separate fragments.

Although it is true that there already exists, at this stage, the first possibility of a connection and that one is right to postulate that one does not completely forget successive experiences, that the state of unpleasure retains a vague echo of the possibility of its opposite and, conversely, this primary 'memory' operates at a minimum. If it is capable, unlike the primal, of linking the scenic fragments, the successive pictures, its mode of functioning is reminiscent of a subject who sticks into an album the photographs that a camera takes successively of itself, a subject who would know that all the photographs were taken by the same camera, that they belong to it, but who would nevertheless be incapable of reading in this the story of his temporality or of foreseeing what he will become in the future.

The importance of mutilation as a prototype of castration confirms that the primary is certainly the creator of prototypes, which the secondary inherits and transforms without ever being assured that they may not regress to their earlier form.

As the mould of Oedipal configuration and precursor of the castration fantasy, the primary is already the establishment of a logic of desire that is concerned with the secondary activity of the mother's psyche and which forewarns the psyche of access to a type of representation that it will make its own. Thing-presentation is the prerequisite for word-presentation to be added to it: *the scenic primary follows the pictographic and prepares the way for the sayable* that will follow in its wake. It is the connecting link between a before, which the subject will never know and which will preserve its sameness and enclosedness, and an after, which will be constituted upon it and be separated from it by repressing that first material that was an essential part of its own flesh.

That is why the productions that one owes to the activity of the primary process consist of two very different groups:

1 The group that we have just analysed under the term of 'scenic primary', whose material is represented by thing-presentations, in the sense that I have given this term – that is, as linked to the body.
2 The group that I shall now examine, in which appears word-presentation, which, linking itself to thing-presentation, will give rise to those mixed productions that show that the primary will take on the task of making its postulate conform to what is 'naturally' alien to it: the system of meaning imposed by discourse. The characteristic of this second group is to be sayable and therefore conscious. It is these productions that will form part of the secondary repression; that is to say, of the repression outside the space of the conscious representations that were part of it.

The analysis of this second group forces me to abandon for ever the fiction that involves analysing the psyche and its productions without questioning step-by-step the role taken by the representative and by the discourse of those who respond to the infant's demand and who, on the other hand, demand that the child conform to an image of the child that occupied the cradle long before its body was placed in it. Word-presentation is not a creation out of nothing; it has its source in that first representative who possessed a 'speaking-milk-breast'. Similarly, the repressing action would remain an enigma if one did not find its source in the words of a representative of the Other, already marked by repression: the indefinite transmission from subject to subject of a 'having to repress' from which no speaking being, neurotic or psychotic, completely escapes.

II THE APPEARANCE OF WORD-PRESENTATION AND THE CHANGES THAT IT IMPOSES ON THE ACTIVITY OF THE PRIMARY

1 The system of primary meanings

The real difference between a *Ucs.* and a *Pcs.* idea (thought) consists in this: that the former is carried out on some material which remains unknown, whereas the latter (the *Pcs.*) is in addition brought into connection with word-presentations. This is the first attempt to indicate distinguishing marks for the two systems, the *Pcs.* and the *Ucs.*, other than their relation to consciousness. The question, 'How does a thing become conscious?' would thus be more advantageously stated: 'How does a thing become preconscious?' And the answer would be: 'Through becoming connected with the word-presentations corresponding to it.'

These word-presentations are residues of memories; they were at one time perceptions, and like all mnemic residues they can become conscious again. Before we concern ourselves further with their nature, it dawns upon us like a new discovery that only something which has once been a *Cs.* perception can become conscious, and that anything arising from within (apart from feelings) that seeks to become conscious must try to transform itself into external perceptions: this becomes possible by means of memory-traces.[6]

Does the psychical inscription of word-presentation require a movement to the secondary process or is its trace already to be found in the functioning of the primary process? To answer this we need to be agreed on how word-presentation functions. If the appropriation of word-presentation and access to the logic of discourse are seen to coincide, which presupposes a fairly complex form of language, then the appearance of word-presentation will have to coincide with the final development of the agency set up by the secondary process: the I. If, on the other hand, we accept the existence of a precocious phase, a transitional stage between the state of infant and that of child, a phase during which the joining of thing-presentation and word-presentation takes place, and a new type of information becomes necessary for psychical activity, while the postulate defining the logic of the fantasy still retains all its power, it might be said, and this is my opinion, that psychical productions, although already represented by a double inscription, may still be used to confirm this postulate.

The hypothesis that I am defending may be expressed in the following terms: for an idea to be represented the psyche must acquire the ability to join thing-presentation to word-presentation, which it owes to hearing, *once* hearing is able to become the perception of *meaning*: the voice of the Other is the emitting source of this meaning. The joining of these 'things heard' to thing-presentation sets up a system of primary meanings that is different from the system proper to the secondary meanings by virtue of the fact that in the first the representation of its relation to the world, based on this system of meaning, remains organised in such a way as to demonstrate the omnipotence of the Other's desire. This demonstration alone may make the fantasiser certain of the truth of his representation, whereas in the second system the truth test becomes a requirement that only cultural discourse, which, in the next chapter, I shall define as the discourse of the group, can provide.

In his *The Philosophy of Symbolic Forms*, to which I shall return when defining the symbolic function, Ernst Cassirer describes how man encounters language as a totality that possesses in itself its own essence, its own relations independent of any individual, arbitrary contribution. This is no doubt the case, but it applies only to a subject capable of using the totality of the linguistic system to reflect upon language. Cassirer also describes the infant's first encounters with language as a series of sound fragments, attributes of a breast that he endows with the power of speech. The first acquisition of meaning that one owes to these fragments is under the absolute and arbitrary aegis of the infant's psychical economy. The temporal gap separating these two stages coincides with the time necessary for the psyche to pass from primary meaning to an ideational activity, the work of the I, which takes account of the secondary meanings and of the interpretative system that they organise.

I must now return to the role played by borrowings made by the primal from the sensory organisations and to the role that I attribute to the erogenous function-zones: this is necessary if we are to understand which is the first form assumed by hearing in the primal itself. The pictogram testifies to the presence of an ability to hear: the vital activity demonstrates from the outset the power of excitation possessed by the auditory zone. Pure meaningless sounds will be a source of pleasure or unpleasure, but only depending on the time of their appearance, which may coincide with a state of pleasure or unpleasure and, on condition, of course, that their intensity does not exceed the threshold beyond which excitation becomes a source of pain.

As long as we remain within the primal the auditory zone obeys the same mode of psychical functioning as any other erogenous zone. If, as I have proposed, there is a need for sensory information whose psychical counterpart is the wish to rediscover the pleasure associated with the excitation of the corresponding zones, we must accept the presence of a pleasure of hearing that at this stage has no connection with the meaningfulness of the noises emitted by the milieu and is connected only to the sensory quality of the audible. This hypothesis ought to have led me to examine the experiences of sensory disconnection in hearing. But, as we have seen, the presence on the psychical stage of the activity of the primal alone can only last an extremely short time, a matter of a moment rather than of a phase.

As soon as the activity of the primary begins, noise, and I would be tempted to add any noise, becomes synonymous for this process with an element that informs it of the presence or absence of the first object that the primary recognises as conforming to the expectation of the auditory function-zone: the mother's voice as the sound attribute of the breast, the voice whose presence will become for the fantasiser a sign of the mother's desire, which the auditory zone experiences as pleasure, unless it is absent.

We shall see the consequences that may result from the presence of a voice that is too often the source of unpleasure. We should stress the first function that the primary will contribute to the totality of acoustic perceptions: metabolising them into a sound sequence that testifies to the presence or absence of the breast-object and of the desire for pleasure, or unpleasure, that this breast, the metonymic representative of the mother, would experience *vis-à-vis* the fantasiser. If the breast is the metonymic representative of the mother and therefore of all objects that give pleasure, any part-pleasure is in turn a metonymic representative of the subject's pleasure *qua* object of the mother's desire. Whether the mother's desire expects the pleasure of this or that erogenous zone signifies to and for the fantasiser that what she desires is his overall pleasure. That is why I said that the presence or absence of the breast will be conceived by the primary as an intention on the part of the object to offer or refuse *pleasure*. It should be added that in this phase the presence of a breast, as a source of unpleasure, and the absence of the breast, as a source of pleasure, probably cannot be distinguished. The corollary of this will be that the presence of a voice as source of unpleasure or the absence of any voice, that is to say, silence, also being experienced as unpleasure, will also not be distinguishable. One of the secondary consequences of this will be to make all silence the equivalent of destructive speech and by this very fact intolerable.[7]

The primary and first meaning of a desire for unpleasure imputed to the breast, *qua* metonymic representative of the world, assimilates this world to an empty space because it refuses to be cathected by the subject, a refusal that finds expression in the disappearance from the scene of the only support that is capable of drawing the libido towards it: the object of pleasure.

The intention projected onto the breast of forbidding the possibility of the state of pleasure is equivalent to the projection onto this breast-world, the all-encompassing occupant of external space, of a refusal of pleasure for the psyche, for it a refusal of pleasure equivalent to a refusal concerning its very existence. In this case the psyche encounters the refusal of the world, it finds itself confronted by a retreat of the living being into its totality. We can understand the dramatic intensity of an experience whose echo is to be found in that end-of-the-world feeling so often found in the beginnings of psychosis. On the other hand, the presence of a breast-world as source of pleasure is signified by the encounter with a 'plenitude', which by the same token concerns all the sensory zones, including the one being examined here: the auditory zone. It would be illusory to wish to set up a hierarchy of value or temporal precedence between seeing and hearing. Although it is true that the primary has thing-presentation as its first raw material, it should be added that the fantasy representation that results from it is a representation of a state of the psyche that accompanies any erogenous sensory excitation. It is because the ear begins by 'seeing' the heard that thing-presentation and word-presentation will be able to be welded together, with the result that the subject will be able to *see* only as long as he can 'think' of himself as seer.[8] If the register of the heard and the voice merits particular attention, it is because of the preponderant place that they assume in the organisation of the semantic system that constitutes the I. What will become the proper of this agency will be whatever is seen, perceived, experienced; it will find expression in a feeling, the necessary condition for this agency for perception to exist, a feeling whose tonality will depend, not on the objectivity of the perceived, but on the meaning projected onto, and interpreted as, the cause of its appearance or disappearance. To remember that language is first of all received as a sound sequence must not make us forget that, for the voice that speaks, this succession is at once message, expression, imputation of a feeling and a desire, and that the possessor of that voice *forgets* that for the infant the effects that will result from it are of a quite different order. The representative of the Other acts in a way that conforms to what he says, the work of the secondary, thus effecting the anticipation that projects onto the child a before-the-event hearing of which it is the indispensable condition.

On the side of the voice, there is from the outset the emission of highly significant messages, expressions that transform the response to need into a response to the mother's feelings, on which in turn she models her response; on the side of the listener, there is the perception of sound elements, which the primary process will metabolise into signs informing him of the breast's desire for him. These primary signs are the nucleus on which language as a system of meaning will be elaborated and organised. This organisation will require a series of modifications by which the voice-object will be transferred from its first status as the breast's sound attribute to its final status, in which the voice will be asked to account for its right to be heard and to submit to the truth test what is heard and said. This slow process, which goes from the perception of a sound to the appropriation of the semantic field, may be divided into three phases, each endowing the heard and the act of speaking with specific functions that will conform to the aims proper to the three processes of psychic activity: the pleasure of hearing, the desire to hear, the demand for meaning, which is the aim of the I's demand.

2 The pleasure of hearing

Proper to the functioning of the primal, this pleasure, which the primary will modify by linking it to the desire 'to hear' the presence of the breast and the Other, is the necessary condition for the cathexis by this process of the activity of hearing. This desire to hear is in turn the indispensable antecedent for the appearance of the desire to hear (and understand) what the voice is saying: that desire to hear implies the activity of the primary–secondary. As long as one regards the primal process, every sound is presented, in and by the pictogram, as the product of a 'sound eardrum-breast' representing, in the register of the auditory function, the two undissociated entities of the complementary zone–object. Hence the same response to the heard as source of an affect of unpleasure: to extend the corresponding organ-zone for self-mutilation. In my opinion, this explains the origin of certain phenomena of psychical deafness encountered in infantile autism and catatonia: the last defence set up by the subject to the voice, in the hope of convincing it of its deafness and in the hope that it might thus, finally, fall silent.

On the phonetic sign, Humboldt writes:

> The phonetic sign represents the material of every process in the formation of language. Indeed, on the one hand, the sound is spoken and as such it is a sound produced and formed by us, but, on the other hand, when received, it becomes part of the sense-perceptible reality surrounding us.

This definition stresses the perennial nature of this double side of the phonetic sign, an object, more than any other, presenting itself to the subject as part of itself that will come back to it from the outside. This is confirmed by the experience, familiar to all of us, of being surprised when we find ourselves speaking in the absence of an interlocutor, an experience that is regarded, if only in jest, as the sign of a 'madness' that has a very special status, since we know, deep down, that no one escapes it. And yet, what is said when one is alone is disturbing, perhaps because it is proof of the split that divides our false unity and suddenly reveals a separation between speaker and listener, between the person giving advice, making a complaint, commenting on an action and the person to whom it is addressed. If we apply Humboldt's definition to this first stage, its truth appears evident: every sound emitted, whether coming from the infant himself or from the outside world, reaches his ear as a production that the world sends back to him, anticipated testimony of the pleasure or pain that will accompany his time on a stage where discourse is master. His own cry or his own babbling erupt once again in his auditory cavity as a sound of hate or love of which an indivisible eardrum-breast would seem to be the emitter. The pleasure of hearing is a first cathexis of language whose only condition is the audibility of the perceived, the cathexis of a single quality of the linguistic sign that ignores its essence. Nevertheless it remains the antecedent that is alone capable of making its way to a second form of perception of the heard, in which pure sound will be transformed into a sign, which will form the basis of the system of primary meanings organising the productions of the secondary process at the point when that process takes account of word-presentation.

3 From the desire to hear to the desire to understand

The appearance of the desire to understand, more than any other psychical phenomenon, demonstrates the radical modification entailed by the primary and the acquisition on which it rests. In the register that I was concerned with, this modification is expressed in its ability to transform the pleasure due to the pure excitation of the activity of a function–zone by the voice-object into a pleasure bound up with a sign proffered by the voice of the Other. This sign refers to the desire of the Other and, from this point on, is responsible for the legend of the scenario that the fantasy represents. This transformation of the cause of pleasure presupposes the acknowledgement of a breast as a separate object. As we have seen, this acknowledgement is necessary if the fantasy organisation is to set up the two poles of a desire–pleasure dialectic that the gaze, outside the scene, contemplates in joy or anxiety. This dialectic also presupposes the precedence given to what in the fantasy is presented as representation of a meaning projected on to the desire of the Other. It is this meaning that has the task of making the affect experienced conform to the logic of the presenter – and also making it of the same structure. These representations of a meaning concerning desire form what I call the register of primary meanings under which the logic of the fantasy functions. The presence of the voice will from this moment be cathected or rejected depending on what the primary makes it say of the Other's desire with regard to the fantasiser. If we take as a marker the presence of a sound emitted in the outside world and perceived by this process, I would say that the pleasure or unpleasure resulting from it depends on the function as sign attributed to it by the primary: what the primary sees and hears is a sign by which the Other communicates to it the intention of its own desire and the unpleasure, or pleasure, that will result from it for the fantasiser. The sign refers, then, in this register, to the cause that the fantasiser projects onto the reason for its appearance, its disappearance or its special nature: it refers to the meaning that the fantasiser imputes to the desire of the Other.

By primary meaning or system of primary meanings, I mean the activity by which the primary will organise word-presentations present in its representations in such a way that they demonstrate the irreducibility of the same postulate: 'The desire of the Other is the cause of what is represented and the cause of the affect that results from it for the observer contemplating the scene.' The system of primary meaning denotes the way in which the primary appropriates word-presentations and subjugates them to a connection that ensures that what they signify will never contradict the postulate on which its 'language' is based. In this 'language' unpleasure may continue to make sense because it is an object targeted by the desire of the Other. That the Other desires the subject's unpleasure poses no problem to the logic of the fantasy. The paradox that, by this fact, the primary succeeds in annulling is that it is unable to misconstrue the possibility of an experience of unpleasure undergone *and* to preserve the certainty that any experience has desire as its cause. I have already analysed the consequences of this solution proper to the primary.

If we come back to it on the subject of the voice, it is because the economic exploit that the primary succeeds in carrying out in transforming unpleasure into that which may be targeted by a desire will be paid for by the appearance of a persecuted–persecutor relation, in which the dialectic between the unpleasure of the one and the desire of the other finds its purest formulation. Clinical medicine shows that the voice-object, more often than others, may play the role of persecuting object: before resuming my analysis of this relation in the section devoted to psychosis, perhaps we should consider why the voice-object possesses this strange privilege.

4 Concerning the persecuting object

Clinical medicine confirms the frequency with which this object appears in sound form: voices, the compulsion to think and to hear that which is thought, the threat perceived in something heard form a set of pathological phenomena that mark psychosis and demonstrate their privileged relation with hearing.

Independently of the nosographical entity that may give it its peculiar form, the persecuted–persecutor relation is never absent from psychotic experience: this certainly shows that this relation retains a power of very intense reactivation. This power of reactivation raises the question as to whether the privileged role that may be held by the voice as persecuting object does not derive from the facility with which, in this case, the mother's response – that is to say, the reality of the 'heard' silence – confirmed the representation that the fantasiser set up of the mother's desire to deprive him of any object of pleasure. This confirmation is substituted for the work of modification that this response ought to have carried out. The mother's silence – whatever reasons motivate it – is an experience that every child has in a repetitive way, an experience that will be fantasised as the mother's refusal to offer the sound object that is a source of pleasure; moreover, this experience is very often something that the mother does not think that she has to justify, that she may impose without knowing that she is imposing it. But if the experience of silence may have such a pathogenic effect in certain cases, it is first of all because of the particular characteristics of the voice-object. The action of these characteristics will be more readily understood if one bears in mind that the specific feature of the persecuting object is indeed to forbid any flight on the part of the persecuted, to require its constant presence, to desire it because it is the sole object capable of realising the desire for persecution that is imputed to it.

Now, if one considers the auditory function, what one notes is the absence in this register of any system of closure comparable to the closing of eyelids or lips, or to the tactile retreat that muscular movement allows. The auditory cavity cannot remove itself from the irruption of sound waves; it is an open orifice in which, in a state of waking, the outside continuously penetrates. Without under-estimating the function that must be given to the work of interpretation in delusion, this particular character of sound waves and their receptacle explains why the first thing heard may so often be the moment at which delusion is triggered off. But this description of the characteristics of hearing and its object would certainly not be enough to explain why the voice-object may so easily become the embodiment of the persecuting object. A much more important factor is responsible for this: I have said that the mother's voice, perceived as a manifestation of the desire imputed to her, will decide which affect may accompany a perception. It only needs a threatening intention to be projected onto that voice for a part-pleasure to be transformed into its opposite. The pleasure of seeing cannot be accompanied by a threatening tone present in or projected onto the voice. Now, the peculiarity of this voice is to be able to erupt while one is experiencing the pleasure of seeing, touching, swallowing: to erupt and to reinforce the pleasure or, on the other hand, make it impossible. The child will now listen out for that sound object, which will assume a higher position in the hierarchy of part-pleasures. The absence of the Other's voice entails a threat to the realisation of any experience of pleasure, which cannot be experienced when accompanied by a state of fear.

As a result any expectation of part-pleasure will also be accompanied by an expectation of the object of pleasure in the auditory zone, the expectation of a voice whose presence ensures that there need be no fear that it will erupt in a form that will forbid the pleasure present in another zone and transform it into unpleasure. It is for these reasons that the voice may become that object whose presence cannot be lacking, the object of a pleasure that must accompany the others, be added to them and perhaps, too, the first part-object of which it may be said that it is expected, on account, not of the pleasure that it offers an erogenous zone but because of its power over *all* the pleasures, a power that will allow it to assume a special place among the part-objects and whose effects will be noted when the subject will have to cathect, not the voice, but the words that it emits as the first rudiments of a knowledge of language, which is necessary in the quest of any knowledge.

Psychosis shows us in what conditions such properties of the voice as 'object-from-which-one-cannot-flee' and 'object-that-one-cannot-lack' may be reactivated; the persecuting object is also that object for which the complement (the persecuted) is a constantly necessary presence, an object that has the power to forbid it any retreat, an object that may erupt unpredictably at any moment. One is reminded of Schreber speaking of God's rays. So the persecuted–persecuting problematic, which can be elaborated only after the recognition of an outside-self in which the Other moves, means that the persecuting action will be expressed in the subject as the prohibition to separate himself from that outside-self, to put a distance between him and the other.

That is why the primal ignores the persecutor, which can only be a construction of the primary.

'Love the bad object' – that is the misunderstood conclusion imposed by the persecuted.[9] This sketch of the relation that the subject will be able to have with the persecuting object was intended to throw light on the relation that the primary activity may have with the voice-object. This, too, is an object that the subject cannot lack as soon as it is given the function of making itself a sign of the intention projected first onto the breast, then onto the mother in her function as representative. That this sign may be the source of an affect of unpleasure is in accordance with the logic of the primary, but the fact that what appears in the outside-the-psyche may not be a sign of a desire cannot be expressed in the language of the primary; the consequence of this will be that everything in that space that cannot be shaped in such a way as to confirm its postulate remains non-existent for him.

5 Signs and the language of the primary

This series of signs informing the primary of the intention of the Other's desire forms the primary system of meanings that gives sense to the constructions that we owe to it. From the primary will open up a way that will be specifically and essentially that of language: that of giving and creating meaning. To the primordial breast perceived as containing all the objects that are a source of erogenous excitation, will be added a final attribute that, added to its predecessors, places them in a relation of equivalence: this last attribute is its power to make meaning, to engender signs that the psyche receives as the message of a desire that, from then on, will decide on the affect of the response given to the excitation whatever it may be. Hearing will be able to be a source of pleasure only if it becomes the hearing of a message of the Other's love: hearing precedes understanding, but the desire to understand the sign decides from then on the effect of what is heard. At the source of the cathexis of language we find a desire to rediscover the presence of a sign concerning the Other's desire – a cathexis that foreshadows that of the linguistic sign, a primary language that has very precise characteristics.

If by primary signifier I understand, in a rather abusive way, the successions of sounds heard that do not yet form sentences, I would say that the proper of these primary signifiers is to connote always and exclusively only two 'signifieds':

- The first embraces an equivalent set of the perceiver's representations: they designate him as the object desired, as the one whose experience of pleasure is the aim of the Other's desire.
- The second embraces the opposite set: the representations by which the experience of unpleasure is presented as the aim of the Other's desire.

This implies a first, if ambiguous, difference between the voice as libidinal object and the meaning of what it says, which may connote two contradictory signifieds. A first fragment of the semantic field gains access to the psyche thanks to those primary meanings to which the analyst owes his own discovery of the meaning to be found in any fantasy. If the I can perceive the intelligibility of the image of a dream, a fantasy, a daydream, even if it is to criticise it for being sense-less, it is because it may discover in it the work of a reason that, while not its own, nevertheless obeys a certain logic. The I may disavow this logic, declaring it to

62

be the effect of a foreign body (the symptom), or misconstrue it; in any case, it knows that, in doing so, it is defending itself against the disturbing strangeness provoked by any phenomenon that is both too close to the human being and too different from the knowledge that it has of him: being and knowledge refer here to the I itself.

That the primary is the creation of meaning is obvious to any analyst. It is more important to stress what will result from a language in which are present primary meanings that give rise to psychical productions that accord with the logic of a fantasy and, side by side with them, productions that take account of secondary meanings, which implies a knowledge on the part of the subject of what the linguistic sign signifies *for others*.

6 Signs and the discourse of others

In order for a gap to appear between the primary sign and the linguistic sign, the psyche must perceive that different signs, and not just two contradictory signs, are emitted by the same speaker. This ability of the same voice to be a source of different messages leads the psyche to appropriate a certain knowledge of the non-arbitrary meaning of what is said; as a result, the linguistic sign becomes the instrument that will be able to be used by a demand that, in addition to the expected object, seeks in the yes, the no, the perhaps, the reason for the answer given. It is no longer the object alone, or the yes or no alone, that satisfies the demand, but what is revealed to it through the meaning that it attributes to the answer. The objects demanded become the instruments by which is manifested a desire that one recognises to be one's own or that of the Other: oneself and the Other are no longer a metonymy of the objects demanded, but denote the agent who desires, demands, rejects, expects, refuses objects: the separation between the register of demand and the register of desire will find its final form only in and by the secondary, but already one can see it infiltrating the field of the primary. Two essential consequences follow from this:

1   The variety and substitution of the objects of demand which desire will make use of. This involves the possibility that the body's part-objects – the breast, the mouth, the look, listening – losing their privileged function as exclusive supports of desire, might nevertheless retain for the psyche their status as living beings, and more particularly, as far as one's own body is concerned, remain living beings whose activity may be preserved. Although it is true that there would simply be no life at all if in one way or another, for one agency or another, there were not present a pleasure in living that is expressed through the cathexis of the vital functions, from the moment when the activity of eating, or some other activity, is no longer exclusively the function necessary to the swallowing of a sign that is a cause of pleasure, there may be a gap between the mouth's feeding function and erogenous function – which will be expressed in touching with the

lips, in spoken words, or in some other action. This gap, it should be stressed, never allows a total de-erogenisation of the alimentary function, which may, in certain cases, rediscover the intensity of its first erogenisation. But it nevertheless makes it possible for the mouth to preserve its psychical existence as part of one's own body and for the search for a sign, or its refusal, to be one of a whole series of other activities and other support-objects of infantile demand. In this way, the subject protects himself from the risk of having to abandon any function of swallowing and places at his own disposal a series of substitute objects that enable him to protect certain pleasures that are essential to life by transferring onto other supports his demand for a pleasure whose possible absence no longer necessarily coincides with the need to refuse food.[10] Just as importantly, these substitute objects allow a more elaborate, more stratified organisation of the fantasy scenario. The fantasy organisation will lay down the markers that will allow the fantasiser to co-habit with different drives, to be no longer fixated on an exclusive representative, to pave the way for an initial mapping out of his successive experiences, a necessary embryo of the subject's accession to temporality, history and the problem of identification proper to the I.

2 In the register of listening, an equally fundamental differentiation will emerge. Although the primary sign referred to a succession of sounds that possessed only two meanings, there will be added to it, in a secondary capacity, the intuition that those signs are not equivalent for her who speaks them, that by her and for her they are linked to a meaning that depends on the type of words actually spoken. Preceding knowledge of the literal meaning of what is said, there thus appears knowledge concerning the possibility of multiple and non-identical statements. This moment of passage marks the movement from the primary sign to the linguistic sign; it also marks the border between a first form of psychical activity governed by the postulate of the primary and a form of activity that foreshadows the one that will follow. In the relation to language, this moment of passage is differentiated by the fact that the statement, as a message emitted by the speaker, may be recognised as different from the meaning given it by the primary sign, whereas one continues to ask the statement, independently of what is understood of its manifest content, to testify to the truth of the speaker's desire, to reveal the message of the non-said.

One may sum up as follows these two successive stages undergone by psychical activity in its access to language:

(a)   The first is itself the result of a series of previously accepted differences:
self/outside-self
mouth/breast
pleasure of the one/desire of the Other.

Whatever the manifest meaning of the succession of sounds may be, it is perceived either as a sign of the desire for the breast, and then of a desire for the Other to offer pleasure, or as a sign of her persecuting intention. There is therefore a perception of signifiers that refer to only two possible referents.

64

(b) In the second stage, it is recognised that the sign may mean different things for the speaker, and may signify them according to the particular material of the statement.

An initial understanding of what is said will result from this; but the fragments of perceived manifest meaning, or the whole of the sentence understood, give way to the question that the listener asks himself concerning the speaker's intentions. Before such questions as 'What is she saying?' or 'What does that mean?', there arise such questions as 'Why is she speaking?' or 'What does the offer or refusal of what she says mean?'

However, libidinal cathexis remains separate from the search for meaning, the first retaining its priority. Whatever the voice is saying, it will always be perceived as a desire for pleasure or as a persecuting intention; libidinal meaning wins over linguistic meaning, but nevertheless the first makes possible access to the second by leading the psyche to accept that this meaning exists, that it is part of the representative's inheritance and that it is not unconnected to the offer or refusal present in her response.

From the time when the psyche recognises the meanings that others give to what they say, psychical productions that merit the term that Freud gave to the fantasy will be set up.

These productions of 'mixed blood' are conscious thoughts that the child may express and does express and which, on one level, respect and take into account the literal meaning of what is heard and said and which, on a second level, show either that what is said succeeds in not being contradictory with the logic of the primary postulate or, on the contrary, that the child also puts his faith in another statement, of which he is also conscious, which confirms this postulate, a statement that for the observer is contradictory with the first. This is a contradiction that the child is unaware of, though for all that he does not repress either of the two statements.

It seems that, during one phase of his existence, the child is confronted by the need to acquire knowledge of language and therefore to know the meaning of the mother's discourse, even though he rejects those same meanings whenever they contradict an interpretation that continues to identify the cause of the world with the omnipotence of desire.

To this contradictory requirement, the child will, for a time, bring an original solution: he will split the meaning imputed to what is said in such a way as to be capable of a response that conforms to the meaning of the demand, while giving his apparently pragmatic response a meaning that he alone knows. This enables him to make his actual response conform to the pleasure principle, while not contradicting the reality principle first encountered as others' requirements.

We shall now see the child, who acts in a way that conforms to the parents' demands and orders, endowing his acts with a meaning that might be called magical and which is simply the result of thoughts that conform to the postulate of the primary. In this way, he will be able to accept that he is not allowed, for example, to play with his excrement, or that he is obliged to sit on the pot at certain fixed times: refusal to do so will be transformed into proof of the Other's desire to regulate his ability to excrete or, on the other hand, the pot will be transformed into a magical recipient that turns his faeces into gold. The contrary is equally true: the words that express the mother's love may perfectly well be heard and interpreted as having a meaning that testifies to a desire for capture.

Parallel with the manifest meanings that the child understands and uses, there unfolds another signifying chain of which he has knowledge and which redoubles the first discourse. The naming of the thing is split: to the name that discourse gives it is added a nickname that childish discourse gives it and makes its own; that is, an object endowed with a beneficent or maleficent power responsible for his affective response. We should stress the co-presence of that double naming: his nickname for the thing and its name for others do not cancel each other out, but split the object in a new way; the object may be either in turn or both at the same time. It is only in a second stage that the two names will become distanced from one another and be inscribed in separate spaces; before that, the split operates within the same, the same thing, the same space, the same consciousness. There will result from this another split, which concerns the speaker and activates a double discourse and a double action: a double discourse, since, when the child agrees to call the father and mother his parents and therefore has access to the meaning of these terms, he continues to call mother her to whom he says openly that he desires to become her husband; a double action since at the same time he may, for example, agree to drink water instead of milk, while declaring that this water has come from the mother's breast.

This double presence of a coexisting secondary and primary meaning during one phase of the child's life is a phenomenon that merits attention. It testifies to another duality: the pleasure principle and the reality principle, whose effects are felt in all psychical productions beyond the primal and show that the secondary certainly begins by cohabiting with the primary and negotiating with its logic.

The first aim of the secondary process may be defined as making the discourse through which reality speaks accord with the logic of the primary. It recognises the autonomous power of discourse, cannot deny that it carries meanings, but will attempt to interpret the whole system that those meanings constitute in accordance with a logic that contradicts that same system. The primary presupposes the recognition of an external world whose presence and separation cannot be eliminated; the secondary presupposes the recognition of a discourse that carries non-arbitrary meanings, informs it of the new logical postulate that it will have to take into account. In either case, psychical activity will first place this information at the service of the aim that preceded its appearance on the scene. The change of aim will be able to take place only when the new aim can ensure that it offers a better form of pleasure – another form, but the same result, guaranteeing a bonus of pleasure.

The primary process denotes the model according to which psychical activity will function when recognition of a first difference between two spaces and two desires becomes necessary: this is the first act of a reality judgement that concerns, at this stage, only the separation that may appear between two desiring supports, the one in which the fantasiser recognises himself and the one by which he represents the Other's desire.

This first perception of the possibility of a duality opens up access to a work of psychical activity whose fruitful moments coincide with the assumption of a series of differences that may, in order of appearance, be listed as follows:

- the difference between two psychical spaces;
- the difference between the two representatives of the parental couple;
- the desire–demand difference;
- the difference between the sexes,
- the difference between primary and secondary meaning.

On each occasion, the recognised difference entails that the psyche reorganises the locus on the basis of which it presents itself as agent of that recognition, which, as a consequence, entails the reorganisation of the representation that it makes of its relation to the world.

We may now illustrate the pleasure principle/reality principle duality, in terms of their relation to the concept of difference, by saying that the reality principle is partly linked to the category of difference, whereas the pleasure principle tends to ignore it. The first requires that any element may be differentiated, be situated in relation to the before and the after, the same and otherness, the unit and the whole. The pleasure principle, on the other hand, organises a field in which difference tends to be eliminated, the after to be presented as the return of the before, otherness as identity, the whole as an amplification of the unit. But what is more important in my opinion, if the recognition of an outside-self precedes, as I have claimed, the activation of the secondary, it follows that pleasure principle and reality principle are present in the primary from the outset. The secondary will have the task of placing the reality principle at the service of a pleasure that the agency constituted by this principle – the I – will experience whenever its construction conforms to a postulate that is differentiated from that on which the logic of the fantasy is based. That which is experienced imposes on the primary a recognition of the elsewhere; that is why I said that it is already involved in a reality judgement; the action of the pleasure principle will be to reshape that elsewhere in order to make it conform to the representation of the world set up by the primary, which will allow it to ignore what made its activation necessary.

The fantasisation that we owe to the primary operates on the basis of a disavowal, but the *raison d'être* of the disavowal is the existence of a fleeting avowal, preceding something known, seen, heard, that is reshaped. At the very foundation of the primary process we encounter the work of the two fundamental mechanisms of psychical functioning: disavowal and splitting. Disavowal of the irreducible autonomy of the outside-self, a splitting between what experience foreshadows and reveals and what representation disavows and conceals from itself.

These two mechanisms, at work as soon as the primary process begins to function, do not weaken, but, on the contrary, confirm the cross-breeding imposed by the consideration of word-presentation.

That is why, from its appearance on the scene, one should speak of a *primary–secondary* process, by which I mean all ideational representations, or thoughts, that are sayable and conscious, even though they may still be subjected to a logic in which precedence is given to the postulate of the primary.

Between primary and secondary, we must postulate the possibility of a compromise signed, at an initial stage, by an agency capable of hearing a meaning that conforms to the logic of discourse and of responding to a meaning that conforms to the postulate that gives all power to desire; it might be thought that this is an 'infantile disorder' of the I, from which it will recover. And it is true that it will be the task of this same I not to prevent the representation of this 'meaning' operating, which is not within its power, but to succeed in repressing this representation when it endangers the coherence of its project. It is true nevertheless that, when the one lends an ear to what the I says, once childhood is over, one realises that this danger continues to pay tribute to a representation of the world that remains the object of a nostalgia that from time to time makes one dream of appropriating it again, of managing to make it conform to one's project and once again . . . subject it to the same failure.

Word-presentation and the cross-breeding that it imposes on those productions of the primary for which I have proposed the term 'primary–secondary', leads me to speak of the I, whose functions and structure I shall now analyse.

What has been said about this stage in psychical activity, during which we witness a temporary cohabitation of the two representations of the subject–world relation, which, in a secondary stage, will have to be separated, explains why this necessary separation is never absolute. Not only can the primary representation of the idea always break into the space of the I, but the I itself remains under the double power of the reality principle and the pleasure principle: the primary meanings, of which the I wishes to know nothing, do not depend on *their belonging to the register of the primary*,[11] but on the fact that they concern 'knowledge', an illusion or a wish from which would flow *for the I* a feeling of unpleasure, because they would entail a risk to its identificatory markers.

The peculiarity of the I will be its ability to *defer* anticipated pleasure and, equally, to avoid its own tension and attention by dreaming of the wished for satisfaction.

This ability to *day-dream* is necessary to the I's functioning, a requirement of its structure, moments of truce during which it suspends action, whether doing or thinking, in order to dream of the uselessness of action, to find room once again, if only for a time, for the illusion of an offer that would precede any demand, a fulfilment that would precede any desire. Even during the most cathected and rigorous theoretical activity, it is in the power of the theoretician, indeed perhaps necessary for him, to lift his eyes and imagine: the theorem demonstrated, the offer of a Nobel prize, a journey to Mars, the return of the beloved.

The essential action of repression, the work of the I, consists of allowing those moments of coexistence in the same agency of the two principles not to be merely 'enclave-moments': reserves of illusions by which the I rediscovers its sources and familiar precursors, plunges back into its own childhood, forgets its acceptance of a deferral that always implies a difference between the wished for and the obtained.

To say that already in the primary is opened up a way to the reality principle, which is present as soon as there is a recognition of an outside-self, confirms the precociousness of the role of prosthesis played by the mother's psyche and by her discourse, which anticipate the I, imposes on the psyche an interpretation of the world that does violence to it and therefore makes possible the reorganisation of a space in which the I may come into being.

This brings me to the end of my thoughts on the functioning of the primary process. My aim has been confined to pointing out the first movements in a game that is played out between the psyche and the elements that provide it with the discourse of the representative, a game that continues throughout life and does not even come to an end with the checkmate imposed on the discourse of the individual subject by death. From the beginning of that game, its successor will be confronted by the memory of a discourse that is preserved by others, a discourse that they impose on the newcomer in the form of a genealogical destiny already laid down by them. The subject will have his own contribution to make to this destiny, but that contribution, even if it expresses a categorical refusal to accept it, will still show that his history, even as constructed by the subject, remains linked to the response that he makes to that prehistory, which is only a resumption of the history of his predecessors.

Between the beginning and the end of the game, play will remain no less eventful and unpredictable: the thought-idea, the represented representation and the pictogram will coexist side by side. The experience correlative with that continuous encounter between the subject and the world is expressed just as continuously by these three productions. None of them ever abandons its tendency and hope to eliminate all competition, to obtain satisfaction that could be total only if it were alone present, and if it could silence the demands of the other processes and psychical agencies.

That is why thought, primary representation and the pictogram retain, more or less overtly, a conflictual relationship. What makes us give precedence to the idea-thought depends on the specific relation linking the activity of the secondary to knowledge and, too, on the paradox proper to that relation. Lacan is right when he declares that the speaking subject is above all the spoken subject, but, in my opinion, this statement throws light on only one side of the phenomenon. Indeed, to what do we owe the discovery of that condition of men and women to be spoken, if not to the speaking subject that succeeds in defining through language what language was partly intended to hide? When I proposed the term 'pictogram', what was I doing if not trying to make it thinkable and sayable by a hypothesis and a construction that are the work of the I? It seems to me that the source of confusion lies in the difficulty for the subject, even when a theoretician, to accept that what is in the power of his knowledge, and therefore in the power of discourse, is not necessarily accompanied by a power to alter, which the illusion of the I would like to transform into a power purely and simply of elimination.

To alter reality – psychical reality or the reality of the world – is rightly part of the I's project, providing it is remembered what alteration means.

Alteration does not destroy what went before. To alter a barn in order to turn it into a library, or a palace to turn it into an hotel, is not to destroy them: it is to respect the characteristics of barn or palace, but to change them in order to make them more inhabitable or more profitable. We have to understand, too, the need for an alteration that allows the world and one's own psychical space to become inhabitable for the I, whatever the limits that its work of alteration inevitably encounters. These alterations, which we owe to the work of the I's sense-making of the world are all the more essential in that this agency may distance itself from its precursors and the secondary activity may reduce the productions of the primary that gain access to its own.

But reduction does not mean elimination: one notes the persistence of the activity of the primary in the secondary and the impossibility for these two processes to avoid the effects of interaction. What will be altered is the ever-smaller place that the secondary will give to a representation of the world that conforms to a postulate different from its own, without ever being able to exclude it permanently.

4

The space where the I can come about

---

1 The organisation of the space where the I must come about

Every subject is born into a 'speaking space', which is why, before approaching the structure of the I, as an agency constituted by discourse, I shall analyse the conditions necessary for that space to offer the I a habitat suitable for its needs.

The infantile state is such that between this individual psyche and the 'psychical environment' a 'micro-environment' – the family or what takes its place – will serve as an intermediary link and, during an initial stage, be perceived and cathected by the child as a metonym for the all. This tiny fragment of the social field becomes for him the equivalent and reflection of a totality whose differential characteristics it will discover only in the course of a series of successive elaborations. Hence the need to define the parameters proper to this micro-environment, the organisation of the libidinal forces that flow through its field and, more specifically, the action, for and on the infant's psyche, of those two essential organisers of family space, the parental couple's discourse and desire.

The analysis of this psychical milieu privileged by the infant's psyche, and which will mark his destiny, will bear in turn on the following factors:

- the 'word-bearer'[1] and its repressive action, the effect and aim of the anticipation proper to the mother's discourse;
- the ambiguity of the relation between the mother and the child's 'knowledge-and-power-to-think';
- the duplication of the violence imposed by what I have called, paraphrasing Schreber, 'the fundamental language' – in other words, that series of 'performative' statements that will name that which is experienced, and which, by that fact alone, will transform affect into feeling;
- what comes from the couple's discourse returns to the child's psychical stage to form the first rudiments of the I; these are the external 'objects' already

71

cathected by the libido, which, *after the event*, give birth to the I by denoting it as that which covets them, possesses them, rejects them, desires them;
- the desire of the father (to have a child, for the child).

2 The 'word-bearer'

This term defines the function given to the mother's discourse in the structuring of the psyche: 'word-bearer' in the literal sense of the term, since it is to her voice that the child owes, from his coming into the world, being borne up by a discourse that in turn comments, predicts, celebrates all his manifestations, but it is a 'word-bearer', too, in the sense of delegate, representative of an external order that communicates its laws and demands to the infant. I have said enough about the voice-object and of the function that the voice owes to its libidinal load, to be able to question, here, the actual discourse of the mother, as bearer of meaning, and to come back to a formulation proposed and left in suspense: the role of prosthesis played by the mother's psyche. In the first stage of life, it is the mother's voice that makes communication possible between two psychical spaces. Of course, one may appeal to the pre-maturation proper to our species, but this merely confirms that there would be no life for the child if, from the outset, the two principles of mental functioning did not act upon the milieu in which he has to live, in order to make it conform to the psyche's needs. We owe it to psychoanalysis to have shown that the need for the presence of an Other is in no way reducible to the vital functions that it must carry out. To live clearly requires the satisfaction of a number of needs that the infant cannot fulfil himself: but, by that same token, a response is required to the 'needs' of the psyche without which the infant may perfectly well, despite the state of pre-maturation that is his, decide to reject life. Whether we are dealing with the primal or the primary, there is no pre-maturation in their principle of functioning. What is surprising is that their production should be complete from the outset: that infant, who will take years to appropriate and constitute the function proper to the secondary, shows in the register of pictographic representation and in that of fantasy representation the perfection and faultless elaboration of constructions that will be faithfully repeated later. But analytic experience proves that the functioning of these two processes requires the presence of raw material shaped by a third form of psychical activity, the secondary process, which acts upon it in a quite different space. The representability of the pictogram, the scenic aspects of representation have as raw materials objects shaped by the work of the mother's psyche. If one is right to declare that representative and presenter metabolise the objects of experience and encounter into products radically different from the 'reality' of the object, it should be added that, in order for those same objects to exert their power of representability, they still have to have been, in one way or another, marked by the activity of the mother's psyche, which endows them with *a libidinal index*, and therefore the status of a psychical object that conforms to what I call the psyche's 'needs'. We can say therefore that the object, which is offered as the only material conforming to the work of the primal and primary processes, must, paradoxically, have undergone a first metamorphosis, which it owes to the mother's secondary processes. This is a paradox, because the peculiarity of the primal and primary, in its first phase, will be to ignore, even to efface, the effect of that work in order to make the represented susceptible to the requirements of their respective postulates, whereas the imprint left by the mother on the object proves to be a necessary prerequisite for those two metabolisations. The contribution of Lacan's theory will be recognised here: indeed it might be said that the object is capable of being metabolised by the infant's psychical activity only if, and as such, the mother's discourse has endowed it with a meaning as evidenced by her naming of it. In this sense 'swallowed' with the object, Lacan was to see the primal introjection of a signifier as the inscription of a single line (*trait unaire*). And it is true that, at the same time, it is always a word or a signifier that the infant swallows. As far as the destiny of this incorporation is concerned, however, I would distance myself from Lacan: the primal ignores the signifier, though the signifier remains the necessary attribute if the object is to lend itself to the radical metabolisation that this process subjects it to. These considerations lead to the central question concerning the work of repression. Although it is true, as I suggest, that it is an object that has first resided in the region of the maternal psyche that the infant metabolises into a pure representation of his relation to the world, it follows that it is a fragment of the world, conforming to the interpretation that repression imposes on the work of the mother's psyche, that is reshaped so as to become homogeneous with the organisation of the primal and the primary. This implies that it is the representation of an object shaped by the work of repression that will be metabolised into a representation which repression has not yet taken hold of. It may be said, therefore, that the psyche takes-into-itself an object marked by the reality principle, that it metabolises it into an object shaped by the pleasure principle alone, but that in this operation emerge a difference (for example, that which separates hallucinated satisfaction from real satisfaction) and a remainder (that which induces the psyche to recognise the presence of an elsewhere-same), which will be inscribed in its space by a sign that testifies not to some physico-objective reality, but, however ambiguous and confused this testimony may be, to the interpretation of the world and its objects proper to the mother. What characterises the human being is to confront from the outset psychical activity with an elsewhere that will be revealed in the form imposed upon it by the discourse that speaks it, a discourse that provides proof of the action exerted by repression. The subject will have to find his place in a reality defined by statements that, as long as one remains outside psychosis, respect the barrier of repression and contribute to its consolidation. That is why, although it is true that the primal ignores the reality principle, although it is also true that the primary process tends to subject it to the aim of pleasure, it is equally true that they are objects *previously* shaped by this principle, which have access to the field of the psyche, and that this principle is by virtue of this fact operational from an extremely early phase of the primary. To say that, by hallucinating the breast, the psyche imposes on it a radical metamorphosis is obvious enough: to say that what the breast represents for the mother is metamorphosed is also true, but different. In this second case, the metamorphosis bears on a representation that is the work of the reality principle, a principle that, opposing its own resistance to the productions of the primary, will gain access to certain of its precursors. Fragmentary and disorganised as they may be, these precursors will nevertheless counterbalance the exclusive, autonomous omnipotence that the primary claims in vain.

The function of prosthesis performed by the mother's psyche makes it possible for there to be a reality, already shaped by her psychical activity and made, by means of it, representable, for the psyche to encounter: for the senselessness of a real that could have no status in the psyche, it substitutes a reality that is human because it is cathected by the maternal libido, a reality that may be reshaped by the primal and the primary only because of that earlier work. It is not the real that is reshaped by the primary or, *mutatis mutandis*, by psychosis, if by real one means that which is unknowable of a thing in itself, but reality as defined by discourse – that is to say, the reality of, and for, the discourse of the Other, which is the only reality capable of lending itself to the work of the psyche, whatever its directing principle may be.

What we are faced with, then, in the infant–mother encounter is a very special dynamic:

- The mother offers psychical raw material that is structuring only because it is already shaped by her own psyche, which implies, by rights, that it offers a material that respects the demands of repression.
- The infant receives this psychical 'food' and reconstructs it as it was in its archaic form for her who had earlier received it from the Other.

One notes the usual oscillation in the offer of an already-repressed transformed into a not-yet-repressed, but which may, in turn, become once again what repression makes it only because it rediscovers, in doing so, a form that has already been its.

The prosthesis effect is manifested, in the infant's psychical space, by the eruption of a material marked by the reality principle, and therefore by discourse, which for me amounts to the same thing, which, very quickly, imposes upon the subject, who does not yet have the power to appropriate this principle, an intuition of its existence. The infant's psyche will reshape this material, while being unable to prevent remainders that elude his control breaking into his own space, remainders that form the necessary precursors for the activity of the secondary. These are rejects of the reality principle, evidence of the presence, the otherness and the discourse of the representative of the Other, which,

74

retroactively, will constitute an agency and mark out its *topos* in the psyche. But this material, which we owe to the mother's discourse, can obviously not be regarded simply and solely as the effect of the secondary, free of all traces of its own past. It is the action of these traces that we shall now analyse, their effect on that demander of objects that is the infant and, by doing so, consider what the word 'mother' signifies for the woman who takes on that function.

3 The violence of anticipation (the spoken shadow)

I shall come back to my concept of primary violence, as practised by discourse, which anticipates any possible understanding, a violence that is necessary however to give the subject access to the human order. Preceding by a long way the birth of the subject, a discourse concerning him antedates him: a sort of spoken shadow, presupposed by the speaking mother, as soon as the infant is there, it will be projected onto his body and take the place of him to whom the discourse of the 'word-bearer' is addressed.

I shall consider in turn the relations existing between:

- the 'word-bearer' and the infant's body, as object of the mother's knowledge;
- the 'word-bearer' and the repressing action.

Analysis will enable us to elucidate the identificatory problematic, which has as its pivot the transmission from subject to subject of a repressed, which is necessary to the structural requirements of the I. The deviations that this process may undergo explain what separates psychosis from non-psychosis and demonstrate the function carried out by a third reference, of which it may be said that it refers to the father, but only if and in so far as he considers himself, and is considered, to be *the first representative of the others*; that is to say, the guarantor of the existence of a cultural order that constitutes discourse and society, an order of which he must not claim to be the omnipotent legislator, but an order to which he subjects himself *qua* subject.

The mother's discourse begins by addressing a speaking-shadow projected onto the infant's body; she asks this cared for, pampered, fed body to confirm its identity with the shadow; a reply is awaited from *her* and it is rarely unforthcoming, since it has been preformulated for her. I hope that I am not being over-optimistic if I say that the word 'mother' will refer here to a subject that I am assuming possesses the following characteristics:

- a successful repression of her own infantile sexuality;
- a feeling of love for the child;
- her agreement with most of what the cultural discourse of her milieu says about the maternal function;

- the presence beside her of the child's father, for whom she has rather positive feelings.

This profile refers to the mother's conscious or manifest behaviour: as we shall see, it is possible to trace a generalisable profile of the unconscious motivations of the woman that we call a 'normal' mother. By this term I mean a mother whose behaviour and unconscious motivations include no elements that might have a specific, determining action in the child's possible psychotic evolution. Indeed it seems to me to be impossible to say anything at all about the pathogenic role that the mother–child relation may play, if one does not reflect beforehand on the experience of that relation outside the field of pathology, if one does not go as far as possible in the analysis of the maternal function, as it ought to be practised, whatever mechanisms of projection the child may impose upon it. Without this previous analysis, one falls into a misunderstanding, very frequent in psycho-analytic discourse, and especially so in child analysis. It is a tautology to recall that any particularly cathected object is at one and the same time that whose possible loss gives concrete expression to the subject's feelings of anxiety, that which, without knowing it, one will not forgive for making one run that risk and, there-fore, that whose death one may unconsciously wish in order to punish it, or to punish oneself, for the excessive love that it arouses. An analysis of the mother's unconscious desire for the child will *always* reveal the participation of a death wish and guilt feelings, the inevitable ambivalence that this object arouses, which occupies on that stage the place of a lost object; a return that is accompanied by that of the affects experienced for that first object whose place it now occupies. To make of this universal fact the cause of the child's psychosis, illness or death is not only nonsense, but an option whose consequences, if present in the analyst's interpretation, may be very harmful. If one does this, one links any event that has really occurred – illness, death, psychosis – to a cause that has nothing specific but its generality. On the other hand, there does actually exist such a thing as a pathogenic family milieu: but how can one know anything about it, if one does not refer to a structure and a milieu that we suppose is not pathogenic, how can we fail to see that the generalisation denies what it wishes to affirm?

That is why my analysis of the maternal role and its effects leaves to one side for the moment what, in this role, results from an obstacle encountered by the maternal psyche, the result of a fault in her own psychical structure.

The presence of what I have called the spoken shadow is a constant in maternal behaviour. It is a shadow cast on the infant's body by the mother's own discourse; it becomes the speaking shadow of a soliloquy for two voices spoken by the mother. The first anchorage, which may, in dramatic circumstances, become the first breaking point, between this shadow and the body, is represented by sex. No doubt the mother will be able to speak in the feminine to the shadow of a body endowed with a penis and conversely, but, in that case, she is not unaware that there is a contradiction between the sex of the shadow and the sex of the body; this may reveal to her the contradiction between the shadow and the body in their totality. This split in the child, operated by the mother, is proved to my satisfaction by the ambiguity of her cathexis of her own body: never will the body-object be so close, so dependent, so much the object of her care, her worries, her interest, whereas it remains merely a support of the shadow that imposes itself as the beloved or the 'to be loved'. The equivalent of the shadow cast by maternal discourse is always to be found again on the horizon of the loved object, but they are separated by a difference fraught with consequences: in the love relation, as it is supposed to be established between subjects, although the shadow represents the persistence of the idealisation that the I projects onto the object, what it would like it to be or to become, it does not eliminate that which, beginning with the object, may be imposed as a contradiction. That is why, between the object and the shadow, the possibility of difference persists. The recognition of this possibility is at the source of what is experienced by the I as doubt, pain, aggression and, conversely, as pleasure, joy, certainty, in moments when it is assured of the concordance between shadow and object.

On the other hand, in the first stage of life, the human being who has not yet acquired the use of speech cannot oppose what is projected onto his person with statements of own identity, which allows the shadow to be maintained for a time protected from any manifest contradiction on the part of the infant's support. But the possibility of contradiction persists and it is the body that may manifest it: first, sex, I have said, then everything in the body that may appear as lack, as a minus: lack of sleep, of growth, of movement, of the ability to speak and, for a relatively short time, lack of 'knowing how to think'. Any fault in its functioning and in the model that the mother privileges runs the risk of being received as a questioning, a rejection, of his conformity with the shadow; and, in extreme cases, there emerges the unacceptable rejection, death, which would deprive the shadow of its physical support. The bodily functions are seen, by this fact, to be given by the mother a value as message, a verdict on what is true or false in the discourse by which she speaks to the infant, their autonomy always running the risk of being felt as the negation of the truth of a discourse, which claims to be justified by the maternal knowledge of the child's body, of its needs and expectations.

This knowledge concerning the body merits some attention. It is found again, together with the work of the maternal defences against the return of her own repressed, in the induction in the infant of the narcissistic cathexis of his functional activities, in the dependence—autonomy conflict that is latent, even if misunderstood, in the very first stage of this relation. It is also the privileged instrument of primary violence and demonstrates what makes it a necessity: the possibility for the category of need to see itself from the outset translated, by the voice that responds to it, into the register of libidinal demand and thus to enter the area of a dialectic of desire.

4 The effect of repression and its transmission

It is the discourse of and for the shadow that allows the mother to ignore the sexual component inherent in her love for her child; it is this discourse therefore that sees to it that what must remain in the repressed does not return. Hence the functional attribute attached to everything in bodily contact that participates in a pleasure whose cause must remain unknown: one rocks a baby because that makes him go to sleep, and sleep is good; one washes a baby because it is hygienic and because the law prescribes it; one feeds a baby according to an established model of good health, etc. Fortunately, this does not prevent the presence of fault lines: the kiss given is surplus to requirements or the infant's sex may be touched with pleasure. Nevertheless everything that in the maternal discourse speaks the language of libido and love is devoted to the shadow. One is tender or severe, one rewards or punishes, according to what one supposes the shadow is expressing through its body; one even goes further, since one imputes to the shadow a desire, unknown to it, concerning its future, which, of the whole educational programme, is that which makes for 'its' good, this good being supposed to conform to what will be the child's future desire. What I call the shadow is constituted therefore by a series of statements that testify to the *mother's wishes* for the child; they culminate in an identificatory image that anticipates what will be said by that body's voice, which for the moment is absent. That shadow, that fragment of her own discourse, represents for the mother's I what the child's body, on another stage, represents for her unconscious desire. It is, therefore, that aspect of the impossible, forbidden object of that desire that has been able to be transformed into the sayable and the lawful. That is why one discovers it at work in the service of the repressing agency. That fragment of discourse is what constructs and cathects the mother's I, in order that the libido should not run the risk of turning away from the actual child in order to return to that of another time and another place. The shadow protects the mother from the return of a wish that has been perfectly conscious in its time, but later repressed: to have a child by her father; but behind it, and preceding it, is encountered an earlier desire whose return would have more serious consequences: to have a child by her mother. The shadow is that which the I has been able to re-elaborate, reinterpret on the basis of the second repressed wish, thus ensuring the foreclosure of the first: it bears its mark and proves to be a re-elaboration of it. The mother begins by addressing that discourse, created by herself, which reassures her I that her cathexes are well founded and not forbidden; the child is he who on the stage of the real testifies to the victory of the I over the repressed, but he is also, and this is the paradox of the situation, he who remains closest to the object of an unconscious desire, whose return would make the child the object of an appropriation forbidden to the I. The whole of the discourse of the shadow may be placed under the heading of *wishes*: to be, to have, to become are wished by the infant; clearly this wish represents what one has had to renounce, what one has lost or what one had forgotten to wish. It is the dream of a narcissistic recovery, but a lawful dream, perhaps that bit of dream that is allowed to lighten up the everyday greyness. It is lawful to wish that one's son should become a great scientist, that one's daughter should marry a prince, even more lawful in that this future retains the privileges of a certain possible without being, for all that, perceived as the possible of madness. It is also lawful that the analyst should read into the wish the reactivation of a narcissistic hope and that he should see, in the brilliance with which the object is endowed, the light whose giver hopes to be illuminated by in return, the over-estimation of the object giving value to its possessor, hence the function as phallic object that our discourse often attributes to the child. But to speak of a penis–child equivalence seems to me to be ambiguous. If one wishes to invest with phallic brilliance any object coveted by a woman and to say of any object coveted by a man that what he demands of the object is the phallic attribute with which he will be able to endow his penis, the term loses any meaning and will tell us nothing about the privileged relation linking the parental couple, and more particularly the mother, to the child, who has come to represent a very special stake in the couple's relationship. On the other hand, if one wishes to isolate the child-object as support of a privileged cathexis, we must admit that it is at one and the same time that which on the stage of the real comes back, at a minimum distance from the object of unconscious desire, and that which, in relation to that same object, is endowed with the maximum repressing force. In so far as it is expressed in the statements of the discourse by which the maternal I makes sense of her identificatory, libidinal relation to her child, the wish comes to occupy, on the stage of the secondary process, a place that, thanks to that wish, is defended against the eruption of unconscious desire and is opposed to its return. That is why the infant, the support of that wish, plays the role of a repressing agency towards the mother's unconscious desire or, rather, becomes a support in the service of her defences. It is the child himself who becomes the rampart that protects the mother from the return of her own repressed, hence the paradoxical and dangerous position held by the child: whereas he occupies the place nearest the unconscious object of desire, it is he who is asked to form an obstacle to its return. The illusion of the future fulfilment of the wish is offered to the mother as a counterpart to the impossible fulfilment of the unconscious desire. The shadow becomes illusion, allowing her to believe that, between the satisfaction of the I's wish and the satisfaction of the unconscious desire, there is an equivalence, an illusion that draws libidinal energy into its field and uses it in the interests of the I's projects, thanks to which the repressed is ignored and left outside the I. The Oedipal wish returns in an inverted form: *that this child may in turn become father or mother, that he or she may wish to have a child.*

In this way one sees the Oedipal statement 'to have a child by one's father' transformed into a statement that is projected on to the child by the formula 'may he become the father or she the mother of a child'.

5 Conjugation and syntax of a desire

I shall leave to one side, for the moment, the role of 'word-bearer' in order to throw some light on an aspect of the dialectic-problematic proper to repression, by which I understand secondary repression. The analysis of the positions that will be taken up in turn by the proposition 'wish for a child', in a syntactical sequence that coincides, point by point, with the development of the proto-identificatory and identificatory positions of the presenter and sense-maker, will show how the dialectic of being and having is elaborated and how the passage from a legend written by the primary to the statements made by the secondary is organised.

I shall take as my starting point, not the primal, but the statement by which the aim at work in the representation of the primary may be translated: to be the object of the mother's desire (of the Other's desire). Taking into account only the maternal problematic, this statement shows the following series of transformations in the course of psychical development:

to be the object of the mother's desire →
→ to have a child by the mother →
→ to take the object of the mother's desire →
→ to be the object desired by the father →
→ to have a child by the father →
→ to give a child to the father → (and from the time when one becomes a mother)
→ to wish that one's own child should become a father (or mother) (so that *a similar 'wish for a child' will be fulfilled in him or her*).

- Three terms of kinship are circulating here: child, father, mother.
- Four verbs are represented in two pairs: to be, to take; to have, to give.

The syntactic analysis of these formulations shows the persistence of the same direct complement of the verbs to have and to be (the child), whereas the indirect complement changes. This change is caused by *the conformity that syntax must preserve with the order of kinship of a given culture.* The subject who desires – to be, to have, to take, to give – will refer of course to the same; in the last statement however the desirer will project onto another a wish that he offers in his own name. The object 'a child' persists as the stake of a desire concerning being and having, taking and giving and, that same object, becomes the support of the wish that one expresses for the child that one has actually had.

The fulfilment of that wish is deferred to a future time: one wishes a child on the child who has just been born. One may wonder if the first function of this wish is not to prove that an earlier wish 'to have a child by the mother', which will become, at the passage to the Oedipal dialectic, 'to desire a child by the father', has remained unsatisfied and been transmitted to another agent. This appears more clearly if the formula 'one wishes to have a child' is transformed into '*one wishes a desire to have a child onto the child*'. The real child is assured of his difference from some mythical 'a child' – the one that the mother could not give and the one that the father refused – but inherits from the outset a wish that is also supposed to concern the child. But which child? I shall now show that this child, introduced by the anticipation of the maternal discourse, condenses in himself his successive representatives and, by that fact, subsumes the latest form that he has to take and the primary, even primal, forms that were those of his past.

The wish places the real child in a position that displays a double analogy: the woman who utters the wish imputes to him her own wish for a child, but, at the same time, she wishes a child on him to whom one cannot give it and by whom it is forbidden to expect it. Thus, in the register of the forbidden, the child occupies a similar position to the one occupied by the first receivers of the mother's desire: her own father and mother.

The repetition of that prohibition – which remains implicit and unknown – separates him onto whom 'one wishes' from those from whom one 'might expect' the gift of the wished-for child. The wish is expressed by a subject who has undergone the impact of repression; it is addressed to a body whose erogenous power one does not recognise, but which that body possesses, in fact, for both partners, and also to a body that cannot, in reality, give or have a child. This impossibility helps to misconstrue the past that the wish exorcises, in order to become compatible with the aim that the I defends in its present project (the maternal project). By the introduction of this wish is expressed a statement that organises, by its formulation alone, all the statements of the maternal discourse that express, 'according to the law', the mother's love for the child: *a similar wish transmits to the child the sameness of the prohibition.*

The wish introduces 'a child' as object of desire, but, in doing so, the mother assures herself and declares that the existing child, her child, is not the fulfilment of the past wish. In wishing a child upon him she separates him from the child that she had wished; she gives, and at first gives herself, proof of the non-transgression of incest. Similarly, by naming him in anticipation, what will become the object of her desire – to have a child – only at a later time, she designates herself as the one who will refuse to give it and to whom it will be forbidden to ask it.[2] In this way the child inherits a wish that proves that he is not himself the fulfilment of the one that was hoped for. This wish dethrones him from the title of Oedipal object, even before he discovers his own wish in this regard; the mother's wish pre-announces that it is forbidden to occupy a place that must remain vacant on the stage of the real. Before being a desirer of a child, he encounters the prohibition of occupying the place of a first desired object, which would identify him with a first 'mythical child-object' whose appearance on the stage of the real is recognised to be impossible. Through the voice of the spoken shadow the mother states to herself and to the child the prohibitions that she has first projected onto him; and by this fact she signifies to him a prohibition that anticipates his own desire. A relation of functional reciprocity is thus established, infant and mother becoming each for the other an agent in the service of repression. This will be confirmed by the temporal evolution of the statements expressing the series of prohibitions: it is not usually forbidden for the baby to see the mother naked, but it will become so at the stage when the child might discover that it gives them both pleasure to discover it, to say it, to say it to one another, with the risk that the child's voice might become that which reveals the permanence of a repressed desire. The maternal prohibitions cover therefore exactly the same field as his own repressed and induce the other's repressed as repetition of the first. The wish that expresses desire *and* prohibition defines an object accessible to cathexis by the I and defends its surface against an intrusion from another stage, an intrusion that might reverse to his advantage the direction of the vector borrowed by the libido and placed at the service of the I's aims.

Thus is constituted what, by repeating prohibitions, repeats the wish and repeats the history of the psychical species: the shadow, heir of the mother's Oedipal history and of its repression, induces the child's repressed by anticipation; thanks to that shadow the infant 'speaks' to the mother as if the repression had already taken place. That first stage shows the transmission of a repressing agency preceding what will have to be repressed, just as the prohibition precedes the statement by which the child will express his desire to have a child by the mother. Thus is transmitted from subject to subject a repetition of the prohibition, which is necessary to preserve the heterogeneity of the two stages present and to constitute the barrier that will reorganise the child's psychical space.

The effects of this transmission take the form of syntactical changes that show how the same initial statement is taken up and reshaped in a final stage, which gives the linguistic structure its definitive form: learn its tenses and conjugations, such is the injunction that the encounter with the Other's discourse imposes on the psyche, as soon as it is able to appropriate its first rough and ready knowledge of the meanings carried by that discourse.

My analysis of this fundamental wish that 'a wish for a child' represents has been focused so far on the formulations given it by the primary and the secondary. We can go back further and reveal its precursor in the primal. To do so we must alter the formula and write it as: '*One desires a state of pleasure.*' That state, expected by desire, is the infant's representative for the infant's psyche: what is desired is the fulfilment of a state of pleasure, the return of a '*living being*' (*étant*), the source and locus of pleasure.

If one accepts, as I have suggested in the case of the complementary object, that, during an initial stage, it is impossible to separate agent and object of pleasure in the complementary object–zone binomial, since each entity is inextricably linked to its complement, it must also be accepted that it is not yet possible, at that stage, to differentiate between these two statements:

'to be the desired of her desire'
'to have the object that desire covets'.

It follows that a single formula – 'let me be the object of her desire' – will express what one wishes to be and what one wishes to have. The first object of which the having is desired concerns a state of pleasure (that is, what the infant desires to be): in becoming the possessor of that object, one is assured of being what one desires to be, of rediscovering what one was when in the state of pleasure. This may be expressed by: '*let me be able to have what I was*'; if the desire to be is aimed at making oneself the desired of the desire and if what the having wishes is to be the possessor of that desired, it is understandable that the having should begin by envisaging oneself as the desired of her desire.

At this point discourse comes up against an unsayable '*having oneself*' (this is not a play on words, but proof that the pictogram cannot be expressed in words), which makes the child the object of an impossible coincidence of being and having.

In a primal stage, preceding the organisation of scenes, which one will owe to the primary, and which alone will allow desirer and desired object to be represented in different supports, the term 'a child', absent from the statement, implicitly supports the desire and refers to the representative itself. This representative is in the unsayable position that makes it the 'represented' of the having that he wishes to be. Being and having, in the register of the primal, confirm that relation of specularity that, for me, is characteristic of that stage.

The term 'a child', the non-said of a first desire to have, finds its origin in what cannot be formulated in a 'having oneself', which might alone allow the position of desired (by oneself and then by the mother) to go hand-in-hand with the certainty of omnipotence over desire; having and being share the same impossible wish. If, as Freud said, 'to have a child by the mother' is the first form of a desire to have a child, it is because that desire is itself the initial translation into the register of the primary of what concerned the primal. The 'a child' in question here remains very close to a self that one might reappropriate as a self-produced desired, which would prevent one ever being dispossessed of what one desires to have. Such formulas as 'let me want myself' and 'let me possess myself' are obviously very close to that which speaks of a desire desiring itself.

What will force the subject to go beyond the madness of such a demand is having to recognise that one cannot have what one is, but that one may, on the other hand, demand and have substitute objects, which will become the signs proving that one is for the mother what she would like to have: the object of her desire.

The first objects, supports of the fantasy representations carried out under the aegis of the primary, have the essential attribute of being able to assure demander and fantasiser that they are what the mother desires to have: a child whose pleasure would be what her desire wishes.

If we return to the mother's statement, it may be said that 'to wish a child to have' is a statement supported by a desire and that this desire certifies to the infant that he is not merely the result of a biological accident. One might add that the desire, of which the child is the unknown fulfilment, must persist, while preserving the gap between the 'desire to have a child' and 'the desire of and for *that* child'. Thus there emerges a gap between 'having a child', the aim of an irreducible desire, and the child who, once there, can no longer claim to remain the object of a fulfilled desire to have (a child). There appear the persistence of a desire 'to have a child' and the impossibility of being, precisely because one is that child, the child that one can have. The recognition of this gap on the part of the child presupposes the gap brought about by the mother herself concerning the child, a condition that allows the child to run the whole course leading to the desire to have 'a child' as object of the Oedipal wish: that the parent should give this child that one can have and that one was unable to be, but which one might have. This formula proves that the subject has had access to the register that separates being from having. But, as long as one remains at a stage prior to the dissolution of the Oedipus complex, this separation is not enough to differentiate between the child to whom one addresses demands and in whom one recognises a power concerning having and the child to whom one attributes a power of designation, concerning the identificatory place that his desire indicates. The child demanded of the father or the mother testifies, without any doubt, to a renunciation of an impossible 'having oneself', but shows that the child continues to hope to occupy in the kinship system the place reserved for the parent of the opposite sex. We shall see later how the child will be able to substitute, for the father and mother, another subject by whom he will have the right, in the future, to have a child and appropriate to himself a deferred wish.

I shall conclude by saying that the wish 'to have a child' inherits a past that makes the statement the formulation of human desire, but that this wish, as spoken by the mother and as she imputes it to the child is, paradoxically, that which allows the mother to present herself as a forbidden giver.[3] Clinical medicine shows what happens when that wish is absent, when the possibility of this future is not anticipated in the child. It is by this wish that the mother establishes the child as heir to a knowledge concerning the difference between the object that fulfils a desire and the object that allows the desire to persist – an object always projected into the future, into the mythical time of a definitive encounter between the desire and its aim. At the very moment when she refuses to let him be the object of her desire, she makes him the successor of the desire that persists and circulates and, by which will be imposed on the subject a conjugation of having and being that will allow the unsayable to become sayable and the statement that speaks the body and the speaking body not to find themselves in a position of absolute difference.

I shall end these considerations on the transmission of repression with a final remark: our theory has rightly put us on guard against any attempt at abusive generalisation, but the analyst believes nevertheless that an interpretation applic-able to a series of fundamental experiences that transcend any individual instance is well founded. This is the case with repression, the erogenous nature of the functions-zones, the 'myth' of the drives. But we can go further: in fact, the theory proposes a model of the normal evolution of the psyche that has, as reference, the similarity of the way to be followed by the subject, from birth to the dissolution of the Oedipus complex. Although it is true that, in the field of the conscious, of action, reflection, pleasure and, more generally, in the field of the I, there is nothing that allows us to see this or that choice, this or that discourse, as more important than another, although we must abandon a 'model' I and a 'model of the I', established once and for all, we do, on the other hand, possess and use a knowledge of what may appear in the I only as the sign of a flaw, because it is evidence of a forcible entry into its field of what should have remained outside its space.

In other words, analysis sees the repressing function as a transcultural invariable and assumes the right to see in what is to be repressed, because it must be excluded from the space of the I, a generalisable and specific characteristic *for a given culture*. It is perfectly clear that when I speak here of repression I am not referring to the primal, which, as I have constantly repeated, cannot have a place in the register of the conscious; by the same token, I hope that nobody will confuse repression, as a necessary factor in the structure of the I, with the facility with which others may bend it to their own purposes, impose an excess that the I will feel, rightly and without knowing it, to be an abusive power whose consequences will cost it dear.

These reflections on repression will help us to understand the risk of excess for which the 'word-bearer' may become responsible.

6 The violence of interpretation: the risk of excess

The preforming and inducing effect on what will have to be repressed is the essential consequence of the anticipatory action that constitutes the mother's discourse, and discourse in general. This anticipation offers the subject a gift, without which he could not become a subject: from the outset he transforms into meaning – love, desire, aggression, rejection – accessible to and shared by the whole, the unsayable and unthinkable proper to the primal. This metabolisation, carried out on the infant's experience, in the first instance by the mother, makes use of and, in her eyes, is justified by the knowledge that she claims to possess of the needs of that body and of that psyche. On one point she is not mistaken: it is certainly necessary to psychical structuring that this radical transformation should take place, a transformation that allows the response that the infant receives to foreshadow the naming and recognition of what will become his objects of demand. This demand will seek the object of need only because it may become a sign shaped and recognised by human desire: a successor that is legitimate therefore, even at the price of a radical difference from what at the outset the psyche demanded. In both cases, what is demanded concerns what the psyche expects and seeks in order for a state of pleasure to be rediscovered and for its desire to find its object in the Other's response. This violence operated by the mother's interpretation of all manifestations of the infant's experience is necessary therefore; it is the paradigmatic illustration of the definition that I have proposed of primary violence.

Its agent is certainly a different desire: that of the mother wishing that she could be that continuous offer, necessary to the infant's life and be recognised by him as the only image that dispenses love. It uses that which for the infant is in two respects a necessary object, that which cannot be lacking, if there is to be physical and psychical survival.

As a result, what the mother desires becomes what the infant's psyche demands and expects: the violence operated by a response that preforms for ever what will be demanded, as well as the mode and form that demand will now take, remains unknown to both parties. If we remained at this stage we could not fail to note an invariable dependent on the laws of psychical structure. But side by side with this there appears another factor that is just as important for the subject's destiny: the risk of excess. Of course, this risk is not always fulfilled, but it is a temptation that is always present in the mother's psyche. In the realisation of the violence operated by the mother's discourse there is inevitably infiltrated a desire that, in most cases, remains unknown and unavowed, and which may be expressed as: a desire to preserve the status quo of that first relation or, to put it another way, a desire to preserve something that, during one stage of existence (and only during one stage), is legitimate and necessary.

What is desired is that the present state should not change, but the mother's inability to abandon this desire for no change is in itself enough to change radically the meaning and extent of what was lawful, just as the specific formulation that it assumed (*'I don't want anything to change'*) makes it easier, for the mother and for others, to be unaware of the abuse of violence that will try to be imposed by that means. How many mothers, who have 'always sacrificed themselves for the good of her child', will be regarded by others as model mothers, whereas the development of the child will reveal, without being able to make itself heard, the abuse of power from which it suffers. The temptation of that abuse is constant, which is why it is so important to understand what the mother would not want to lose, even if she agrees that she must abandon it, and the danger that lies at the source of that temptation to excess.

What she would not want to lose is relatively easy to demonstrate in an analysis of even the surface of the phenomenon: a place that nobody else can give you, that of a subject giving life, possessing the objects of need and dispensing everything that is supposed to be for the other a source of pleasure, satisfaction, joy. I have said that, during an initial stage, it is in the good functioning of

86

the body's activities that the mother seeks, and finds, a response that confirms her right to claim this triple power for her function. But, very quickly, a new activity will appear that has also – it must not be forgotten – been expected for a long time and foreshadowed by the mother's discourse: *the activity of thinking*.

Health and intelligence, *mens sana in corpore sano*, become the last fruits expected of that cared for, fed, caressed, educated body, in the hope, it might be said, that it offers optimum support to the activity of thinking. Not that health and intelligence lose all their value: but they may preserve it only if, and as long as, the mother is assured that the child's 'capacity to think' corresponds, at the very least, to the norm and, if possible, goes beyond the norm. The first consequence will be that the power of intellection is expected as the last arrival that will confirm for the mother the success or failure of her maternal function. As a result, the part functions-objects, which have served as stake in the pregenital mother– child relation, will find their definitive status in the meaning that will be given to this latest arrival, which, after the event, decides on a retroactive meaning concerning them. The second consequence will be that the time preceding the manifestations of the thinking process is never experienced in a neutral way: not only will a number of varied signs be interpreted in advance by the mother as proof that her child thinks, but the first actual manifestations of this activity, the learning of the first few words, the pragmatism of the first answers, will be awaited as guarantee that they have avoided the major risk: that he, or she, would not be able to think.

If we went no further than this analysis, we could not fail to understand one of the privileged forms that may be assumed by maternal anxiety and the over-cathexis that knowing-how-to-think may enjoy. One essential fact would remain in the shade: the mother knows through her own experience that thought is pre-eminently an instrument of disguise, the hidden, the secret, the locus of a possibly undetectable (and undecidable) deceit.

One cannot hide the fact that one is refusing to eat or sleep; one cannot hide the fact that one has defecated; but one might be able to hide that one is pretending to love, to hear or, on the other hand, not to hear or not to desire the forbidden. Unlike the activities of the body, the activity of thinking is not only the latest function, whose value will take precedence over all its predecessors, but it is the first whose productions may remain unknown to the mother and also the activity by which the child may find out that she has lied to him, under-stand what she would not like him to know. So what we see being set up here is a strange struggle in which the mother will try to find out what the child is thinking, to teach him to think 'properly', as defined by her, whereas the child discovers the first tool of an autonomy or a refusal that does not directly put his survival at risk.

One cannot, at least without paying the price of one's life, refuse for long to eat, to excrete, to sleep: one may try to preserve a solitary, autonomous space in which one can think what she does not know or what she would not want one to think. It is worth remembering that, at the beginning of this analysis of the mother's role, I presumed that it was possible to define what would be normal behaviour, by which I meant behaviour that, if taken in isolation, would not encourage psychotic reactions in the child (which does not mean that the child would be protected from such reactions by this fact alone).

In this behaviour I stressed the constants that were most likely to induce a psychotic response, infantile or not, because they were the most susceptible, simply by stressing their function, to that which in the mother's, or others', desire, entails an excess of violence, which the child's psyche may not be able either to avoid or to overcome. One notes how slender is the gap, at this stage, between what is necessary and what is excessive, what is structuring and what is destructuring.

The analysis of the mother's relation to the child's activity of thinking brings out the special characteristics of this relation. It reveals what is aimed at in excess, whenever it appears and whatever form it takes. From the moment when excess takes place, which generally precedes the child's 'ability to think', this aim is always to succeed in making that activity of thinking, present or future, conform to a pre-established model imposed by the mother: this activity, in which secrecy must remain possible, will have to become an activity subjected to the mother's ability-to-know and only those thoughts that the mother's knowledge declares to be lawful[4] will have the right to reside there. In those cases, which are fortunately most of them, in which the mother has been guilty of no excess, one notes that the appearance of the activity of thinking arouses in the mother three constant responses:

1 This latest manifestation of a new activity that the child has acquired follows on from other bodily functions, which at the outset had been endowed by the mother with a meaning allowing them to pass from the functional to the libidinal register. That is why it may be said that the thinking zone and its object, thought, begin by occupying for both psyches a position similar to those proper to the other part object–zones.

2 This analogy is defective in one respect: a hierarchy is imposed and attributes to that latest function the ability to crystallise all the responses that the mother expected of the body, as evidence that she carried out her maternal function correctly and efficiently. By this fact, the child's thinking becomes the royal way indicating to the mother the response, whether refusal or acceptance, that the child gives to what she expects.

3 This activity is perceived by the mother as coextensive with a risk. Long before it assumes its canonical form, which will entail the acquisition and handling of language, it is expected and at the same time feared by the mother. What she expects is proof par excellence of the value of her function; what she fears is being for the first time confronted, before the child, with an undecidable:

'What does he really think?' It is a question that she rarely asks so explicitly, but one that undermines the terrain on which she accompanied and made possible his first steps. As soon as he thinks, she knows, while forgetting it, that transparency of communication has been lost, together with that power over need and the body's pleasure. The verdict of analysis is that such transparency and knowledge are purely illusory. The mother usually begins by believing in them; and it was necessary, partly at least, for the illusion to exist and for her to believe it.

These three responses are always present; it is enough for one of them to go beyond its legitimate duration or sin by excess, in relation to the other two, for one to pass from lawful, necessary desire to that *desire for no change* that will endow it with the power to dispossess the child of any autonomous right to be, by forbidding him the right to think autonomously.

Indeed these responses play their proper role only if they themselves respect the same *invariant* concerning their destiny: *to renounce having a place in the future development of the mother–child relationship*, to agree to encourage the variability of the relationship, to renounce a function, which had once been necessary to him, in favour of change and movement in the future relationship. This future will radically change what is at stake in a game that will require that other partners take part in it, that the stake circulates and that, if there is in the future a return to a privileged partner, it is no longer the one who held the role before, nor another who takes over a similarly exclusive role.

This invariant that ought to be respected by the future of the relationship may be rejected by either the child or the mother, or by both. A refusal on the part of the mother always has as its cause the tenacity with which one of the three responses refuses, or all three refuse, to accept change. The persistence of their presence gives rise to what might be called 'the invariant' of family structures most likely to see developing within them a way of life that may be seen as psychotic. It should be added that in this case the term 'invariant' is an abuse of language: one cannot, in effect, speak of an identical relationship. What *does not vary* is the mother's refusal to accept that her way of relating to the child must change, a refusal that her statements may be questioned or questionable, an inability to see in change anything other than the destruction of the present and of any future: this maternal demand will be echoed by the child's inability to coincide, or at least to reconcile, what the mother actually says (which may vary) and the referent that what she says claims to designate and find in reality, whether that reality refers to the reality of the world or to the child's psychical reality. In this particular type of family structure one always finds a contradiction between what is actually said by the mother and what she claims to be referring to, on the one hand, and, on the other, what the reality of family experience imposes on the child as recognition of an impossible truth – impossible because to recognise it would undermine everything that the mother says.

In the final part of this work I shall take up once again the analysis of the effects and causes of this contradiction.

7 The reduplication of violence: the basic language

As we have seen, the forces organising the external psychical space that the I will have to occupy make the family milieu a necessary locus of passage. Hence the importance given in my analysis to the twin pillars that support it: the parental couple and their discourse. But beyond its boundaries one encounters the action of a third factor to which the infant, the couple and others are equally subjected: the action brought about by the effect of discourse. Analysing the function of the mother's discourse and of her anticipation I gave precedence to that element of the mother's desire, of her prohibitions, in short, of her personal problematic that may be used by her voice. I drew a distinction between what might be termed necessary violence and that which results from excess, the effects of which, negative for the I, will be manifested in the psychopathology of the subject undergoing them. This structurally *necessary* action of primary violence will operate in two successive stages, a temporal rhythm that recalls the one proposed by Freud for the problematic of castration. As we know, Freud differentiates in that case between two factors and two moments: the moment when the mother threatens castration and designates the father or the father-substitute as the agent of its possible realisation and the moment when that threat becomes effective and operant for the child confronted by the sight of a different sex. Personally I believe, as far as castration is concerned, that this schema would be worth revising, though I feel sure that the 'heard–seen' relation plays an essential role in it. If I referred to it, it was because, in the register of primary violence, one is effectively confronted by an action in two stages, the second giving its final form to that initiated by the anticipation of a discourse that speaks of the infant well before the infant can speak. This reduplication will complete the work of discourse in the field with which we are concerned here: *to permit and induce the passage from affect to feeling.* This action, too, is a structural *requirement*, a counterpart to the linguistic prematuration specific to the human subject. The appropriation by the child of his first knowledge of language marks a decisive turning point in the subject's relation to the world; it reduplicates an earlier mouth–breast encounter, the desire of self/desire of the Other, by bringing face to face *the affective experience and the name that one will have to appropriate* if it is to conform to the fulfilment of the demand. From that moment demand becomes the fundamental anaclesis, even if it is illusory, to which desire must subject itself in its quest for the object. Anticipating what was in question, I showed what separates, from the child's side, the effect of signification from the effect of meaning, and the originality of the first response that he gives. We shall now analyse what I then left to one side: the action of discourse, this time *independently* of the shifts that the desire of those who speak it always operates on it.

To affirm that there exists an already-there of discourse, about whose origin we can say nothing, has as corollary the presence of *the limits defining the space within which the I will find its identificatory statements*. These limits, which contain all the identificatory positions that the I may occupy in a given culture, including the positions of the so-called psychotic subject, cannot be crossed. It is this uncrossable character that conditions the possibility of psychosis. That is why it forms part of the phenomena that define the human being: insanity is the extreme form of the only refusal accessible to the I. Enclosed in a place that, no more than any other, the I cannot transgress, there remains to him the power to refuse the order of relation that for others governs all statements; he cannot go outside space, but he can refuse to cross it according to a predetermined route, he can ignore the 'one-way' signs and choose to lose himself in ways that lead nowhere: no less, but no more.

The basic language (the limits imposed on identificatory statements)

For me, all discourse has a *de jure* identificatory function. Nevertheless, if we study its mode of action, two subsets stand out in that set of terms that play a fundamental role in the identificatory register:

- The first comprises the terms used to name the affect that, by that utterance, is transformed into feeling.
- The second comprises the terms that designate the elements of the kinship system for a given culture. Here, too, the utterance of a single term implicitly involves the total order of the system and designates the relational position linking the term named to all the other elements.

These two subsets form what I call the *basic language*, which Schreber describes as that archaic language spoken by the divine voice; the choice of this term is not only a homage paid to Schreber's intuition, but also a way of stressing that by which the essential power of language as identifying act is exercised.

In this part I shall be dealing only with the first subset, and for three reasons:

- In temporal terms, it seems to me to be the first.
- The essential consequence of its appropriation by the subject takes the form of a deferred action to which we owe the I's first identificatory markers.
- The analysis of the subset that refers to the kinship system requires to be inserted into that of the symbolic register that is inextricably linked to it.[5]

In this infrastructure of the linguistic field, I distinguish between what concerns the naming of the affect and what concerns the naming of the elements of the kinship system: this must not make us forget that they are necessary if the identificatory action proper to what we call the basic language is to be carried out.

The naming of the affect and the identifying deferred action

Language, and no longer the mother's voice, imposes on the subject a series of terms that may alone make it possible to *speak* the affect experienced, to communicate it and, in doing so, obtain from the Other a response that conforms to what will be, from now on, the demanded and no longer simply the manifested.

Love, hate, envy, joy, pain, sexual pleasure; who can claim that the experiences of those who claim to be in their grip are identical? All we have is a law, pre-existing all subjects, linking one of those signifiers to a signified that is supposed to be that affect. Thus is isolated a linguistic sector in which the same sign refers to referents whose equivalence is guaranteed by nothing, which will reduplicate the violence that 'having to speak' exerts on the psyche. When Schreber describes the 'basic language' as 'a somewhat antiquated but nevertheless powerful German, characterised particularly by a wealth of euphemisms' and when, by way of illustration, he chooses 'reward in the reverse sense for punishment, poison for food, juice for venom, unholy for holy',[6] we rightly think that what is echoing in his ears is the confused memory of a first series of significations by which he had been forced to define an experience by its opposite: what Schreber discovers as the special quality of God's language is 'the ineptitude' of a term that denotes by its opposite what it claims to name.

The richness of euphemisms refers him to the malignity of a divine voice that in his opinion betrays the order of signification. What it calls food is poison, the satisfaction of need is effected by the destruction of the body: beyond this there stands out the violence that forces one to call love, reward, joy what accompanies the representation of one's body torn apart by the desire to destroy of Her who provides the food. It is in the register of the naming of affects that a God, who has, 'by nature, only a knowledge of the corpse-body', exercises intolerable abuse; what follows is the collapse of the function of signification. The most everyday experience shows us that, for any subject, in the register of the affects, expression and meaning remain the shifting ground on which he moves forward, anxiously awaiting the act that will bear out the truth of the statement.[7] In this sector, the shadow of doubt hangs for ever over the linguistic sign. The subject easily accommodates himself to knowing that nothing will assure him that what he sees as 'red' or 'green' is identical to what is seen by another; he is willing to call table, glass, dog, the objects that others call by those names. On the other hand, he has learned, at some cost, that when he says 'I love you' or someone else says it to him, he cannot be sure that it means the same thing or is to be believed, but he can say nothing if he refuses to have recourse to these terms.

Hence his search for signs that prove the truth of the libidinal statement. But, once encountered, what do these signs refer him to? To what certainty? Objectively they can only refer him to what they represent, depending on the affective problematic, the culture, the way of being of him who is their agent.

In the final analysis proof is based on nothing but confidence, the credibility that the subject grants to the statement in the name of criteria that are subjective, and never objective, whose history, the history that privileged them for him, he is unaware of. That is why the subject swings between moments of certainty and moments of doubt, and signs a compromise with that sector of language that safeguards at best the economy of his cathexes, in the field of affects and in the field of meaning. Let me open a parenthesis here in order to stress one of the features peculiar to sexual pleasure: a privileged experience in which the proof of the statement would be guaranteed by a certainty of the body, the deceptive appearance of an ensnaring coincidence, which is one of the reasons for the strange relation between the subject and the enigma that the pleasure of the other sex poses. Valued as proof of the desire of which one hopes to be the object and the giver (hence the frequency with which subjects imagine the pleasure of the opposite sex to be always superior or more triumphal), it remains the enigma whose presence one can forget during the act of sexual pleasure. To wish to know what is being experienced by the different-from-me-other, who uses the same term to designate what cannot be the same: an otherness that deprives me of the certainty of a proof that the body alone might have been able to provide, and which gives new impetus to the search for what might confirm that the linguistic statement conforms to the affect of which it speaks. If it is still possible to achieve sexual pleasure, it is because, at the moment when pleasure is achieved, the subject forgets the question that he will ask himself only after the experience. During the fleeting union of two bodies, a term to be understood in the strict sense of one part of a body filling an opening in the other, the subject may cease to distinguish between what is happening in one and what is happening in the other. What a man experiences in his body through his own sexual organ and what his partner's body experiences thanks to the same organ may, while the pleasure lasts, be expressed in the form of the identical, which, *effectively*, abolishes the space separating two bodies. It is only later that the question will recur with its load of doubt and anxiety. The ravages that they may cause, beyond a certain threshold, may be explained if one sees them as the consequences of an experience that may be forgotten, but the scar from which never disappears (an experience that may in certain cases lead the subject to the frontiers of madness).

What is responsible for that scar is what resulted from the form of link that the basic language imposes between signifier and signified, voice and statement, the naming of the feeling and the affect that it names. As soon as the subject agrees to conjugate, if only in the present, the verb to love, he comes up against an alien territory that will accept him only if he completely forgets where he originally came from. Feeling, far from being reduced to the naming of an affect, is *an interpretation of it, in the strongest sense of the term*, that *links an experience* in itself unknowable to a cause that is supposed to conform to what one experiences. As we have seen, what one experiences is also what has first been interpreted by the discourse of the Other and of others, by recourse to what might appear as a series of false syllogisms that refer everything that is manifested under similar appearances to one and the same thing. The statement: 'all people dressed in black are in mourning' would make one smile; but in what way is it different from the following: every satisfied need is a source of pleasure, every cry is an appeal to her who is absent, every movement is a sign of intelligence addressed to the mother? In a sense, they are equally abusive and forced, but in another sense far from being reducible to a false syllogism, they represent the price that has to be paid for the gift and creation of meaning proper to language. The desire for conformity between affect and feeling entails the illusory belief that it would be possible to know something that is doubly outside language.

Indeed, it was a question not only of knowing what belongs to an outside-language, but also of possessing a knowledge that might not belong to the sayable: it is obvious, and I have stressed the importance of the fact, that there exists an interpretation of the world and an inscription of experience that precede and are ignorant of word-presentation; but this does not prevent the I, or the analyst, whenever he is confronted by his own psychical world, from discovering that for him knowledge and sayability coincide, that to abandon saying what one has experienced amounts to abandoning experiencing the experience as an adventure that concerns the I and not as an accident that happens to it, like a foreign body, incomprehensible because unsayable. The transformation of affect into feeling is the result of that act of language that imposes *a radical break between the pictographic register and the register of sense-making*: that break is in itself independent of the voice and of the voices to which the subject owes the acquisition of language. If one regards the voice as the metonymic representative of the subject, it may be said that the libidinal load that it adds to the language entity is necessary in order to become a subject, but that independently of that action and that overload, there appears, in that space in which the I comes about, the equally fundamental role of the identifying action of discourse. What we have here is an autonomous action carried out by the linguistic institution and from which no subject escapes. Its autonomy is even more evident where the mother's discourse has characteristics that induce a psychotic response. The mother's words inevitably reach the limits of her power in her need, in order to make the infant's psyche intelligible, to speak of the infant's love, pleasure, obedience, naughtiness. That is why the more she claims an exhaustive power and knowledge over that other, the more she will be forced to transform everything into the sayable. And the more she transforms into the sayable the totality of what she says she perceives, the more she finds herself caught in the trap, unless she is herself delusional, of the gap that will appear between the meaning that her discourse claims to convey and the meaning that other speakers may convey back to her. The more a discourse wishes to be faultless, unambiguous, unquestionable, and tries to present itself as a complete construction, the more there appears at work what I shall call the autonomy of logic proper to the linguistic system. In this case, meaning can no longer prevail over the wealth of metaphor, play on nonsense and humour – that is to say, that set of procedures that make communication the locus in which interpretation and questioning remain possible. This possibility is sacrificed by the mother's ambition to acquire the type of certainty that is claimed by scientific discourse. The triangle is reminiscent of the Oedipus complex; in the demonstration of the theorem, that association is trivial both for him who is demonstrating it and for him who hears it. Paradoxically, the autonomous and autonomised power of language is all the more active when the speaker claims to possess the totality of statements referring to the field of meaning of what he wishes to demonstrate. Outside mathematical discourse, in the strict sense of the term, which may allow itself to create its own postulates, discourse must obey postulates over which the subject has no power; as a result, the possibility of getting others to accept a conclusion that is contradictory to that resulting from the sequence of successively spoken statements eludes him. Whenever discourse opposes the heard to what others may relativise, in that they assume the right to accept it, while telling themselves that this or that statement has a double meaning and may, without invalidating the whole, be understood by them in a different way, whenever therefore discourse makes claim to this type of exhaustive objectivity, it is forced to demonstrate an absolute conformity between the object of which it speaks and what it says about that same object.

It is clear that this conformity is unsustainable in the register of the affects, the register in which the listening of interlocutors is always affected by their own particular problematic. We are confronted, therefore, with the special role that will be played in the identificatory economy by the terms of affective language:

• Naming imposes a status on what is experienced. This status transforms in a radical way the relation of subject to experience, imposes a pre-established meaning, one over which the subject has no power.
• This status and meaning, in turn, will add a signifier, shared by all subjects speaking the same language, to signifides that from that moment have as referents only other signifiers (the signifier 'loving' will be able to designate its referent only by appealing to other signifiers such as the desirer, the giver, the other's hope for happiness, the state of expectation, etc.; in this sector the linguistic term refers to another term, which in turn refers to another and so forth).
• This subjection of the referent to the signifier of the linguistic sign has two consequences: on the one hand, it preserves the illusion of the existence of an identity between referents and, on the other, it inevitably introduces the risk of a break, a conflict, between the utterer and the signification of the linguistic sign. Indeed if, in this reference from term to term, the subject encounters only

a series of terms that repetitively expose him to the contradiction between its referent and that of others or, which amounts to the same thing, show him that others refuse to recognise that it signifies to them something other than what they claim to hear, the subject will see in the set of linguistic signs only the locus of the lie and the basic language will assume the signification that it had for Schreber.

The proper of discourse, then, is the break that it imposes between the represented and the statement. Words describe what was not sayable and by this fact allow the upsurge of an utterer. The appearance of the understanding and appropriation of language imposes on the subject the consideration of a model that transfers into this register, and hence into that of the secondary process, a cause of the affect, which *qua* affect would be unknowable for the I. Paraphrasing Freud, one might say that in acceding to language the subject becomes a theoretician in spite of himself and that, confronted with the unknowable of his experience, language declares: 'At this point something occurred of which we are totally unable to form a conception, but which, if it had entered our consciousness, could only have been described in such and such a way.'[8]

At this cost the unknowable takes on meaning and becomes sayable: words will define what moves the subject and of which he would know nothing except by recourse to that displacement in the register of the sayable; and it is true that *this displacement is the subject itself* qua *I*. It remains outside knowledge that pain is repetition, that this other that I love and who is not there recalls a lost object responsible for an initial wound, that it is this mourning that is revived on each occasion. What language defines as love allows us to construct a coherent, 'reasonable' model of it that separates the present other from the past breast, which conceals their consanguinity, and which so arranges matters that the avowal that one needs its presence as the earth needs water is heard as a poetic metaphor, which reveals nothing about the first relation of absolute necessity that bound a mouth to a breast. It should be added that there is not only a use of metaphor here, but a re-elaboration of the subject–object relation: the necessary and the absolute are no longer the inevitable properties of a single object, thanks to which may operate the reorganisation of the economy of the cathexes required by the secondary process. This reorganisation involves the appearance on the psychical stage of identificatory statements that one owes to the linguistic statement that names the affect: the linguistic sign will identify the affect with what the cultural discourse defines as such: to love refers to what the term 'love' designates *and* to an image of the lover of which discourse becomes the only possible referent. This leads the subject to accept, as proofs of the truth of the statement, those that the cultural discourse sets up: to love one's mother is to be kind, obedient, strong, handsome and whatever else is decided by the cultural models.

The truth of loving ought therefore to be proved by the identity of the subject with the image of the lover[9] as transmitted by the culture: a link will be established between the concept (to love) and the cultural forms that prove the truth of the affect that assumes the name of feeling. The passage from the representation of the affect to the naming of the feeling entails the abandonment of a representation by the image of the bodily thing in favour of an image that refers to the lover. When I say 'I love you' I show that I accept that this statement, of which the I wishes to be the agent, can find its confirmation only in the model that discourse proposes of it. There is, in a sense, a subordination of the action of the verb to the discourse that defines it: one might also say that action in this register is subordinated to that which discourse designates to it as motivations, aim, limits. The refusal of this allegiance will be called alienation: and it is true that to break off those relations set up by culture between experience and its signification is to reject it, to go back or to go elsewhere, a source of alienating strangeness for anyone considering the plight of the traveller.

What I have said about the basic language and the naming of the affect enables us to show in what and why its identifying action is at the origin of the I.

8 The deferred action of the naming of the affect

The particular relation that links the referent to the signifier of the linguistic sign in the register that I am concerned with here means that the first can be defined only by recourse to other signifiers that try to define the thing ever more closely, yet only ever find the spoken thing: this relation has, as its deferred action, the uprising of the I. In order to understand this process it must be remembered that the naming does not concern, in this case, an object perceived in a neutral manner, but, on the contrary, an object that has been previously and particularly cathected and is already a libidinally loaded support. As soon as naming concerns the affect, it is *ipso facto* a naming of the object and of the relation that links it to the subject: to name the other with the term of beloved is to designate the subject who is naming by that of lover. This simple example may be extrapolated to all namings that define the child's relation to others cathected by him. In the register of the affect the act of utterance designates a relation and it is this relation that one designates by a single term. The precathexis of the object does not have the I as agent, but a psychical activity that pre-exists it; the naming does not concern this first mode of relation, but that which is present between an object and an I that is recognised in that named person: *the act of uttering a feeling is therefore at the same time the utterance of a self-naming by the I.*

What I have said about the signifier–signified relation[10] in this register will be manifested in the identificatory field by an operation in which every signifier implicitly designates as its privileged referent a naming that identifies and constitutes the I. Indeed the constitution of the I follows, step by step, the succession of namings by which the Other names its affective relation to the subject, namings that the subject will in turn await, induce or reject. The space in which the I must

97

come about, which is also the only space in which it can come about, shows that its organisation is placed under the aegis of a series of linguistic signs – those proper to the affect and those proper to the system of kinship – which, naming a thing or an element, define the relation present between the object being named and that which appropriates and states that naming. It is therefore in and by the deferred action of naming the cathected object that the I comes about: the discovery of the name of the object and of the naming of the link that unites it to the subject gives birth and meaning to an agency that defines itself as desire, envy, love, hate, expectation . . . of that object. The I is nothing more than the knowledge that the I may have of the I: if my formula is correct, it also implies that the I is formed by all the statements that make sayable the psyche's relation with those objects in the world invested by it that become identificatory markers, emblems recognisable by the other I's that surround the subject. We shall come back to this aspect of the problematic of the I; what I want to do here is simply to throw light on the role played, in the space outside-I, by the act of language as an identifying operation that has the strange power to create a named that might have existence for the I outside that naming.

9 The desire of the father (for a child, for that child)

Before turning to the desire of the father and its relation to the cultural we should remember what, in the functioning of the psyche, is on the contrary transcultural. The 'anatomical destiny' is accompanied by a 'psychical destiny' whose first manifestation is imposed on the child as soon as he has to recognise, and every child, wherever he is born, will have to accept this fact, that in his first relation to his mother he misconstrued the irreducibility of the following elements:

- Men's bodies possess an organ that women's do not have.
- That object gives women pleasure and is necessary for procreation.
- Every infant discovers that the first object cathected by the whole of his libido does not respond to it in the same way, that the mother desires something other than he can give her, that her sexual pleasure has another support.
- The mother respects, fears or venerates the discourse of another or others. His desire and his demand are not enough to get the response that he wants. Hence his attempt (and here again we remain within the universal) to try to know who she desires or who dictates the law to her. In our culture this attempt brings him up against the father and his desire.

Encountering the father's desire the child also encounters the last factor that allows the space outside the psyche to be organised in such a way as to make possible the functioning of the I or, conversely, the setting up of an obstacle to it. It is astonishing to note the ambiguous place given by psychoanalytical theory to the agent of this desire. As referent of the law, holder of the keys that give access to the symbolic, giver of the name, the Name-of-the-Father, already in Freud, even if the term is not used, assumes an even more central place in Lacan's theory. Its foreclosure will designate the cause of the psychotic destiny; its absence or, rather, its non-recognition by the mother's discourse, will be said to be responsible for the contradiction between the subject of the statement and the desiring subject. This same theory allows us to go a step further. A privileged signifier, the phallus, the only one, according to Lacan, that can refer only to itself, is set up as the central point necessary if the gravitation of the signifying chain is to follow an orbit in accordance with the law and not to sink into a disordered movement that would bring chaos to the world and chaos to language. But, side by side with the role assigned to that name, one notes how little importance is given to the analysis of the father's desire, whose action seems to be reduced to the response that the mother gives to it by her recognition or rejection. At best, the schizophrenic's mother apart, stress will be laid on the analysis of the parental couple and their relationship; concerning the action of the father's desire on the child we find nothing but a strange silence. This is to forget that, unless we share the infantile illusion as to the mother's omnipotence, the exclusion of the father implies on his part a wish to exclude himself, that the mother's possible desire to castrate him makes all the more possible, that he encounters in the partner a desire to play this role of victim. Added to this is what is revealed by clinical medicine: the importance of the problematic of the father, his violence, his maternal attitude and, more generally, what he does and says to manifest his desire for the child on the stage of the real. In the syntactical analysis proposed above, I said that both boy and girl inherit a wish for a child transmitted by the mother's wish that they become in turn father or mother. The fulfilment of a desire for paternity finds its source in a wish transmitted by the mother's discourse. It is true therefore that the father's wish for a child is closely related to wishes concerning the mother's sphere and the period of her power. The anticipation proper to her discourse, when it concerns a son, will transmit to him an identificatory wish – to become a father – which concerns a function that she does not possess and which she can only refer to that of her own father. In this sense her discourse speaks of a function that passes from father to father: her wish combines two positions and two functions, that occupied by her own father and that which the infant may occupy as a future father. Between these two links is situated the child's real father, to whom the child will look in an attempt to know what the term 'father' and the concept 'paternal function' mean.

The meaning of the term 'paternal function' will therefore be framed by three referents:

• the interpretation that the mother gives herself of her own father's function;

- the function that the child attributes to his father and the function that the mother grants that same father;
- that part that the mother wishes to transmit of this function and that part of it that she may wish to forbid.

It follows that the mother's wish, inherited by the child, condenses two libidinal relations: the relation that the mother established with the paternal image and the relation that she lives out with the man to whom she has actually given a child. The fact that the child may become a father may refer to the hope that is repeated by her own father's function as well as to the hope that the child may take up on his own account the function of the man who is his father. In fact, there is an interaction between these two wishes. It is unusual for a woman's negative relation to her father to allow a positive relation to the man. But since we are speaking of the father here, I shall make the same optimistic hypothesis about him that I made in the case of the mother: a subject who has heard that wish, who has himself taken it up, and who has wished to fulfil it, with a woman who agrees to recognise his function for her desire and for their child.

If we situate this couple in our culture,[11] we note that, although, in Lacan's words, the mother is the first representative of the Other on the stage of the real, the father is, on the same stage, the first representative of others, and of others' discourse (of the discourse of the group).

Our culture offers a model of the mother's function, a law that decides in what circumstances the man may or may not give his name, the rules and the benefits laid down by the kinship system: this set of prescriptions establishes a model of the relation of the parental couple and of their relation to the child, in which the father inherits a power of jurisdiction, exemplified by Roman law, which, originally, went so far as to give him the right of life and death. It is true that this power has lost many of its attributes, but nevertheless it has preserved its function in the register of the transmission of the name, with all that it entails. In the family structure of our culture, the father represents him who allows the mother to designate to the child, on the stage of the real, a referent that guarantees that his discourse, his demands, his prohibitions are not arbitrary, but are justified by their conformity to a cultural discourse that has delegated to him the right and duty to transmit them. If the reference to the father is the one most likely to testify to the child that it is a question of delegation and not of abusive, absolute power, it is because, here again, we find that specific feature of psychical functioning by which knowledge, or re-cognition, is preceded by a precathexis of that which is to be recognised. Furthermore the child's access to the category of the concept shows the usefulness of an intermediary link that offers him a first embodiment of the symbol, with which he will be able, at a later stage, to separate the concept from what was its first support on the stage of the real. The man who will be able to become a father begins by recognising the representative of that function in the man that the mother's discourse designates as such, but also, and it would be a serious error to forget this, in the actual discourse spoken by the father's voice. In the encounter with the father we may distinguish two stages and two experiences:

- the encounter with the father's voice (from the child's point of view) and access to fatherhood (from the father's point of view);
- the father's desire, by which we understand the child's desire for the father as well as the father's for the child.

10 The encounter with the father

I have already approached that encounter in my analysis of the transmission from the primal couple to the parental couple. I might recall that what first appears to the infant's gaze and what is offered to his libido is that 'Other-without-breast' that may be the source of pleasure and more generally the source of affect. What marks its specific, differential feature, as opposed to the encounter with the mother, is that the encounter with the father does not take place in the register of need; that is why the father is no doubt he who induces the first breach in the original collusion that made the satisfaction of the body's needs inextricably linked to the satisfaction of libidinal 'need'. This breach will induce the infant's psyche to acknowledge that, although this presence is desired by the mother, it remains totally alien to the field of need.[12]

This 'unknown' desired by the mother, if one places oneself at that very early moment in psychical life when the infant's gaze discovers it, is first of all placed, in its relation to the mother, in a position that is the reverse of the one that it will assume at a later stage. I have said that it is to the father that the mother will refer in order to demonstrate the reality of her models; on the other hand, during this first stage, it is from the mother that the infant seeks and finds the reasons for the father's existence. It is that 'elsewhere' desired by the mother that represents the father on the scene and it is that desire that confers upon him his power, whereas, in a second stage, it is because the father desires the mother and presents himself as the agent of her pleasure and legitimacy that he assumes the place of him who has the right to decree what the son may offer the mother as pleasure and what it is forbidden to him to offer. For that double reason the father will present himself to the child both as an object to be seduced and as an object of hate.

An object to be seduced. To hope to be desired by the father is to hope to play the same role as the mother in the register of his desire: by decreeing an equality between the child and the mother as objects equally coveted by his desire, the father's gaze would allow that common attribute to be transformed into a proof of identity between those two subjects. What lies at the bottom of the child's desire to seduce the father might be expressed as: what the father desires in me is my mother's desirability.

To desire the father, to seduce him, to be seduced by him may therefore be analysed under the following formulations:

- to offer oneself as the equivalent of what he desires in the mother, that is to say, to be recognised as identical to the 'desirability' that she thus proves she possesses;
- to keep the mother for oneself by offering oneself to the father as an equivalent of pleasure;
- at the cost of the seduction induced and submitted to, to pay for the right to continue to share the maternal objects; to be like the father's wife, at that stage, does not mean to lose the penis – a meaning that will occur only at the phallic stage – but to offer oneself in the place of what is desired in the mother and which she therefore possesses in the same way as the child's body;
- the man's desire of femininity finds its precursor in the desire to be able to identify penis and the woman's desirability. He begins by repeating the child's wish as he had formulated it to himself: to be him who carries out the impossible castration of the first Representative of the Other.

The object to hate. This stage of the encounter is followed by the need to recognise the difference of the sexes, the non-absolute character of maternal power and, on the other hand, the power exerted by the father, which first takes the form of a prohibiting voice, a voice that the mother herself seems to obey. The major consequence of this will be that he who embodies that voice comes onto the stage of the real to make sensible – by allowing its cause to be found in the outside-self – the hate without object and the unsayable of a desire for non-desire whose effects repetitively invade the psychical field.

It is the father who begins to make bearable the discovery of maternal betrayal, before this betrayal is seen to be an unavoidable truth. If she does not desire me, when everything seemed to suggest that she did, if she says that she does not find in me the object of her pleasure, it is because she is obeying an order, coming from the father, that she simply has to submit to.[13] This first rationalisation of disappointment, whose traces will never be erased, allows a state of temporary complicity between mother and child, and makes it possible to transfer outside the couple that they form the verdict of a law that appears, at first sight, to be iniquitous. Moreover, the *desire for death*, transformed into a *desire to murder*, finds in the father a substitute as well as a reassurance: indeed the wish that he should die is counterbalanced by the image of a force far superior to his own, a superiority that, for him, goes some way to justifying a wish that he has little chance of carrying out. It is true, none the less, that the scandal of the discovery of psychoanalysis, far from being reducible as is often claimed, sometimes with the complicity of analysts, to the discovery of the sexual where only innocence was seen, is all the more intolerable in that it affirms that the subject begins by wanting to kill his father, that he is a parricide *in potentia*. There is something intolerable for every human being in that image, whose presence, after the event, is made bearable only by the playful dimension that is still used to cover its immodest nakedness. To the child's 'I'm going to kill you', the adult replies 'I'm going to eat you', which, by reducing the first statement to a game, conceals the non-metaphorical meaning that it conveys. It is striking to note, in the current interpretation of unconscious guilt, the place given to incestuous desire and to the fear of retaliation, as opposed to that given to the desire for the father's death. It is as if that desire were merely the logical consequence, a secondary evil effect, of the desire to possess the mother: it is nothing of the kind. In fact, here, too, we encounter the reduplication of a psychical operation of which we can see no more than the second stage. It is obvious that during the Oedipal stage the little boy sees the father as a rival whose death is wished in order that he be left free to be alone with the mother, but this is only the secondary form of an earlier wish for the father's death. Before occupying the place of the Oedipal rival, the father is presented to the psyche as the embodiment in the outside-self of the cause of his inability to preserve the state of pleasure in a perfect and autonomous way: by this fact he has allowed the death drive to be caught in the trap of a reason for the unpleasure experienced that would be *outside* the presenter, a reason responsible for an order of the world that resists the orders of the psyche. On the stage of the real appears he who imposes himself both as the first representative of others and as *the first representative of a law that makes unpleasure an experience from which one cannot escape.* Unless we consider that stage prior to the Oedipal wish, which is marked by a desire for murder, we cannot understand what is particularly involved in the problematic of the father's desire for his child. The effects of his presence, his absence and his specificity will be grasped more clearly if we consider the context proper to fatherhood:

• The father's uncertainty concerning his procreative role. Doubt about it is always possible; the certainty of fatherhood cannot be compared to the corporal relation enjoyed by the mother.
• Fatherhood is directly bound up with a naming that, in the name of the law, designates him or those who may be called fathers. This explains that the father's procreative role may not be recognised in certain cultures, in which the man becomes merely an intermediary between the woman and the spirit who impregnates her.
• In the child the father meets the proof that his own mother transmitted to him a wish concerning his function and the laws of its transmission. It follows that the child becomes for the father the sign and proof of the phallic function of his own penis.
• By giving him the child his wife shows him her desire to transmit a function that passes from father to father. By accepting that gift the man may finally consider that his debt towards his own father, a debt that his son takes over in turn, has been settled. Echoing the maternal voice, and thanks to its presence,

there now resonates the discourse of the fathers, a series of statements that by their very transmission ensure the permanence of the law governing the system of kinship.

In our culture, the real subject, who for the son has been the representative of the fathers, has also been, since the constitution of the Oedipus complex, the object of a desire for secondary murder. The memory of that wish may remain present or be rediscovered if it has been repressed, a characteristic that distinguishes it from its predecessor.[14] As a result, on becoming a father the subject runs the risk of seeing in the son what Laius saw: the man who will desire his death. Death will therefore be doubly present in the father–son relationship: the father of the father being he whom long ago one wished to kill, and his own son he who will desire your death. This double death wish can be repressed only thanks to the link that is set up between death and succession, and between the transmission of the law and the acceptance of death. A death wish, repressed in the father, will have to be replaced by the conscious wish that the son should become, not him who will remove you from your place, but him to whom one gives, in the profoundest sense of the term, the right to exercise the same function in the future. What the father offers by the mediation of his name, his law, his authority, his role as referent, is a right of inheritance over those gifts in order that they may be passed on to another son. In doing so he declares his acceptance of his own death. As long as the father occupies his place, between the subject and death, there is a father who by his death will pay his tribute to life: after his death it is the subject himself who will have to pay with his death others' right to life. In the relation between father and daughter, things will be different: there is less risk of reminding the father of the wish for repressed hate. Furthermore, on his death, it is not she who will occupy his place, but possibly his son. The relationship between father and daughter entails less direct rivalry. We have the contra-proof of the fact that she poses less danger to the return of the repressed in that she is able to lull the vigilance of censorship. The fact that the father senses that the daughter's wish, contrary to that of the son, will be to seduce him and not to kill him seems in certain cases to encourage in him the desire to be seduced, a desire that, given the age gap, seems to him to be 'innocent'. There results from this a sort of more or less latent eroticisation of the relationship, with the danger nevertheless that the latent may become manifest, hence the frequency, greater than in the case of the mother–son couple, of incest, due to the eruption in the conscious mind of a desire that makes the daughter her who allows him, in an inverted form, to fulfil the incestuous wish. The son being unable to take the mother from the father, it is the daughter who will take the men.[15] To return to the father–son relationship, it might be said that the son may convince him that the law and the paternal function have a meaning.

The relationship in the flesh is in itself meaning: in every species of mammal there is a definite persistence of an immutable maternal function. Things are very different in the paternal function: as a result of its dependence on cultural institutions it can preserve its function as pivot in the register of the kinship system only if it can be guaranteed a succession. It is especially endangered if the son refuses to accept this inheritance: to that threat the father responds by projecting onto the son a sort of positivised castration. The child is he to whom he proves and proves to himself that by accepting castration one has access to that place where, becoming the referent of the law on incest, one discovers that he never set out to castrate him, that his fears were purely imaginary. But access to that place requires of the subject that he discovers his own mortality: to recognise the value of what is to be transmitted presupposes that you know that you are there only temporarily, that you are only the transitory occupant of a place that another had occupied before you and that another will occupy after you.

To conclude, I would say:

- The father's desire cathects the child not as a phallic equivalent, which it could be in the case of the woman, but as a sign that his own father has neither castrated nor hated him, hence the importance of the proof that the son brings him of the phallic function of his penis.
- Consequently the father will recognise that he will die not because of his son's hate, nor in order to be punished for hating his own father, but because, agreeing to recognise himself as a successor and as having a successor, he accepts that one day he will leave his function to that successor. It follows from this that the father's desire envisages the child as a voice, a name, an after: he sees him as him who confirms to him that death is the consequence of a universal law and not the price that has to be paid for his desire to kill his own father.

This mode of cathexis of the child by the real father is confirmed by what we learn from everyday experience about the extreme difficulty experienced by a father in accepting that his son refuses to share his values, contrary to what may well occur in the case of a daughter.

Similar confirmation is provided by the violence of the disappointment that may be aroused in him by the sexual, ethical, physical weaknesses of a son and by the aggression that he may feel when challenged in his authority, which is always put into question by his function and his desire to make his son the guarantor of a tradition.

These remarks illustrate the difficulty and ambiguity that appear as soon as one tries to separate what is a support of the psychical structure and what is a function of the peculiarities of a given social system.

It may be said, quite rightly, that every society privileges what encourages the status quo of its models, a status quo that is defended at first by those who are privileged by those models. But it must be understood that no society would succeed in doing so if it could not use the force and violence that it exerts (and

105

its stability will depend on the greater or lesser success with which they are used) in order to preserve the illusion that what, in fact, is at the service of its conservative intentions conforms to the needs of the psychical structure.

If one tries to formulate the broad outlines by which the mother's desire is differentiated from the father's desire for the child, we may note the following characteristics:

- The father's desire sees the son as a successor to his function, he promotes him more rapidly to his place as a future subject. He at once privileges in the son the paternal power and the power of future succession.
- The narcissism projected onto the child will be supported, more than that of the mother, by cultural values.
- The child's passage to the status of adult will be felt less as a separation or loss than it is in the case of the mother. Indeed one often sees the opposite. Through the child, he who is cathected by the father is the future subject who, taking a similar place to his own in the register of function, reassures him regarding his paternal function and his role as transmitter of the law. But we also see the risks of such a relationship and the rivalry that it reveals. That is why to become a father may arouse an intolerable anxiety that may, on a clinical level, go as far as phenomena equivalent to those associated with a puerperal psychosis.

I have indicated above the ways in which the psyche defends itself against these risks, that is against the effects of a return of the repressed; risks caused, at the assumption by the man of the paternal function, by his confrontation with the child's unconscious.

On the side of the mother, as on the side of the father, one meets the same need to keep outside the field of the conscious what infantile amnesia had effaced.

This brings us to the end of my analysis of the forces at work in the organisation of the familial micro-field that constitutes the space in which the I may come about. We shall see, in the case of psychosis, the damage caused by the father's desire when the father has been unable to resolve his own problems with his mother, or his father, and why his power, which can induce the beginnings of a psychotic response is in no way inferior to that which may be exercised by maternal desire.

The narcissistic contract[16]

One last factor that is responsible for what is played out on the *extra-familial* scene should be taken into account. Although its effects are felt throughout the field of analytical experience and act with the same force on both analyst and analysand, its analysis is more difficult than that of the factors encountered so far. It is to its presence that we owe what I shall call the *narcissistic contract*.

The mode of action proper to the basic language obliged me to make a first incursion beyond the familial space. Very little could be said about the effect of the mother's and father's speech if one did not take into account the law from which they are inseparable and which is imposed by discourse. The narcissistic contract confronts us with a final factor acting on the couple's mode of cathexis in the child. What I shall say about it must be understood as a mere sketch based on a few hypotheses concerning the metapsychological function performed by the sociocultural register. By this I mean the set of institutions whose functioning shares the same characteristic feature: it is accompanied by a discourse on the institution that affirms how well founded and necessary it is. For me this discourse designates the ideological discourse. It is evident that in speaking of institution and ideology I am appealing to concepts that go well beyond our discipline, and I accept that they have never had a place in it. That is why I wish to stress that, although I may deal with certain concepts in what may seem a rather cavalier fashion, slanting their usual meaning in a particular direction, it is not because I do not recognise their complexity and extraterritoriality, but because I have a precise aim in view. In fact I wish to show that:

- The relation between the parental couple and the child always bears the trace of the relation between the couple and the social milieu (the term 'milieu' referring, according to the couple's particular problematic, to society in the broad sense, or to the subgroup whose ideals the couple shares).
- The social discourse projects onto the infant the same anticipation as that proper to the parental discourse: long before the new subject is there, the place that he will be expected to occupy will be pre-cathected by the group, in the hope that he will transmit the sociocultural model unchanged.
- In his turn, the subject seeks and must find in that discourse markers that will enable him to project himself into the future, so that his distance from his first support, the parental couple, will not be translated into the loss of all identificatory support.
- The conflict that may exist between the couple and its milieu runs the risk of confirming for the infantile psyche the identity between what takes place on the external scene and his fantasy representation of any situation involving rejection, exclusion, aggression, or power. The reality of social oppression for the couple, or the dominant position that the couple exercises in it, will play a role in the way in which the child will elaborate his future identificatory statements. It is no coincidence that the history of the families of a large number of those who will become psychotic so often repeats the same social and economic drama: this reality, which has a direct, unmediated effect, plays a role in the destiny of those children that society, in a second stage, sends off to various institutions to repair the damage for which it is certainly responsible.

The discourse of the group

I shall represent the social group – by which I mean a group of subjects speaking the same language, governed by the same institutions and, when this is the case, having the same religion – metonymically as *the totality of voices present*. This group may issue an indeterminate number of statements: among these a special place will be given to the series defining the reality of the world, the group's *raison d'être*, the origin of its models. As a result this series includes all statements that have the group itself as object; this more or less complex, more or less flexible set of statements, always has as its infrastructure, unchanging for a given culture, a minimum series that I call *the statements of foundation*, but may also be termed *the foundation of statements*, the one inevitably including the other. Depending on the type of culture, this series will be constituted by mythical, sacred or scientific statements. Whatever their differences these statements share the same requirement: their function as foundation is an absolute condition if a harmony is to be preserved between the social field and the linguistic field that will allow the interaction that is indispensable to the functioning of both.[17] For these statements to perform this function they must be accepted as *unquestionably true*: if this attribute is lacking they will be abandoned and replaced by a new series; in any event the function will never remain vacant.

Sacred discourse and ideological (profane) discourse are obliged to offer these points of certainty, which may be different in form, but which will be identical in their basic role in the sociolinguistic field. It should be added that, whatever group defends, proposes or imposes a model of the social, it will always be a model that conforms to the ideals of those who defend it. It is the discourse based by and on the ideals of the utterer that I shall call 'ideology', for want of a better term, in order to remind ourselves that the subject is necessarily the recipient of a certain theory concerning the foundations of the social: it is by the ideal image favoured by his theory that he measures the reality of the world as it appears to him. As a result any subgroup in conflict with the dominant model will be constituted around its own model: if I stress this point, it is because it will have a direct action on the anticipatory effect of the discourse of others on the infant.

In these reflections on the social field, I have chosen to illustrate the functions of the discourse of myth, science and the sacred, with the example of those of the sacred, of which I shall consider here only *the few characteristics that may be extrapolated from the other two*. One characteristic of this discourse is that it always involves statements that speak of the origin of the model, that origin implying in turn a definition of what ought to be the aim towards which the model tends. The model of origin implicitly bears within it the model of the aim that it is proposing: any change concerning the aim envisaged entails therefore a change of the first.

For a very long period in the history of our culture it was the divine voice that was set up as the original utterer of the model. In a sense, it was a voice outside the group, but one that was its founder: the group's prehistory, far from referring to the primal horde, refers to the sacred. As soon as belief in a mythical founder disappears, there emerges what Leroy-Gourhan calls 'the myth of monkey man'. The difference is not a small one, but here again we find two common features:

- the preserving of a certainty as to origin;
- the idealisation of scientific knowledge that would make it possible to predict and to act on the possible future of evolution.[18]

The statements of foundation under the aegis of the sacred show, quite overtly, what the discourse of science preserves while concealing it. The characteristics common to this second discourse are to be found in the register of the sacred in the form of the following givens:

- The original voice is supposed to state the eternally true. By means of this postulate a sector of absolute certainty is established in the register of discourse.
- It assures the I of the existence of a series of statements, those present in the sacred text, which will guarantee an identity between the uttering I and the I that guarantees the truth of that discourse.
- It allows the I to appropriate a fragment of discourse whose truth is independent of any confirmation or questioning of it by the individual interlocutor. When the I repeats the sacred discourse, it assumes the right to claim a priori the recognition of its truth by the group and to exclude anyone who contradicts or rejects a certainty shared by the society as a whole.

I have stressed that in the function carried out by the discourse of the sacred I isolated only those few characteristics to be found in any culture's founding discourse, whatever the theoretical reference chosen. These characteristics establish what I call the narcissistic contract.

The narcissistic contract

Let us consider a group 'X': its very existence implies that the majority of subjects, except during very brief moments in its history, accepts as true a discourse that affirms that the laws governing its functioning are well founded, that they define and lay down the aim envisaged.

We can regard these laws as the canvas that supports the representation that subjects give themselves of the ideal group: it follows that the relation of subject to group depends on the subject's cathexis of the statements of foundation. In adhering to the social field, the subject appropriates a series of statements that his voice repeats; this repetition brings him certainty of the existence of a discourse in which the truth about the past is guaranteed, with as its corollary a belief in the possible truth of predictions about the future.

The cathexis of this future model is a necessary condition for social functioning: I said that it is directly related to the model of origin. Any decathexis of the first will have repercussions on the second: if the subject ceases to be certain about the origin, he loses, by this fact, that point of support that the utterer must have if the discourse is to be offered as the locus in which the possibility that a truth may find a place in it is guaranteed by the assent of the entire collectivity of voices.[19] In becoming a lawful appropriation of the subject, the discourse of the sacred, and its successors, cathects the subject as group subject: the statement of foundations comes back to the subject as the statement establishing his position in the group. This designation must be separated from the identificatory register in the strict sense:[20] it is coextensive with it, follows a parallel path to it, but is not identifiable with it. It allows a mapping that will frame the identificatory problematic and so arrange things that this problematic is not totally ensnared in the imaginary relation. This designation defines for the subject what transcends the singularity proper to the relation between two speakers, it points out, in each voice, the statements that each has the right to repeat and to affirm as true, and to which it claims a legitimate right of inheritance. Although I consider the real group to be represented by the totality of existing voices, I would say that it can be preserved only in so far as the majority of subjects cathect the same ideal group; that is, a group in which the subject may project himself into the place of an ideal subject.

The ideal subject is not identical with the ideal ego or the ego ideal: it refers to the group subject; that is, to the idea (a term that is more legitimate here than that of presentation) of itself that the subject demands of the group, as concept, a concept that designates him as an element belonging to a whole that recognises him as a part homogeneous with it.

In return, the group expects the subject to lend his own voice to what was stated by a voice now silent, to replace a dead element and ensure the immutability of the group. A deal of exchange is thus set up: the group guarantees the transfer onto the new arrival of the same recognition enjoyed by the individual who has disappeared; the newcomer commits himself – through the voice of others playing the role of social godparents – to repeating the same fragment of discourse. In more economic terms, one might say that the subject sees the group as the support offered to part of his narcissistic libido; that is why he makes his voice the element that is added to the chorus that comments, in and for the group, on the origin of the play and announces the aim envisaged. In exchange, the group recognises that it can exist only by the voice being repeated; in this way, it places great value on the function that it demands of him, transforms the repetition into a continuous creation of what is, and can continue to be, only by this means. The narcissistic contract is established thanks to the pre-cathexis by the group of the infant as future voice that will take up the place assigned him:

by anticipation the group endows the infant with the role of group subject that it projects onto him. The existence of the group presupposes that the majority of its elements sees in the requirements of its functioning what, if they were entirely respected, would make it possible to attain the ideal group. Belief in this ideal will be accompanied by a hope in the permanence of the group. The subject will now be able, without entirely succeeding in doing so, to establish an identity between the possible permanence of the group and his own desire for permanence; measured by human time, the first is presented as achievable, which is why at the source of the cathexis of the ideal model we find the participation of a desire for immortality, for which this cathexis is offered as a substitute. We see that, independently of the function that may be played by what Freud calls the group leader and the ideal ego, it is the very condition of the group's existence to be supported by an ideal model, drawing towards it part of the subject's narcissistic libido.

The narcissistic contract has as signatories the child and the group. The cathexis of the child by the group anticipates that of the group by the child. Indeed we have seen how, from his coming into the world, the group cathects the infant as a future voice that will be asked to repeat the statements of a dead voice and thus guarantee the qualitative and quantitative permanence of a body that would continuously regenerate itself.

In exchange for his cathexis of the group and its models, the child will demand that he be guaranteed the right to occupy a place independent of the parents' wishes, that he be offered an ideal model that others cannot repudiate, without repudiating at the same time the laws of the group, that he be allowed to maintain the illusion of a timeless permanence projected onto the group and, above all, onto a group project that his successors will be expected to take up and preserve.

The discourse of the group offers the subject certainty as to origin, which is necessary if the historical dimension is to be retroactively projectable onto his past, which will thus be removed from a reference of which the knowledge of the mother or father would be the exhaustive and sufficient guarantor. Access to historicity is an essential factor in the identificatory process; it is indispensable if the I is to attain the threshold of autonomy required by his functioning. What it is thus offered to the individual subject by the group will lead the subject to transfer part of the narcissistic stake cathected in his identificatory game onto that group, which promises him a future bonus. This future, in which the subject knows that he will have no place, he can now represent to himself as a continuation of himself and of his work, thanks to the illusion, which makes him believe that a new voice will give back life to his discourse, in identical fashion, and thus avoid the verdict of time.

The definition given of the narcissistic contract entails its universality: but although it is true that every subject is a co-signatory, the part of the narcissistic libido that he cathects in it varies from subject to subject, from couple to couple and between the two elements of the couple. The quality and intensity of the cathexis present in the contract linking the parental couple to the group, and the peculiarity of the markers and emblems that it will privilege in this register, will act in the space in which the child's I must come about, in two ways:

- The emblems and roles valorised by the couple, which in doing so ensures the agreement and often the complicity of other subjects in the group, may make it possible to disguise from the parents and the child a desire that, thanks to them, finds this additional justification that will give them a place in the register of the good, the lawful, the ethical.
- They impose on the child's I his first knowledge of the relation between the two elements of the couple and the social field, and of the relation of others to the position occupied by the couple.

As long as we remain within certain limits the variations in the couple–milieu relation will play a secondary role in the destiny of the subject, who will be able to establish in a second stage an autonomous relation with these models that is directly marked by his own psychical evolution, his peculiarities and the individuality of the defences set up.

It is very different when these limits are no longer respected: either the couple rejects the essential clauses of the contract or the group imposes a contract that is vitiated in advance, by refusing to recognise the couple as elements of the group as a whole. Whether responsibility for this lies with the couple or with the group, the breaking of the contract may have direct consequences on the child's psychical destiny.

In this case, two types of situation will be observed:

- The situation in which, on the part of the mother, the father or both, there is a total refusal to be committed to that contract; a decathexis that in itself indicates a serious fault in the psychical structure and reveals a more or less compensated psychotic kernel. Over the past few years, stress has been laid, from several sides, on the enclosed character of certain families of psychotics, microcosms that, while keeping their madman, preserve an unstable equilibrium that is more or less maintained, as long as any direct confrontation with the discourse of others can be avoided, by silencing anything that is said outside. The risk that the subject then runs is to be quite unable to find outside his family a support that would make it easier for him to obtain that degree of autonomy necessary to the functions of the I. This may not be the cause of psychosis, but it is certainly an inducing factor often present in the schizophrenic's family.
- Equally important, but more difficult to define, is the situation that results from the breaking of the contract, for which the group – and therefore social reality – is primarily responsible. I reject the various socio-genetic conceptions of psychosis, but, on the other hand, I do believe in the essential role played

by what I call *historical reality*. In that reality, I give equal weight to events that may affect the body, to what has actually taken place in the life of the couple during the subject's infancy, to the discourse directed at the child and the injunctions addressed to him, but *also* to the position of excluded, exploited victim that society may have actually imposed on the couple or the child.

In the final part of this book, we shall see how, whenever the historical reality of a child's life is telescoped with a fantasy construction of his perception of the world, their collusion may make it impossible to replace the fantasy by an act of sense-making that will relativise it. In a number of the cases of anamnesis among psychotics one is struck by the reduplication that social reality operates: rejection, mutilation, hate, dispossession, all those situations to which the psychotic problematic refers us, turn up again, transformed into acts, and not only fantasy acts, in the relation between the group and the couple. As soon as the I discovers the outside-family, as soon as his gaze seeks a sign there that would give him a rightful place among his fellows, he can only be met with a verdict that denies him this rightful place, that offers him only a contract that is unacceptable, since to accept it would imply that he is abandoning in reality the possibility of becoming anything other than a valueless cog in a machine that does not hide its determination to exploit or exclude him. This verdict reduplicates what, in the relation between the I and the couple, had been perceived as a refusal of any autonomy, a prohibition of any wish to contradict what has been said: it is evident that these two verdicts are not identical. To posit an identity between social repression and psychical repression, between economic exploitation and appropriation by the mother of the child's thinking, is a nonsense: but, on the other hand, because the child begins by projecting onto the social scene the pattern of his problematic in relation to the occupants of the familial space, he may see inscribed on that scene the reduplication of the same dialectic in which he now finds himself doubly trapped.

These considerations concerning the function and omnipresence of the narcissistic contract conclude my analysis of the space in which the I must come about: I have indicated the conditions that must be respected if the I is able to inhabit it and those that may make it incompatible with that function. Before approaching the most dramatic consequence of that incompatibility – psychosis – and in order to understand what expropriation it entails for the I, I shall now consider a function that specifies that agency, once it has been able to come about: one that makes possible the conjugation of a future tense compatible with that of a past tense.

The I and the conjugation of the future: concerning the identificatory project and the splitting of the I

By identificatory project I define that continuous self-construction of the I by the I that is necessary if that agency is to be able to project itself into a temporal movement, a projection on which the I's very existence depends. Access to temporality and access to a historicisation of experience go hand in hand: the appearance of the I is at the same time the appearance of a historicised time. I have indicated the factors responsible for the organisation of the space in which the I may come about; psychosis will enable us to see at work the dramatic consequences of their absence or deviation. What has been said about them and what I shall add, with the help of psychosis, defines my conception of identification[21] and marks the point at which my thinking came to a halt: now I shall simply stress the characteristic proper to the 'I that has come about', the characteristic whose absence marks psychosis. Psychosis does not eliminate the I; it would be truer to say that it is the work of the I; but it shows the reductions and expropriations with which the I pays for its survival in this case, the most obvious manifestation of this being the relation of the I to a temporality marked by the collapse of a future tense, with a resulting sameness in experience that will place the I in the grip of an image of itself that one is tempted to describe as having 'passed away' rather than belonging to the past.

The I is nothing more than the I's knowledge of the I. To the definition that I gave above a corollary may now be added: the I's knowledge of the I has as its condition, and as its aim, to ensure that the I has a knowledge of the future I and of the I's future. The 'I that has come about' denotes by definition an I that is supposed to be capable of assuming the trial of castration. That is why that image of a future I will be characterised by a renunciation of the attributes of certainty. It can only represent what the I *hopes* to become: that hope cannot be lacking in any subject, indeed, it must be able to designate its object in an identificatory image valorised by the subject and by the group, or by the subgroup, whose models are privileged by it. The ability of the I to cathect identificatory emblems that depend on the discourse of the group, and not on the discourse of only one other person, is coextensive with the alterations that the identificatory problematic and the libidinal economy undergo after the decline of the Oedipus complex. From then on, new markers will shape the image to which the I hopes to be able to conform. This image is constituted in two stages. It appears at the moment when the child is able to say: 'When I grow up, I . . . ' This is the first formulation of a project that demonstrates the child's access to the conjugation of a future tense. As long as one remains at the stage preceding the castration trial and the dissolution of the Oedipus complex, what one says will refer to formulas that may be summed up as:

- 'I'll marry mummy.'
- 'Everything in the world will be mine.'

114

In the next phase, the sentence would be completed by: 'I'll be . . . ' (a doctor, a barrister, a father, retired). Whichever term is used, and which one is never unimportant, the important thing is that it will have to designate a possible predicate and above all, and before all, a predicate that conforms to the kinship system to which the subject belongs.

That conformity proves access to the symbolic register and to an identificatory problematic suitable to him.

The formulations of the first phase show the ambiguity of the child's relation to the future tense: a tense in which the mother would become once again the person who was once thought to be the privileged object of desire, a stage at which one might finally possess everything coveted by her and by one's own I, and be absolute master of it. The time that separates the here and now from a future to come is identified with the tense that would be necessary for the return of something that would be otherwise lost. The I first opens itself up to the future only because it can project into it the encounter with a past state and a past being. But this presupposes, nevertheless, that it has been able to recognise, and to accept, the difference between what it is and what it would like to be, an acceptance that will be possible only if that encounter with knowledge concerning the difference between two human beings, who are of particular concern to him, is accompanied by an offer of the right to hope in a future that might conform to the identificatory wish. Although that future is illusory, and there can be no doubt about that, the discourse of others, on the other hand, must offer the *non-illusory* assurance of a right to see and a right to speak about a future that the I claims as its own, only if the psyche is able to valorise what 'by nature' it has a tendency to flee: change.

Whether it is a matter of the support objects of libidinal demand, identificatory markers or the mode of cathexis, the possibility of seeing change as the instrument of a bonus of future pleasure is a necessary condition for the coming into being of the I. This agency *must* be able to respond whenever the question[22] of what the I is is asked – a question that will never be silenced, which accompanies the human being throughout life and which cannot, except at fleeting moments, come up against the absence of any response without the I dissolving into anxiety. The project is the construction of an ideal image that the I proposes to itself, an image that could appear in a *future* mirror as the reflection of the observer. This image or ideal is concerned above all with what is said: although it is the successor of the image of the mirror stage, it is *also* what the reflection becomes, once it must respond to the requirements of what may be said and of what may be made meaningful. What the I wishes to become is inextricably bound up with the objects that it hopes to have and those objects, in turn, draw their brilliance from the identificatory statement that they send back to him who possesses them. As long as one remains at the stage preceding the dissolution of the Oedipus complex, the ideal will be dependent on the idealisation enjoyed by the first objects: the identificatory demand is directed at a future image that conforms to what those same objects are still supposed to expect of the subject. The I hopes to become what will once again be able to respond to the mother's desire: it will renounce this or that instinctual satisfaction by means of its belief in a future that will amply compensate it or, on the other hand, it will offer the mother that ideal, in accordance with her discourse, in exchange for the gratification obtained in the present. We can see to what extent the ideal participates, at this stage, in infantile narcissism and in a pleasure principle that it preserves more than it contradicts. But the time will come when understanding will be mandatory: the prohibition of being able to enjoy the mother is directed equally at the past, the present and the future. One must renounce belief in having been, of being, or of being able to become the object of her desire; the coincidence between the Other and the mother will be definitively dissolved. To such questions as 'who am I?' and 'what must the I become?' the mother's voice no longer has the right, or the power, to give an answer that is endowed with certainty and excludes the possibility of doubt or contradiction. To these two questions, which must necessarily find an answer, the I will respond on its own behalf by the continuous self-construction of an ideal image that it claims as its inalienable right and which assures it that the future will prove to be neither the result of pure chance, nor forged by the exclusive desire of another I. But in order for the cathexis of the future to be preserved, the subject will still have to be able to make a deal with the paradox proper to the identificatory demands as they are reshaped by the dissolution of the Oedipus complex. The future cannot coincide with the image that the subject constructs for himself of it in the present; this non-coincidence, which is constantly experienced by the subject, must nevertheless substitute for lost certainty hope in a possible future coincidence, if the cathexis of a future, from which the I cannot subtract itself, is to preserve all its strength. In order to be, the I must find support in that wish, but that future time, once reached, will have to become the source of a new project, in a referral that will end only in death. *A gap must remain between the I and its project*: what the I thinks it is must reveal a '*less than*', which is *always there* in relation to what it wishes to become. The future I and the present I must maintain a difference, an *x* that represents what would have to be added to the I for the two to coincide. *That x must remain lacking*: it represents the assumption of the castration trial in the identificatory register and it recalls what that trial leaves intact: the narcissistic hope in a self-encounter, always deferred, between the I and its ideal that would permit the cessation of any identificatory quest. It is therefore a compromise that the I makes with time: it renounces making the future that locus to which the past might return, it accepts that fact, but it still hopes that one day that future will give it back possession of the dreamt-of past.

To preserve that compromise is the task of the I that has come about: the space that it inhabits will be organised in such a way as to reinforce its stability. The factors making this organisation possible have already been analysed, in the context of the action of the parents' discourse, when the parents, having been able to assume the castration trial and repress their Oedipal desire, have handed on that possible assumption and repression to the child. But castration anxiety, which no subject can escape, must nevertheless not go beyond a certain threshold. What Freud denotes by that term is simply the anxiety that overcomes the subject when he discovers that the I can exist only by finding support in the good things that he cathects, that he is dependent, in part, on the image that the other's gaze sends back to him, that the satisfaction of his desire requires that the Other's desire reciprocates his desire, whereas he discovers at the same time that there is no guarantee of the permanence of either the desire or the life of the other, or of the permanence of his knowledge concerning identification or of his belief in its ideology. At a stage preceding this trial, the I has been able to believe in the immutability of the libido's fixation on objects emblazoned by the Other, to believe, too, that the obligation to make meaning imposed upon him offered a guarantee of certainty and that the reference to others' discourse could only confirm a posteriori the obligation to make meaning that he had accepted.

This series of certainties collapses when the subject discovers that the mother does not see her pleasure as a response to his desire, that the objects that benefited from the brilliance given them by virtue of belonging to the maternal field had usurped her. The confrontation between the child and the father's discourse and, more generally, the discourse of the group, for which an agency other than the father may play a mediating role, reveals to him that what he thought about his relation to his mother, and about his mother's relation to him, was a deception. He finds himself back in the position of a usurper who was unaware, not only that he occupied a place to which he had no right, but, more seriously, that he was alone in believing it to be his. The parental discourse and, through the parents' voices, the discourse of others, placed him elsewhere, in that place to which he had not yet come. Castration may be defined as the discovery in the identificatory register that *one had never occupied the place that one had thought to be one's own and that, on the contrary, one was supposed to occupy a place where one could not yet be.* Anxiety arises when one discovers the risk, implied by knowing that one is not in the eyes of others in the place that one believed one was occupying and that one could no longer know from what place others are speaking to one or in what place he who is speaking to you situates you. One must then agree to recognise that the markers that assure the I of its identificatory knowledge may always come up against an absence, a mourning, a rejection, a lie, that force the subject into a painful reassessment of his objects, his markers, his ideology. That is why castration is a trial that one may enter, but from which, in a sense, *one does not emerge*; one may refuse to enter it, one may make a desperate retreat, but it is an illusion to believe that one can emerge from it. What one can do is assume the trial in such a way as to preserve for the I some fixed points, on which one may find support when an identificatory conflict arises. To believe in the possibility of a world in which men and women would be spared the anxiety deriving from their dependence on the desire of the Other or the price that has to be paid for a desire of omnipotence and a desire for death, which are unremittingly engaged in their discreet, but endless struggle, is to believe in a myth or to understand nothing about the psyche. Although identification anxiety or castration anxiety (the two terms mean exactly the same thing) is particularly crystallised for men, at least in most cultures, in the fear of being deprived of the sexual organ, and for women in the fear that men, discovering that women have no penis, will find that what women have to offer their desire is without value, it is because being *either* a man *or* a woman is the first discovery that the I makes in the field of its identificatory markers. This first division of the subjects of the world informs the I that 'to be' is always accompanied by an *either/or*, that there is a destiny according to which one will never know what the pleasure of the other sex is, that auto-eroticism itself depends on the introjection of an image of the object that embodies a fantasy. This is the origin of a kind of knowledge, whose achievement will allow the subject, at best, to renounce the fulfilment of a desire recognised as impossible and to maintain a hope that one day the desire might become objectless. Castration anxiety is the tribute that every subject pays to the agency that is called the I and without which the subject could not be the subject of his own discourse.

Castration and identification are two sides of the same thing; once the I has come about, anxiety will return whenever the identificatory markers show signs of vacillating. No culture can protect the subject against the danger of this vacillation, just as no structure can protect the subject from the experience of anxiety. On the other hand, it may be argued that in the familial structure, as in the social structure, there are forms that are particularly anxiety-inducing and, as a result, particularly likely to induce in the subject either psychotic reactions or forms of behaviour that, in a more or less camouflaged way, are close to them. Access to the identificatory project, as I have defined it, proves that the subject has been able to overcome that fundamental trial that forces him to renounce a group of objects that, in the earliest phase of his life, represented the supports both of his object libido and of his narcissistic libido, objects that have enabled him to posit himself as a being and to designate the objects that he covets. There is no doubt that castration anxiety may be manifested in certain cultures by a different statement, that the object whose loss one fears may not concern the sexual organ directly, but nevertheless it refers, at bottom, to a castration fantasy; that is to say, to the fear felt by the subject when recalling wounds and bereavements whose trace remains ineffaceable. His pleasure has not been the same as that enjoyed by the first representative of the Other; sexual pleasure is at the mercy of an impossible knowledge of the desire and pleasure of the other sex; one can have no hold on one's own body. What the I 'is' can be known only through the mediation of what it thinks it knows and, above all, of what it thinks it *has* as self-knowledge, this possession concerning his knowledge being essentially revealed as the locus of an impossible certainty. To agree to renounce that certainty and to preserve the cathexis of the I and its coming about are tasks that are the responsibility of the project, the presence of this project implying that the I has been able to run over all the stages from his entry on the psychical stage to the dissolution of the Oedipus complex.

The need to preserve this project is responsible for what I define as the concept of the *unconscious I*, the effect of the repressing power exerted by the project, at the expense of the statements in which the I has successively recognised itself and which it represses outside its field, whenever they endanger the coherence of the identificatory project that the I cathects. In its totality, the I embraces all the identificatory positions and statements in which it has successively recognised itself. These statements will be able to be maintained or rejected: they may preserve part of their cathexis or be only the cathected memory of a stage in its existence. Thus the effect of the project is not only to offer the I that future image towards which it projects itself, but also to preserve the memory of past statements, which are simply the history by which the I constructs itself as a narrative. On the other hand, that part of those statements that will be rejected outside the space of the I coincides with *that part of the I itself that must be excluded if that agency is to be able to function in a manner that conforms to its project.* It may be said therefore that the I is constituted by a history, represented by the set of identificatory statements that it remembers, by the statements that manifest *in its present* its relation to the identificatory project and, lastly, by the set of statements on which its repressive action is exerted in order that they remain outside its field, outside its memory, outside its knowledge. What remains *unconscious for the I* – and I mean unconscious in the fullest sense of the term – is *the repressing action that the I exerts and which succeeds in repressing part of its history*; that is to say, the statements that have become contradictory with a narrative that it *constantly* reconstructs and every statement that would demand a libidinal position, which it rejects or declares to be forbidden. A split takes place between the I, as identificatory knowledge that is intelligible and may be expressed in *statements that conform* to the laws of discourse and the kinship system, and part of the set of statements representing stages in the I's libidinal history: it is this part, belonging to this second set, that by the I's repressing action constitutes the *I's unconscious*. If the I coincides with its knowledge of the I, the unconscious I represents the effect and consequence of the action exerted by that knowledge; it represents a necessary condition for the existence of that knowledge. It comprises the major part of past identificatory statements, the very ones that could alone reveal to it who the I was, what were its desires, what were the objects that it has had to mourn.

The function that I have attributed to the project as a way of access to the category of the future has as its corollary the action that it exerts in constituting a past tense that is compatible with the cathexis of a becoming. That is why I have been able to say that the appearance of the I is coextensive with the appearance of the category of time and history. These two categories, in turn, can become an integral part of the functioning of the I only through the presence of a project that gives them their status in the psychical field.

If it is right to argue that one of the effects of the castration trial takes the form of the assumption by the subject of a knowledge of his own death, it should also be added that this assumption has as its prerequisite the appropriation of an identificatory project, which is inevitably a temporal project. It is a project in which the dream of an ever-deferred tomorrow continues to have a place, a project that would finally allow desire to encounter the object of its quest and the I to cancel out the 'less than' that separates it from the ideal of which it *dreams*.

The project shows the limits that the I imposes on that dream, but also the limits that it continues to reject, once it has been able to overcome the various trials that mark its history from the moment of its appearance on the psychical stage to the moment represented by the dissolution of the Oedipus complex.

In an explicit and perhaps even more in an implicit way, the concepts of the imaginary and the symbolic have had a central place in the conceptualisation that I have proposed of the identificatory process and its mechanisms: hence this annex.

Annex: what I mean by the concepts of symbolic and imaginary

We owe to Lacan the place that the concepts of the symbolic and the imaginary have come to occupy in analytical theory; and it is also to him that we owe a calling into question of psychoanalysis in general and, in particular, of a theory of identification, from which I have borrowed most of my own. If theoretical borrowing is to be anything other than mere repetition of another's thinking, it cannot but entail a subjective interpretation of the material borrowed. I am convinced that if we are to think another's thought, which is really the only way to pay homage to it and to recognise its value, we must never reproduce it in an identical fashion. There would be little point in referring the reader to Lacan's *Ecrits* with a view to understanding what I mean by the concepts of imaginary and symbolic.

In this particular case there is another difficulty, bound up with the concepts themselves: their long history in philosophical discourse, their semantic overload, the meanings that other authors have already given them, which cannot be ignored, mean that, by using them, the analyst always runs the risk of introducing with them concepts belonging to other disciplines and which the history of ideas has long associated with them. The analyst-author may be tempted either to make a *tabula rasa* of the past or to create an amalgam that may turn out to be a source of confusion: in either case the reader will have difficulty in understanding, being unable to determine what the terms designate in the text that he is reading.

It seems to me that there is a particular danger of this in much of the writing of Lacanian inspiration; this is especially apparent when the writer is dealing with the concept of the symbolic, where it is difficult to see whether he is referring to the function proper to all language, to written signs, to mathematical language, or to the metaphorical dimension that the sign must safeguard. When reading such writers I have often had the impression that the term 'symbolic', whether used as a noun or an adjective, defined at one and the same time the function of language, a particular property of the sign, specifying an enigmatic relation to the phallic signifier, the Name-of-the-Father as organiser of the kinship system, access to a law and many other things, one gaining emphasis over the others according to the needs of the argument. This demonstrates the real difficulty posed by the use of these concepts, but what makes their use even more abusive is when they are transformed into a sort of master-key that can in fact turn the locks only of doors that are already wide open or, on the contrary, give another turn of the key to any lock that dares to resist the analytical key. It is in the hope of reducing this danger that I felt the need to explain the use that I am making of these two concepts when applying them to the register of identification.

The concept of symbolic

The peculiarity of the symbolic function, of the linguistic sign and of language, if we accept Ernst Cassirer's definitions of these terms,[23] is to create a symbolic relational configuration that may produce a shaping of the real that allows us to pass from the individual to universal values. The singularity of the elements contrasts with the universality of the relations linking them; in naming them, language is the creator of the meaning that these relations produce; this power is manifested through what will now be declared to be the law of the relation between the elements.

If we are to understand by *body*, not the chemical body, but the body inhabited by the speaker, it may be said that there exists a sector of language whose terms no longer designate the body according to what it is and the way in which it is presented, but grasp it as a set of possible reactions, causal relations and possible relations governed by universal laws.

This way of grasping the body, which designates the individual as the support of a symbolic function, is the one at work in the term *kinship*, which lays down and produces the relational law present between the totality of the terms of the system. So if the symbolic function of signs is a property inherent in them taken as a whole, if that function is always intended to pass from the singular to the universal, we encounter in the field of discourse a fragment made up of a particular series of signs, whose function is expressed in a direct and privileged way by *the naming that defines the subject's place and function in his familial network*. The terms 'father', 'son', 'mother', 'ancestor' designate a function that has meaning only through the relation that the function posits between a term and the set of terms of the kinship system. That function is independent of the individual subject who embodies it during the brief duration of his existence. To the mobility of the occupants are opposed the fixity and identity of the concept of the function defined by the symbol. It is to this sector of the linguistic field that I am referring when I use the terms 'symbolic' or 'symbolic function', *in the identificatory register*.[24] I believe that clinical medicine allows us to operate that division: it shows us that it is certainly that subset that may prove to be an obstacle to the subject's accession to the function of language and, more importantly, that this linguistic sector possesses a power of self-naming that explains why, in most cases, the psychotic can still name a mathematical symbol, often in a perfectly correct way, whereas he is incapable of knowing how the concept of father, mother or ancestor relates to him.

A split occurs between the subject's continuing ability to recognise himself in the term that designates him as *this* son of *that* mother, of *that* father, or as brother of *that* other person, and his inability to appropriate the symbol for himself, in other words the function as concept, an appropriation that would require him to recognise the permanence of a law of transmission that transcends any temporary, particular occupant. It now becomes impossible for the psychotic to separate the empirical support from the element of a concept, which must refer to a class; it is no longer the class of fathers or sons that defines the paternal function independently of this particular father, but, on the contrary, that individual element will be identified with the category of the class. The universal is annulled in a particular, accidental element: the concept loses all universal meaning and, by the same token, any ability to symbolise; it becomes a prisoner of the physical thing that embodies it. Although the psychotic knows that there are such things as fathers, he can conceive of the function of the class, and therefore the concept of paternity, only as a mere extension of the relation existing between himself and that father or between himself and that absence. It is no longer in his power to represent to himself the whole set of elements of the system as an autonomous structure and, therefore, to see in the kinship structure a law to which all subjects are subjected. Such a representation would imply the subject's capacity, on the basis of the position that he occupies in the network, to relate the whole set of actual elements, past and future, to one another, whether or not he has any empirical knowledge of them. The fact that one has actually known a grandfather, an uncle, or even one's own mother, must become an accident independent of the fact that it remains in the power of the I, on the basis of the position that the term 'son' imposes on him, to reconstruct a relational network in which each place is defined by the term designating the kinship relation proper to the system. The psychotic cannot declare himself to be a filial '*function*'; he cannot go beyond a designation that pins him down as the son of that couple. As a result, the meaning of son or daughter remains a prisoner of the recognition, or the non-recognition, that he can no longer expect, except from the Other identified with a real referent; hence the conflict, of which death is the stake, that may oppose him to the discourse of the Other, a conflict justified by his absolute dependence on a meaning subjected to the arbitrary whim of him who recognises or annuls him by refusing him that recognition.

The term 'foreclosure', as proposed by Lacan, as pathognomic of the register of the psychotic problematic, designates, in my opinion, not the foreclosure of the symbolic function of language in general, but the impossibility for the I to separate the statements that refer only to the specular image, with all its accompanying precariousness, randomness and impermanence, from a name that might designate him as having a right to a kinship function independently of any arbitrary action. He can appropriate an inherited symbolic function only if he has the right and duty to transmit it to his successor. As a result, any possibility of presenting himself as the representative of a class, as guarantor of a function and as guarantor of a transmission of which he has been the effect and of which he will become the agent, is foreclosed to the psychotic. The symbolic function of the kinship system has the task of framing the space of the imaginary, which marks off the limits that the imaginary must not transgress: any statement that contradicts the coherence and order of the kinship system, itself coextensive with the linguistic system defining a culture, will be excluded.

In the psychoanalytic field, the symbolic function should designate three functions proper to the linguistic sign belonging to the kinship system:

- it should link each term to a law and to a relational system, which is universal for a given culture;
- it should indicate the designation that is opposed *qua* universal meaning to the *necessary* individuality of the I's identificatory and imaginary markers, an individuality in which the individual could not be differentiated from a whole, a species, a kinship class, a sexual category, in which he would no longer see himself as anything other than one element interchangeable with any other;
- it should allow the I to find its place between a before and an after in which it may recognise itself: those who preceded him, whether he knew them or not, occupied the same position in the system, just as those who will follow him will take over the same place and exercise the same function. Between these two limits is deployed the imaginary field, on the stage of which identification in the strict sense will take place.

The imaginary

The relation of the I to the image, in which it recognises itself and becomes alienated, comes about at the moment defined by Lacan as the mirror stage. It is a decisive encounter between the observer and his reflection, but an encounter that can assume its full meaning only if one takes account, as Lacan put it in his

123

seminar for 1961-62, of 'that movement of the small child's gaze discovering himself in the mirror, which takes him to the mother's gaze, in search of confirmation for the beauty of the image, before returning to the mirror and to his own specular reflection'. The specular experience comprises three stages:

- the appearance in the mirror of an image that the psyche recognises as its own;
- the turning of the gaze towards the mother's gaze where a statement is read to the effect that this image is the object of her pleasure, that it is the image of the loved, the good, the beautiful . . . ;
- the return of the gaze to the image present in the mirror, the gaze that will now be constituted by the junction between the image and the legend concerning it, as perceived in the mother's gaze.

It will be this junction that sets up the imaginary register and designates the stage at which will appear that which heralds the arrival of the I: the stage at which a summons takes place between the specular image and the identificatory statement that the Other, at an earlier stage, utters concerning the specular image.

What the child encounters is not just the objectification of self as image, but also the designation, which is sent back to him by the Other's gaze, indicating to him 'who is' he whom the Other loves, names and recognises. What the subject discovers in the mirror is the image of the thing that is the subject of the discourse spoken by her and by those who speak to him, a discourse that begins by identifying the subject with the identificatory statement of which that same discourse is the agent. As we have seen, these statements will have to become, during a second stage, the property of the I: their diversity and profusion will require that what has been constituted in the mirror stage as a specular marker, and which will become a point of anchorage, remains cathected and accessible to the subject.

Imaginary identification presupposes that the subject can name himself by an identifying statement that may be referred to his image, by which I mean that image of himself that accompanies him throughout his life. The relation that any subject will have with that image testifies to the conflictual dimension that runs through the entire field of identification.

To begin with, this is because the subject demands of the image what it is impossible for it to give him: to be for himself an autonomous, independent reference in the way in which he is seen by the gaze of others. This independence would allow him to oppose what may be unsustainable in the image of oneself that is sent back to one, one's own judgement on one's reflection. Experience will prove to the subject that the image is incapable of forcing the other to see it as one imagines it, and as one would like others to see it. It should be added that the subject can never be content unless the mirror tells him, as in fairy stories, that he is the most beautiful of all, because it is for the other's look that he wishes to occupy that place and, under that gaze, all mastery eludes him. The omnipresence of that conflict reveals the ambiguity of the link that, in the identificatory register, unites the seen of the image to the statement that decides what is to be seen in it:

- The image offers a point of anchorage to the identificatory statements; its presence is indispensable if the statement is to be offered as a legend specifying the image of an I, which may recognise in the statement that which expresses what it desires, what it demands, what it is.

But once this summons has taken place, the I, which is Hegelian without knowing it, finds itself confronted by a double image:

- that which its gaze sees in the mirror;
- that which appears to it on others' retinas.

Any contradiction between them leads to an identificatory conflict the results of which run the risk of bringing about the destruction of one or the other, and ending in the mutilation of the I itself. Indeed, the I may function only if it can be assured of the stability of those two markers; namely, its recognition of itself and the recognition of itself through the gaze of others. This conflict, which forms for the I part of an ever-recurring experience, will bring about a reorganisation of the identificatory problematic that will displace its centre of gravity from the specular support to what I have called identificatory knowledge or the I's discourse on the I. I shall say no more on this matter, except to remind the reader that, from this moment on, the truth of statements referring to and defining the I, is no longer within the exclusive power of another's discourse, but is expected from the discourse of the group, which alone will have the power to decide in what conditions the I's knowledge of the I may be declared to conform to the truth test recognised by others in general, even if it is refuted by *an* other.

It is to this same discourse that we owe the valorisation of a series of value-emblems, hierarchised in the name of a set of imaginary values, but under the aegis of the sociocultural field. The term 'imaginary' means here that the definition concerning the reality of the thing named gives way to the function of identificatory value that it will possess. One may define the concepts of physical strength, erudition, wealth, fidelity, but what represents for others a strong, erudite, rich, faithful subject will always share in the imaginary value that the cultural discourse gives these terms. The value and identificatory function of those emblems require the consensus of the group or subgroup to which the subject belongs. The valorisation of the emblem by the subject himself dispossesses the emblem, in this case, of its value as identificatory marker. The fact that the consensus operates totally in the imaginary register does not mean that it

125

represents only the possibility offered the subject to endure his non-recognition by a fellow human being, even if that person is particularly cathected, without having to destroy him or accept being destroyed oneself.

I would say that the register of the imaginary defines the set of statements that have the function of identificatory emblems *and* the specular image that must serve them as a point of anchorage.

These emblems are presented to the I as identical to his 'qualities': these 'qualities', in turn, are defined by the message that, beginning with them, returns to the subject telling him 'who' he *is*. To be like the image that others admire or to be like the image admired by those whom the I admires are the two formulations that the narcissistic wish borrows from the field of identification.

If the specular never loses its rights, if it remains a necessary point of anchorage, one also notes that the image may maintain its brilliance only as long as the subject believes that it conforms to statements that declare that it possesses the values that it claims to display, and as long as the subject thinks that these values are seen and recognised as such by others.

Once the organisation of the identificatory field is in place, we shall see throughout the subject's life a double mapping:

- In the register of amatory cathexes will persist the demand for recognition – to be the lover or to be the beloved – which brings two I's face to face; the fact that others in general recognise that the I is behaving as a loving subject has little weight in the face of the beloved's statement that 'it isn't true that you love me'. In this register recognition, for both partners, falls under the aegis of a particular statement that may or not coincide with the one in which the subject recognises his truth. But, even in this case, recourse to others is not totally excluded; the subject will be able to have recourse to them, in case of danger, to prove to himself that, in spite of everything, his choice or his rejection was well founded.
- On the other hand, in the field of the narcissistic cathexes, the I deals with markers that must be shared and valorised by the discourse of the group; this has as its result the quest for a guarantee, for and by the I, that discourse and truth may coincide.

Perhaps it has now become clearer what I meant by the framing of the imaginary, which one owes to the symbolic function and designation. The set of identificatory statements designate who is I and the objects that he possesses, what he dreams to become and what he wishes to have; to keep that power – of substitution, invention of other markers and new emblems, change – which these statements show, and also to give place to that element of dream that is necessary to the functioning of the I, remains the task that falls to them. The fact that man allows himself to be caught in the trap of creations of his own imaginary is another matter. But this inventiveness, which always verges on excess, finds, and must

126

find, boundaries that show the subject that to dream the impossible does not mean making it possible, or making impossible the existence of the I. These boundaries are neither the work of the subject himself, nor that of the imaginary register: the subject encounters them in a discourse that guarantees him the existence of a series of non-arbitrary statements independent of any particular psyche. It is to them that the subject will appeal, not in order to define what he hopes to be or to have, but to designate the relation that links the hoping subject with the earliest recipients of his most fundamental demands. Whether the response given by these archaic interlocutors has been affirmative or negative, the symbolic designation declares that it has no effect on the rights that the subject may claim as a member of a particular class, as a necessary link in the transmission of a kinship system or a linguistic system, on which he depends, just as those two systems depend on the transmission carried out by each new subject.

I hope I have made clear the meaning that the terms 'imaginary' and 'symbolic' have in my work. I also hope that I have justified my choice of those terms.

PART TWO

The interpretation of violence and primary delusional thinking

Concerning schizophrenia: the potential for psychosis and primary delusional thinking

Schizophrenia, paranoia, primary delusional thinking: general considerations

Whatever criticisms one may rightly make of this entomology of human beings and the thoughts about them offered by psychiatry, analysts continue to use the same labels, even while transforming the meaning proper to them. Do we do this out of force of habit or as homage paid to our predecessors' gifts of observation? Probably both. But this borrowing is not without its dangers and one may well wonder if it does not conceal an ambiguity in the relation of psychoanalysis to psychosis. I shall leave the question unanswered and simply say that the forms that psychotic discourse assumes for the observer are never the effect of mere chance and may be understood simply by analysing the mode of defence that they privilege. They derive from a time when psychical work came up against an insuperable obstacle, forcing it to abandon well trod paths, and they provide an insight into the particular nature of that obstacle. Nevertheless, psychoanalytic theory generally assumes the right to speak about *psychosis* (in the singular) or the psychotic structure and to postulate, beyond the diversity of its forms, the presence of a minimum series of features, a common background to the various clinical pictures. The elements that each author will isolate in the series, the interpretation that he will offer of them, define in turn the various psycho-analytic constructions that seek to account for the psychotic phenomenon. The homogeneity that these options often claim is illusory, though each author usually appeals to the same key concepts of fixation, regression, reality loss, foreclosure, to cite only the principal ones. Much more than in the field of neurosis one is struck, as soon as the question of psychosis arises, by the facility with which one assumes the right to create an amalgam in which will be found a jumble of

Freudian, Kleinian, Lacanian concepts, and more recently ones deriving from Bateson, Bion and that other amalgam called anti-psychiatry. Now most of these authors would be the first to declare that, in our discipline, one cannot appropriate a concept, especially a key concept, without accepting its consequences and the prerequisites that depend on the theory that forged it and from which it cannot be extracted. I am not defending any sectarian dogma or orthodoxy, but the confusion that so frequently arises in analytical discourse, as soon as it is applied to psychosis, creates a smokescreen that should be denounced: in such cases, Harlequin's costume scarcely conceals the holes and hasty patching up that are all too apparent in all our interpretative models when applied to psychosis. Yet another slide into the theories on psychosis or the psychoses seems inevitably to be taking place: to bracket out the questions that psychosis poses in favour of *a* question that is more approachable and which therefore can be identified as *the* cause; this will allow us to declare all those questions to which we have no answer to be secondary. What we have here is a reductionist tendency, two characteristic examples of which are the Kleinian concept of projective identification and the Lacanian concept of the foreclosure of the Name-of-the-Father. It seems to me that such inappropriate concepts adopt, without knowing it, a similar position of rejection concerning the specificity of a message that embarrasses and disturbs. Like the road to hell, the roads of theory are paved with good intentions: they cannot hide the extent to which a will-to-knowledge displays a lack of respect for the individual on whom one imposes an interpretation that merely repeats, in a different form, the violence and abuse of power of an earlier discourse. It seems to me that nowadays psychosis very often serves interests that have nothing to do with it; all too often when speaking in the name of the mad, one is merely denying them once again any right to make themselves heard. One uses language that one imputes to them in order to show how well founded is a particular discipline, ideology or struggle, which actually concerns the interests of the non-mad, or of those who claim to be so. The apologia of madness, the apologia of the duty not to intervene and not to cure are modern forms of rejection and exclusion that we do not even have the courage to recognise, which makes them at least as oppressive and harmful as their predecessors. If we are to approach the frontier of madness, we must agree in advance to move into that place where a drama is being played out for which the observer, without exception, pays neither with his pain nor his reason, and also to recognise that we cannot expect too much of our adopted theories. This last statement is a warning addressed to my readers: my reflections on psychosis do not avoid the danger of making the theoretical construction on which they are based, and without which they could not have been formulated, seem more complete than in fact it is.

Before examining this construction and defining what I mean by the concept of 'delusional thinking', two things should be made clear. The first concerns the sense that I give the term 'necessary condition', which will often recur in what

I say; the second is the place occupied by clinical example in this work and more generally in analytical writings:

1   To speak of 'necessary conditions' is not the same thing as to speak of sufficient conditions. We can define the first and show that they are very common; it is not within our power to declare them sufficient. If we could pass from one term to the other, we would be in possession of a model that accounted exhaustively for psychotic causality: we simply cannot do this. Between the necessary and the sufficient is to be found not only that which eludes our knowledge, but also that which makes psychosis a destiny in which the subject has a role to play, and not just an accident passively submitted to. In my introduction I wrote that psychosis never allows itself to be reduced to a minus quantity in relation to some correct measure of the 'normal'; if there is a minus quantity, there is also difference and a plus quantity. That plus quantity is enough to invalidate the various theories that set out, on the basis of the mother's desire, social oppression or the double bind, to reduce psychosis and more particularly schizophrenia to a passive response created and preformed by others' desire, discourse, madness. The presence of these factors is not enough in itself to create the child's madness; it is enough to put in place the conditions that make it possible.

2   As for the role generally played by clinical examples in analytical writings, one thing is obvious from the outset: any case history or fragment of case history is always chosen by the author to support a particular theoretical hypothesis. We all know that there are privileged examples and others that lend themselves much less easily to that demonstrative function: we may well wonder to what extent extrapolation remains valid at all.

As far as the examples that I use are concerned, the reason for their choice is obvious: they are 'exemplary' because they prove the function proper to the elements of reality on the basis of which psychotic discourse has constructed the interpretation that we call delusional. In case histories where those elements seem to be absent, even though one hears identical interpretations from the subject, I assume the right to deduce from them, not that they have certainly taken place or that only the memory of them has disappeared, but that experiences *actually* undergone by those subjects have led them to interpret their historical reality in the same way as if those elements had been present. At the end of this book, I shall show the role played in the case of a paranoiac by the manifest hate between the parental couple. Such an example does not allow me to conclude that in every family in which the child presents paranoiac features the manifest discourse would indicate, if it were known, a similar hate, but I believe the hypothesis by which the child, in all cases, has perceived something in that relation that enabled him to unmask that element and to hypostasise its presence is a legitimate one. In other words, psychosis is never reducible to the projection of

133

a fantasy on to a neutral reality; in this sense, it differs from neurosis. This fantasy projection quite obviously exists, but the role that it may play in the beginnings of a psychosis is due to the telescoping that takes place, in these cases, between the fantasy representation and what in fact appears on the stage of reality. The exemplary case, therefore, only shows, in a crystallised form, what was very probably played out in other cases. When Monsieur R . . . told me how his father had forbidden him to learn the language spoken by his mother, how as long as he could remember his father had condemned and shown contempt for his mother's race and that his mother refused to learn his father's language, I knew that, from a theoretical point of view, I was in a privileged situation.[1] But, on the other hand, when I observe that the discourse of various paranoiacs that I have been able to listen to, and not only that of Monsieur R . . . , have proved the subject's need to see himself as the fruit of hate, to posit an identity between hate and the state of being a couple, and to create, on that basis, a history, his own, that may continue to make sense, I conclude from this – and it does not seem to me to be abusive – that the history of Monsieur R . . . exemplifies a situation that, in a more partial, more veiled way, was present in all the histories experienced. I should add that, within the limits of my experience, this hypothesis, has so far proved true. My sensitivity to this type of phenomenon certainly played a role in it; I hope that it has not led me to hallucinate something that does not exist.

Primary delusional thinking

Under the terms of schizophrenia and paranoia I designate those two modes of representation that, in certain conditions, the I can construct out of its relation to the world, constructions that have the common feature of being based on a statement of origins, which is substituted for that shared by the group of other subjects.

By delusional idea I mean any statement that proves that the I links the presence of a 'thing' – whatever that thing may be – to a causal order that contradicts the logic according to which the discourse of the group functions, a relation that remains unintelligible therefore for that group discourse.

That is why I apply the term 'delusional' to the statement of origins around which is elaborated the logic of the schizophrenic and paranoiac discourse, and it is also the reason that allows me, within the usual sense of the term and within an initial mapping of the schizophrenic problematic that is concerned only with those characteristics that we think may be generalised, to speak of a psychotic construction or of a delusional construction when defining the response given by the subject to a particular organisation of the space in which the I ought to have come about.

The analysis of the factors responsible for this type of organisation, which forces the I to work out a construction that appeals to a 'delusional' causal order, will present us with two discourses, that of the 'word-bearer' and that of the father, both of which have turned out to fail in their tasks. This failure may be overcome by the subject without his having to have recourse to an order of causality that does not conform to that of others, which is why the necessary is not the sufficient. In all other cases one will observe the presence of a statement concerning the alien origin of our mode of thinking: this is what I call *primary delusional thinking*. It is a consequence of the encounter between the I and a specific organisation of the space outside the psyche and of the discourse that circulates in it, and it becomes itself a prerequisite for the possible elaboration of the manifest forms of schizophrenia and paranoia.

The presence of this prerequisite is for me synonymous with what I shall define by the concept of psychotic potentiality.[2] By this I do not mean a latent possibility common to every subject, but an organisation of the psyche that cannot but give place to manifest symptoms, and which reveals, whenever it can be analysed, the presence of a primary delusional thinking that is encysted and not repressed. This cyst may manage to burst its membrane and pour its content into the psychical space: when this happens one passes from the potential to the manifest.

Primary delusional thinking or psychotic potentiality therefore act as a hinge between two orders of causality; that is why, before embarking on an analysis of the conditions to which they respond, I shall elucidate what I mean by these terms.

By primary delusional thinking I mean the interpretation that the I gives to itself of what is the cause of origins – the origin of the subject, of the world, of pleasure, of unpleasure: all the questions posed by the presence of these four fundamental factors will find a single identical response thanks to a statement whose function will be to indicate a cause that makes sense of their existence. By this creation the I maintains access to the field of signification by creating meaning where, for reasons that we shall analyse, the discourse of the Other has confronted it with a meaningless or inadequate statement. On the basis of this thought it will be possible to set up a system of meanings that conforms to it, to operate a particular form of splitting that takes the form of what I call the encystment of that thought, an encystment that allows the subject to function in accordance with an apparent, fragile normality or, again, that thought will give rise to no system-atisation but will act as a single, exhaustive interpretation covering any experience that is loaded with affect and therefore meaningful: what eludes the grip of this single interpretation will be decathected and ignored by the subject and by his discourse. The first case finds its completed form in the paranoiac system, the second constitutes psychotic potentiality, the third marks the schizophrenic experience. Systematisation and extrapolation may occur as soon as the primary delusional thinking is in place: it will then be confronted by the infantile forms of schizophrenia and paranoia. They may occur later, following the failure of the compromise that hitherto protected psychotic potentiality. A special place must be given to precocious infantile autism, in which it is the primary delusional thinking itself that has been unable to develop. This first setting up of the concept of primary delusional thinking would be enough to show the importance that I give to the function of the I in psychosis: far from being the great absentee, the I is the artisan of a reorganisation of the relation that it will have to maintain with the other two processes that share its own psychical space and with the discourse of the representative of the Other and the representative of others. On the basis of the psychotic phenomenon in both discourses under consideration, I posit this original creation of a meaning that fills a gap in the discourse of the Other. This is not, as might be thought, a substitution of one meaning for another that one rejects because it is frustrating or contrary to the pleasure principle, but the creation of a new meaning that might be formulated if one respected the logic and causal order proper to others' discourse. A paradoxical example comes to mind: let us imagine a mathematician who, claiming that his theory conforms to the rules of mathematics, declared that two plus two make five; let us imagine a subject forced to count according to the rules of mathematics and to accept that contradictory postulate. The subject might be able to respond to that injunction only by inventing a new theorem proving that in certain cases four and five are synonymous; he would have to create a non-existent demonstration in order to make the proposed postulate probable. The same goes for the subject that we call psychotic: in order to succeed in speaking the language of others, and usually he does do so, he must first invent an interpretation that makes a meaning imposed upon him, which he cannot reject, conform to reason, without endangering the foundation of his statements. He is then free to reconstruct the totality of the mathematical system, to reconcile this demonstration with others contradictory to it, to discover the existence of an undecidable, or to abandon mathematics in favour of a single, exhaustive demonstration.

Delusional thinking assumes the task of demonstrating the truth of a postulate of the 'word-bearer's' discourse that is clearly false. Implicitly or explicitly, this postulate concerns the origin of the subject and the origin of his history: the first words heard that speak of that double origin have proved for the subject to be contradictory with his affective and actual experience. Between the commentary and the commented a contradiction has appeared. To accept the commentary, to take it over as his own, would entail appropriating a history without a subject and a discourse that would deny all truth to sense experience. To reject it would involve remaining face-to-face with an unsayable experience, something unnameable. In order to escape these two impasses, an escape that is nothing less than guaranteed, the I can always interpret the commentary. By doing so it may hope to coincide, always in a more or less shaky, forced way, the sequence of his history and a first paragraph written by primary delusional thinking.

The construction of an I that wishes to preserve its relation to discourse, but which, in doing so, like the sorcerer's apprentice, invents a magic formula that always has the power to assume autonomy and to impose a radical defeat on him.

To see this primary thinking as a result of the subject's encounter with a statement of the discourse has two corollaries:

- to situate in that phase in which the infant becomes a child by acceding to the register of meaning the moment when primary delusional thinking may be constituted;
- to grant a privileged role to the special factors present in the discourse that the child encounters on the stage of the real. It is the texture of this discourse that brings with it the conditions necessary for that space to become a locus in which primary delusional thinking will come about.

The question concerning the origin

To understand the consequences of the absence in the texture of this discourse of a statement concerning origin, or of the presence of a statement that refers the child to a meaning that his I cannot assume, forces us to consider in a different way the role that must be given to infantile sexual theory and, above all, to that which conceals and condenses the question, apparently so simple, posed by every child: 'Where do babies come from?'

Freud showed us the way by linking that question to that other question posed by the child concerning the sexuality of the parental couple, the enigma of their pleasure and of what might be the cause of their desire. If we continue along that path, we observe that at the moment when this question appears, the answer that the child expects concerns previous questions and, in particular, the question posed to the I by the presence in his field of effects of psychical productions of which he is not the agent and with which he can cohabit only if he can link them to a cause made knowable to him. This being the case, and we have already seen why it is a requirement for the functioning of the I, an equivalence will be established between knowledge of the supposed cause and recognition of an effect and of an affect of which one would be the agent. To simplify, it might be said that from the time when the I is able to state 'I feel pleasure or unpleasure because . . . ', he makes pleasure or unpleasure that which would depend on the knowledge that he has of its cause and in doing so transforms it into an effect that would fall under his jurisdiction.

At a first rough attempt, I would say that the question 'Where do babies come from?' is equivalent to the question 'Where did I come from?' and that the second waits for the answer to give the text of the first paragraph of the history in which he must be able to recognise himself, since it alone can give meaning to the series of identificatory positions that he must in turn occupy.

Now, whether we are dealing with a particular history or the history of subjects in general, the two share the same requirement: they cannot admit that they know nothing about their origin. The first paragraph cannot be presented as a succession of white lines: if this were the case, all the others would be exposed to the risk that one day one word, on being written down, would declare them to be completely false. That is why in the register of subjects' history it may be said that any myth, which is always a myth of origin, serves as a guarantee for the existence of that first paragraph.

In the register of a subject's history, that first paragraph cannot remain blank: what specifies its texture is that, in this case, it can be written only thanks to a borrowing made necessarily from the discourse of those others, who may alone claim to know and remember what the author is supposed to have experienced at that time long ago when the words 'I was born . . . ' were written. Of that first moment necessary for the history to be written, the I can know nothing, any more than he can do without the guarantee that he will be able to discover the answer through the discourse of the Other and of others.

The discourse of the 'word-bearer', therefore, has the task of offering the child a first statement concerning that origin of history: it would be enough to show the danger for the I of a failure to respond to that question or by an unacceptable response to it.

But equally determinant for the I is the power of extrapolation with which it will endow that response. If the question proves the link between the I's questioning as to the meaning of its own existence and its intuition that, at the same time, it is questioning the desire and the pleasure of the couple, it is because, by that same question, the I is questioning what might be the original cause of the experience of pleasure and unpleasure. If what the child experiences might have no meaning, the I itself would be unable to make sense of its own existence.

'Where do babies come from? – Where does the I come from? – Where does pleasure come from? – Where does unpleasure come from?' Here we have four formulations of a single question that seeks a response that ought to posit the relation between birth–child–pleasure–desire.

'At the origin of life is the desire of the parental couple to whom the birth of the child gives pleasure.' Whatever the explicit formulation of the answer might be, it must be able to refer implicitly to that concatenation of questions. Not only because that concatenation is the only thing that can bring a meaning that conforms to the logic of the I, but because that answer given as to the cause of its origin will be retroactively projected by the child onto the original cause of all experience of pleasure and of all experience of unpleasure.

The cause of pleasure, of all pleasure, will be linked by, and for, the I to the pleasure that the couple experiences by the fact that *he* exists and, just as the logic of the I will have to obey the principle of non-contradiction, the cause of unpleasure will be able to be separated off and to contradict the postulate of the primary process for which everything that exists is an effect of the omnipotence of the Other's desire. This separation will allow the I to make unpleasure compatible with its belief in the love that is felt for it, by accepting that unpleasure is no longer solely an experience decided by the Other's desire, but that which may be imposed, despite and contrary to that desire, and have as its cause the reality of the body, the existence of others, a mistake, a lack of knowledge.

We can now see how the statement by which the 'word-bearer' believes that he is answering the question concerning origin will be metabolised by the child into a meaning on the basis of which he develops his own theorisation as to the cause of everything concerning origin: of himself, of pleasure, of unpleasure, of the world.

The meaning that, for the I, makes sense of its existence is the only one that may also make sense of its experiences. The other side of this will be that any meaning that makes the cause of pleasure or unpleasure meaningless also makes meaningless what might be the cause of the I.

A final remark should be made as to the role assumed in this problematic by indices that give reality to the supposed conformity between the statement that bears meaning and the experience to which that meaning refers. To tell a child that his origin lies in the parents' desire and the pleasure that his birth brings them is a proposition that the I can appropriate only on condition that pleasure has a place in the child–couple relation – the pleasure felt when they meet, the pleasure expressed by the 'word-bearer' when stating that proposition, the pleasure that one expects to be felt by the person to whom it is addressed.

As soon as the postulate proper to the logic of the secondary process finds its place in the psychical organisation, any experience of the pleasure of the I requires that there be a concordance between the feeling that expresses it and the experience that the feeling names.

As for the experience of unpleasure, in order for it not to be deconstructing for the I, the representative must *first* recognise that this has actually been experienced by the child and that, later, it provides him with a meaning that is not contradictory with the logic of discourse, which means that this cause is different from that given for pleasure.

That is why, if ever the answer given to the subject concerning his origin leads him to understand that his existence has been a source of unpleasure for the 'word-bearer' and the couple, he runs the risk of positing as the cause of unpleasure the Other's desire to impose it on him, thus taking over the fantasy interpretation, interpreting pleasure as the effect of a mistake, a lack of knowledge, some misdeed: as a result, an inversion takes place between the two causes that ought to have been attributed to pleasure and unpleasure respectively. In the absence of this inversion the attempt to make meaning of these two experiences will come up against the paradox of having to attribute two contradictory effects to the same cause: in each case pleasure and unpleasure will probably lose all meaning, and be unable to be 'spoken'.

This parenthesis on the question of origin shows why, if the I cannot find a 'thought' in discourse that it might appropriate as an initial postulate for its own theorisation of origins, all that remains for it is to create one, otherwise he will have to abandon any attempt to preserve a psychical space in which its functioning is possible. Whenever this 'thought' can no longer be thought,[3] the conditions responsible for the acting out, in the sense that I have given this term, will be met. If I come back to this it is because, after defining the aim of primary delusional thinking, it seemed to me to be logical to recall against what danger such thinking has to defend the I.

In order to prevent a return to a situation in which 'it would act', the I must continue to be able to think what it is doing or experiencing. As long as a particular kind of thinking allows it to define itself and to protect, if only a pitiful fragment of, the I's knowledge of the I, it will be able to keep for itself a space compatible with its mode of functioning: if it finds itself unable to have thoughts, the I itself will disappear from the scene. The I must have at its disposal a sign that attributes a cause to its feelings that is intelligible and expressible, even if it makes sense only to it.

If, in the absence of meaning, an interpretation could no longer be projected onto what appears on the stage of the real, the I would find itself unable to know its own experience, to name the feeling that it feels, to project a knowable cause outside itself. Things that appear in the space of the real, rejecting any attempt to makes sense of them, will become once again pure things without name. Whenever reality no longer has a statement that can speak it, this silence will entail, as long as it lasts, the silence of any source capable of emitting a statement on the I: any representation of an I–world relation will become impossible. A similar difficulty will be encountered by the primary process: as we have seen, it, too, entails that what becomes a sign of the existence of an external space occupied by things confirms the postulate by which everything that appears is proof of the omnipotence of a desire. Thanks to that silence, only the primal encounters the world in its usual form: a container of things capable of reflecting the pictogram. The result will be a closing of the gap that usually separates pictographic representation from fantasy and ideational representation. The world no longer has any other representation than that which makes it the reflection of the pictogram, a reflection on which will now be projected the affect that can no longer be linked to other representations that might have made it possible to alter its aim and to relativise its intensity.

We see how serious is the risk against which the I protects itself by the setting up of primary delusional thinking. We shall now move on to an analysis of the factors responsible for an organisation of space outside the psyche that may make necessary the creation of that thinking. Among these factors, we must distinguish those that act in a manifest way on the reality that the infant and child encounter whenever they are confronted by the mother's behaviour and discourse, and those that are responsible for those manifestations and which themselves depend on the particular organisation of the parental I.

In this chapter on schizophrenia, I shall pay particular attention to the function of the 'word-bearer'.

The space in which schizophrenia can come about

In order not to expose myself to the same criticisms that I have made of certain psychoanalytic views of psychosis, perhaps I ought to make a few things clear. In my original project, and even at the time that I was writing those two chapters, I was thinking that they would be followed by others. Given the time in which its function is carried out, it was understandable that I should begin by questioning the discourse of the 'word-bearer' with a view to examining its consequences on the infant's psyche. The father's discourse and desire, the reasons why they have facilitated the psychotic response when they ought to have offered the child a support that might help him to relativise the shortcomings of the 'word-bearer', play just as determinant a role in the organisation of the psychical space encountered by the infant; only by analysing them will we be able to understand the action that is exerted on the child by others' psychical reality and the risks that the child may be exposed to as a result. This chapter deals only with the first part of a question, which I leave in suspense, in the hope of taking it up later.

To begin with, I shall consider what it is in the mother's behaviour and discourse that forms part of 'manifest' reality, as revealed to the infant by that behaviour and in that discourse. Both will be marked by the presence, recognised by the mother, of a *non-desire of a desire*, or a *non-desire of a pleasure*, which concerns either 'a child' or *this* child. In the first case the mother will say quite openly that she did not want a child, in the second that the act of procreation that gave birth to the child was not a source of pleasure and that she felt no pleasure during pregnancy, which was often a painful experience that she resented. Once the child is born, the mother will be able to express the desire that he will survive, but this desire will usually take the inverted form of a fear that he might die, with the result that this fear justifies and makes impossible the 'pleasure of having him', which is replaced by the 'unpleasure of always having to run the risk of losing him'.[4] In the first case, and also in the second, as soon as we pay attention to what is said to us, we note that both the rejection and the particularity of the cathexis correspond to the same cause: *the absence of a 'wish to have a child'* that may have been transmitted by one's own mother and which one may transmit to one's own child. We shall see in the next paragraph the reasons for and the effects of this non-transmission; I shall stress here what is its first manifest consequence: the impossibility for the mother, at the time of birth, to cathect the act of procreation in a positive way; everything that tends to prove that by giving life one engenders a 'new' being, which is the return not of a 'child' that had already existed, nor a moment in time that was merely being repeated. Such women may well have what I call a *'desire for motherhood'* that is the negation of a *'wish for a child'*: a desire for motherhood, in which is expressed a desire to relive, in an inverted position, a primary relation to the mother, a desire that will exclude from the register of maternal cathexes everything that concerns the moment of the child's origin, a moment that would prove that, by abandoning her body, the child has also 'abandoned' the maternal past, which he will later represent as a point of departure, the beginning of a new time, whose progress no subject can reverse. We see the mutilation practised from the outset by the mother on what in the child is a sign and a reminder of the peculiarity of her body, of her time, of her destiny. Before any fantasy representation by the infantile psyche of the primal scene, the 'scene of conception' – by which I mean the real situation experienced by the mother – is marked by a rejection of its essential meaning: it can be cathected not as an act of creation, but, at best, as an act that might repeat a moment experienced in the distant past by her own mother, an act that might take her back to the time that was her own.

It is the first factor that may lead to schizophrenia: the subject whose birth should normally have been evidence of the fulfilment of a wish meets with no wish that concerns him as an individual human being. The subject is born into a psychical milieu in which his desire, constituted at a very early stage as a desire to be desired, can find no satisfactory answer: either no child was desired or if a 'child' was desired, the mother's desire refuses to cathect that which in *this* child speaks of his origin, and would prove that he is the origin of a *new* life. The fact that the infant does not immediately have access to an understanding of this problematic does not prevent him from suffering its effects, which will be manifested in the mode and form of the answers that the mother gives him, first by what she does, then by what she says. From the earliest encounters, a split, a discrepancy, a too much or a not enough, are evidence of the conflict that the arrival of the infant has reactivated and revived. That is why, at the time of his encounter with the outside-psyche, any representation relating to rejection, nothingness, hate will prevail: the pictogram of rejection is universal, it is the representation that the primal makes of whatever may be the source of an experience of unpleasure. In a milieu in which the encounter with the child, for the woman who experiences it in a repetitive and necessary way, is actually experienced as a cause of unpleasure, the representation of rejection, aggression, snatching away will be more likely to be induced, whenever the displeasure of the Other actually diverts what is being played out in the encounter. The satisfaction of need and the experience of suckling will become that which silences need, but which express loud and clear the privation of a libidinal pleasure that the mother cannot or will not give. The same consequences are to be found in cases in which the mother acknowledges that she did not want a child and in cases in which there *appeared* to be such a wish, while in fact what was desired was the return of what I have called the mythical child of a primary desire. What the mother wants is still 'the mother's child'; she expects *the return of another herself*, as a source of maternal pleasure. In such a case the child can continue to be the object of her desire only if she is able to pin him down in an untenable position in which he represents someone who re-embodies a fantasy position that concerns *her*; in this way she is able to identify him with a rediscovered image of herself, which enables her to live out in an inverted way an incestuous, archaic relation with her own mother. The

142

rejection of the father's desire by the mother, or her inability to desire that desire and the pleasure that it might offer in the sexual act *qua* act of procreation, has little to do, it seems to me, with the 'phallicism' imputed to that type of woman: it is not the father that she is expropriating, but the child directly. This 'castration', long before it concerns the sexual desire and pleasure that the child might claim for himself, is aimed at dispossessing the infant of *everything that may designate him as an individual human being*, as the object of a pleasure and desire that might claim to be different from anything that existed in the mother's past. For the same reason it is not simply that the couple's desire can never be designated by this discourse as primal cause of the child's existence, but, more radically and more dramatically, the mother's discourse will refuse to recognise that there was a time when the *original* came into the world. As a result everything in the existence of the child that takes the form of the unexpected, of a question to which she does not already know the answer, *as well as* anything that might remind her of the participation of a father and therefore the desire of a *third party*, which constitutes an obstacle to a relation that would be repeated from mother to mother,[5] is for her a source of unpleasure. This 'non-desire of a desire' that finds expression in a refusal to find any pleasure in anything that is individual about the child *will be expressed in the register of the I*: if the maternal I does not know what is being played out in her unconscious, that same I knows and says that the act of procreation either was not supported by a desire or refused to recognise in the father a legitimate wish for a child that he had a right to be fulfilled. This 'consciousness' will be manifested in an attempt to take over the child and to negate the third party, and in a discourse that cannot give the subject a statement concerning origin that would link his birth to the couple's desire. In the first paragraph of the history recounted by the 'word-bearer', and in the perceived truthfulness of what is heard by the child, the event of birth will be overtly designated as the source of a conflictual situation, as the failure of the mother's desire not to be a mother, as a biological accident that has to be borne and, in any case, as an event in which the father's desire has been unable to play a valorising role.

Strangely enough, and it is seldom a matter of pure chance, to this first factor marking the reality that the infant encounters are often added, at an early stage in life, experiences that are inscribed in the child's bodily experience and which reinforce, in the child, the perception of hostility and ambient threat: the mother's bodily space and psychical space will become equally responsible for an experience of unpleasure that will make the autonomous cathexis of one's own body very difficult. Hence the importance that I shall give to what is manifested in an attack on the body, involving a state of organic pain, which the psyche will experience as a further, sometimes unbearable expression of a pre-existing or concomitant affect of unpleasure, an affect for which the mother's response was responsible.

In what I shall define as experiences of historical reality responsible for an effect of reduplication that transforms them into 'psychical traumas', physical pain plays a determining role. It prevents the infant being partially able to defend himself against the ordeal imposed upon him by the reality of the milieu, by a hypercathexis of pleasure and of the functioning of the sensory zones. There is a failure in the attempt to foreclose the outside-self and its messages, by means of this hypercathexis, an attempt that would make it possible to postpone the moment when inevitably they will force their way into the psychical space. The pleasure of hearing may try to postpone the moment when it will be necessary to *listen*; for there to be pleasure, these sounds still have to exist, the excitation of the eardrum must not be a constant source of pain, the auditory nerve must be able to function without hindrance. But, if we make an exception of serious cases of somatic pain, a malformation or mutilation of bodily functions, we must stress the role played by what, after the event, the child *will hear* his mother say about the meaning of those experiences. If the experience itself reduplicates an affect of pre-existing unpleasure caused by a failure of maternal desire, this experience becomes, in turn, traumatic, in the sense that I shall give the turn, only when it is *added to what is heard*, to what is expressed in the causal explanation that the mother tries to impose on that experience, which, very often, precedes the mother's commentary on it. This goes to prove that the effect of the experience depends, without exception, on the context of the situation in which it arises: according to the characteristics proper to that situation, the fantasisation of the person experiencing will be strengthened and fixed, one might say, or, on the contrary, forestalled by an act of giving meaning that re-elaborates and reshapes the experience itself. It is never on the side of the fantasy representation that some feature specifying psychosis will be found, but in the consequences of its encounter with the meaning that the mother's discourse claims to give of it. The psyche no longer finds in that discourse statements on the basis of which it could accord value and faith to evidence deriving from its own experience and to its memory of it and, *at the same time*, give the person experiencing it a new meaning that makes it possible to describe and master unpleasure. At the end of this chapter I shall come back to the analysis of the effect of reduplication operated by historical reality. This first sketch of the mother–child relation makes it possible to conclude that primary delusional thinking reshapes *the reality of what is heard* concerning experiences that have actually been imposed on the subject, and which concern:

- the encounter with the mother that manifests and expresses the notion that the origin of the subject may have as its cause neither the desire of the *couple* that gave him life, nor a pleasure 'to create something new' that she might acknowledge and valorise;
- the encounter with bodily experiences, as a source of pain, which confirm that the individual who has been brought up in pain can only encounter the world with pain;
- the encounter with the mother's discourse, which either refuses to

acknowledge that unpleasure was part of the subject's experience, or imposes a commentary on it that makes that experience and any later pain meaningless.

The task of primary delusional thinking will be to forge an interpretation that remodels the experience coextensive with these three encounters. It is a reshaping of three ordeals for which is responsible, not a universal *ananke*, but, on the contrary, the particular desire and discourse with which the psyche has been confronted. 'Reconstructing' *a fragment of the mother's discourse*, primary delusional thinking, and therefore the I, tries to make up for the abuse of power for which the same discourse has been responsible.

After indicating what, in the mother's behaviour towards the infant, is a manifestation of the lack of a 'wish for a child', I shall approach the register of the latent in order to try to understand the reasons for such a 'lack' and its effects on the activity of the child's thinking. I shall analyse in turn:

- the failure of repression evident in the mother's discourse;
- the excessive violence that results from this;
- the prohibition to think;
- the passage from primary delusional thinking to primary delusional theory as to origins;
- the referent that this thinking must find on the stage of the real if psychotic potentiality is not to become manifest.

1 The failure of repression in the mother's discourse

In this case, a *primary meaning* of the subject's relation to his own mother could not be repressed by the mother's I; this prevented access to the concept of maternal function and its power of symbolisation. In the part dealing with the symbolic function, proper to the terms of the kinship system, I showed that its task was to separate the individual occupant from a function of the concept that must be transmitted by that function. A distinction must be drawn between the meaning of 'being a mother' and what might have been the relation to the particular mother that one actually had; access to the concept makes it possible to prevent a repetition of the sameness of the experience.

Primary delusional thinking has as its essential cause the presence of the discourse, communicated by the mother's voice, which uses concepts that *seem* to accord with the group's discourse, whereas, in fact, the 'concept-that-refers-to-itself' is lacking in it. The meaning of 'maternal function' refers the mother to the only primary meaning that this function had for her: the feeding, frustrating, dominating, absent mother, the image that she had given herself of her *own* mother's desire in her regard has assumed a universal value – universal, not delusional. It should be remembered that generally, and it is with these cases that

I am dealing, the schizophrenic's mother is not delusional in the clinical sense; she has been able to compromise between others' discourse and a discourse, her own, in which, however, a statement testifies to a failure of repression. If the function is reduced to a single attribute – to feed, to educate, to protect her child, and to let him be – this attribute remains part of the totality of attributes that others give the concept. As a result, the definition that she defends will seem ridiculous, exaggerated, partial, but may still make sense in terms of others' discourse. What those others do not understand, or understand imperfectly, is that this partiality has shattered the concept and retained only a small fragment of it, which has little to do with the original totality – misheard and misunderstood, because perhaps this version of the concept is a risk that every mother incurs. It is a different matter for the individual who will be expected, as a child of the 'attribute', to define himself or herself in turn in relation to that *same, sole* attribute. This reduction of the meaning of the concept, which is in fact its negation, may make it impossible for the child to find a place in the kinship system that will open up to him access to the symbolic. The power to force-feed, to frustrate, to reject, or any other form of power, always refers back to a 'power to be' and a 'power to do' possessed by the mother alone; this power says nothing about what can take place only through the participation of others and above all of the father. It is as if in these cases the mother could have a '*desire for motherhood*', while being unable to convey in the proper way the '*wish to have a child*'. The fulfilment of this desire for motherhood would allow her to relive in an inverted position the relation experienced with her own mother and to prove to herself how well founded was the meaning of the maternal function that she had imposed. This meaning had organised, in a way conforming to it, the identificatory markers of the I of the girl who, in turn, may become a mother. It is understandable that this desire for motherhood cannot give way to the father's desire and to the pleasure that she would feel in becoming for the father the woman who enabled him to become a father, since it is a matter of rediscovering the pleasure that one's own birth is supposed to have given to one's own mother and to her alone. The pleasure that the mother may feel in the fulfilment of that very special desire for motherhood[6] cannot be linked to a pleasure dispensed by the father: if this were the case the mother might have to reshape her own identificatory position in her relations to her own father. The participation of the father in procreation is acknowledged; what is rejected is the idea that it may have been motivated by a desire and that it was a shared desire that gave birth to the child. This rejection is proved by the frequency with which one observes a substitution in the terms referring to the mother–child relation; sacrificing oneself for one's child involves nothing more than renouncing pleasure in favour of the person resulting from the sacrifice; loving him would involve the acknowledgement of a pure gift that gives pleasure and the presence of an exchange, and not a potlatch in which nothing remains, to either, but to give one's life in order to put an end to the challenge. When the first identificatory statements are heard, when the mother's voice still possesses that power of truth with which her libidinal cathexis by the child has endowed it, the child's I receives the injunction to appropriate a statement that defines him in such a way that he confirms the statement by which the mother defines herself as mother. Now, in its quest for meaning, the I is motivated by a very precise aim: to find a response that may give meaning to what was at the source of its entry into that place that it now has to inhabit.

On the question of origins, we have seen that it is only if the I is able to find an answer that it can name, and that it can cathect, to the question regarding the cause of the existence of the I itself, that the I can make the fundamental statement about it that will enable it to make sense of its view of the world and of its relation to the world. Now, to the question concerning its origin posed by the I, the mother's statement responds by a rationalisation that ill conceals the fact that she has no answer, for the simple reason that for her the child's I is not an I. The child does not have the right to a system of meaning that would not be a mere echo of the mother's system. One of the most disastrous consequences of this will be that, when they have to use the system of meanings in order to express the experience of the affect in terms of feeling, with a view to making it knowable, and therefore partly controllable, by the I, these children will have at their disposal only the mother's commentary on an experience that she interprets according to her own problematic or, which is more usually the case, that she declares *does not exist*. The child has either to accept this verdict, which dispossesses him of any right to claim the truth of the experience, or to reject it and be confronted by the terror of a representation of the experience that entails hate, rejection, death. To his question concerning origin, the first response is usually a comment on the act of asking: 'It is forbidden to ask.' On the other hand, he must accept an answer that precedes the question and which is intended to make it useless by imposing in advance an untruthful meaning. Because the mother is not delusional, she cannot have recourse to thoughts that would speak the truth of her desire, freeing them from the system of meanings shared with the discourse of the group. She is therefore forced to fill a void with her own discourse on the reason for the child's existence, using meanings borrowed from the discourse of others. But she is not unaware that this is a forced, abusive borrowing; she knows that she is trying to forget, and to make someone else forget, by a series of rationalisations justifying the verdict of guilty that she pronounces when confronted by any request from the child and the verdict of absolute truth that she demands for any statement coming from herself.

In the mother's discourse, the experience of pregnancy and the encounter with the infant have provoked what, metaphorically, might be called a 'puerperal psychosis' in the sector of the kinship system. As long as there is no child the mother is able to ignore the fact that she lacked the statements that make sense of the concept of the maternal function: in the presence of the child it is incumbent upon her to become the mediator between the function that she embodies

147

and the concept to which she ought to refer and which is lacking. What she embodies can now refer only to the thing embodied; the circuit closes upon itself in a vicious and sometimes lethal circle. At the time of pregnancy and the fulfilment of a wish for a child, the mother experiences the consequences of an omission in the discourse of her own mother: what was not said or not heard, because for her it cannot be heard, concerning the transmission of a wish to have a child that would have made the mother her by whom is transmitted a right to the desire, but also her from whom it is forbidden to expect its object. This non-transmission may lead to the silencing of any desire for motherhood: there will then be a refusal to have a child, which, for these women, is no doubt the most economic solution for their own identificatory equilibrium. If this solution fails, if the desire for motherhood persists, the mother will find herself confronted by the following paradox: she cannot acknowledge what is the cause of this desire, that is to say, that it is to 'a mother' that she wishes to offer pleasure, but nor can she acknowledge that the child would be the fulfilment of what actually has no place in her problematic: a wish for a child. She now has recourse to a rationalisation that excludes desire as the cause of the existence of children: one becomes a mother as a result of duty, sacrifice, ethics, religion, because of men who impose this ordeal, because of chance . . . The child finds himself confronted by a discourse in which no statement gives meaning to his presence, links him to the couple's desire and to behaviour in which the signs of desire that are manifested – the desire to feed him, to protect him – are not addressed to his I and deny that I any right to any autonomy and demand that he make room for a ghost. Where the project ought to be constituted, where the notion of the future ought to allow the I to move in an ordered temporality, the return-of-the-same stops time and replaces it with a repetition of the identical, inverts its order since he who is becoming and must come about discovers that he has been preceded by a past, and by a dead person, who imposes upon him the place and the time to which he ought to return.

The spoken shadow does not anticipate the subject; it projects him regressively to the place that the representative had occupied in the past.

This inversion of the anticipatory effect of the mother's discourse deprives of all meaning the answer given to the question concerning origin. Indeed, for the mother, birth is not the origin of a subject, the initial moment at which a new life emerges whose destiny remains open, but, on the contrary, the repetition of a moment and an experience that have already taken place. It should now be clear why one of the characteristic features of schizophrenic experience is non-access to the order of temporality, the inability to measure and to count a 'time' in which is lacking the marker necessary to fix the point of departure from which an ordered succession might be established.

2 Excessive violence: the appropriation by the mother of the child's activity of thinking

I would willingly propose the title given to this second part, 'The interpretation of violence', as a definition of any delusional discourse: the interpretation that the subject gives or gives himself of the excessive violence for which the discourse of the 'word-bearer' and, generally, the discourse of the couple were responsible. In taking over the task of primary delusional thinking, delusional discourse tries to make sense of the violence committed by the 'word-bearer' at the expense of an I that did not have adequate means of defence. It should be added that, although a meaning could not be reinvented, the I would encounter a single desire: that of subjecting the same violence upon the agent of the discourse, which would imply that he decides to hate her and him who gave him birth. But to hate that couple at the moment when he is still the exclusive representative of others and of the world would mean that the same hate is thrown back onto everything outside-self: the I as effect of that which comes back on to the psychical scene, beginning with that locus, could only be revealed as worthy of hate, hated and hating. This is an untenable situation, and one that the death drives would have quickly exploited to their own advantage. What primary delusional thinking succeeds in carrying out is to interpret violence, to link it to a cause that uses the mother as a necessary libidinal support. I shall not go back over what I have already said about the activity of thinking, but I shall try to explain more clearly the danger that it represents for the mother of a child who might become schizophrenic; my summary of the problematic of his identificatory markers may be of help in this. As long as the child does not speak, the mother is able to preserve the illusion that he is actually thinking what she believes he is thinking; similarly, she declares that she knows what his body expects and demands, a necessary illusion during that first stage of life; she may claim to know what his 'brain' is thinking and, above all, what it expects and demands as 'knowledge'. Indeed she is willing to offer him and impose upon him a 'knowledge' concerning the language necessary for him to acquire speech, but only on condition that she can at the same time insist that he hear only what *her* language claims to mean.

From the access of the child to the order of discourse, the mother awaits proof that nothing is lacking in her own discourse. Here again we see the normal process become inverted: the appropriation by the child of explicit, and above all implicit, injunctions, present in the mother's discourse, ought to have the task of reinforcing the barrier of the mother's repression and so preserve her I from the return of a repressed concerning the primary representation of the object of desire, whereas, in this type of relation, proof is expected from the child that the non-repressed did not have to be so, that it is therefore legitimate to ask him to embody a lost image of herself, to repeat a libidinal relation under the aegis of the primary, to which the situation gives back all its impact. So he has to think what she thinks, for, if he came to think of his I as an autonomous agent with a right to think, it would prove to her that the past cannot come back, that the desire of the same is unrealisable and unthinkable, that her discourse lacks a concept. In order to avoid this risk, a number of options are open to the mother.

The first is to privilege the other part functions, to hypercathect the body as a set of different functions, an eating, excreting, sleeping, seeing, hearing body . . . in accordance with a model of correct functioning that she will seek and find in what is said about the body and its functions by medicine, hygiene, religion or science. The peculiarity of the corporal model proposed to the I will be the fragmentary aspect of the functions whose activity she supervises: eating, to take one of many examples, is a matter not of future growth, but of what is to be eaten now until the menu is changed according to a programme that lays down what the menu is to be at the ages of two, three, five, etc.

The child may respond to the mother's concern for correct functioning by a similar hypercathexis of his body as a machine. He will cathect the activity of different apparatuses 'in themselves', without cathecting a project that would transcend them and alter their aim. The pleasure of seeing, hearing, excreting, eating will result from the eroticisation of the activity and not from its purpose. With a body in bits and pieces before it is a fragmented body, each bit may be a source of pleasure on condition that the child does not ask himself what purpose the action is serving: the answer could be given only by an integrating project that postpones the purpose and cathects the wait. A frequent consequence of this will be the presence of hypochondria in both child and mother: once one bit does not work, there is a loss of all pleasure. In such circumstances, instinctual pleasure will gradually lose the integrating, irradiating function that it possessed when it first appeared. The more the child perceives that the mother is asking him to do something and expects him, as the only possible source of her pleasure, to eat, sleep, or see 'properly', the more he perceives that any failure of one of the functions of his body will be seen by her as an intolerable rejection, and the more he loses the ability to offer her the spectacle of him 'seeing properly' at the moment when she was expecting him 'to eat properly', 'to excrete properly', rather than 'to hear properly'. If the mother awaits the manifestations of his body so anxiously, fearful that the value of what she claims to know may be undermined, it is because in fact she cannot allow herself, without incurring major risks, to acknowledge that something may be lacking in her 'knowledge of the body's needs', that the unexpected may have a role to play in them, that something might emerge in that body that will distinguish it from any body that she has known in the past. If that happened, she would be forced to conclude that an encounter was taking place between her and a living I that would show her what eluded repetition, the already known and the already seen. That is why what she fears above all is the unexpected and that is why she cannot bear there to be any alternative to the response that she expects. It is a bitter and serious discovery and it does not help the child to show her that he knows how to smile just when she is expecting him to show her that he knows how to swallow or go to sleep. Anything unexpected is dangerous: the ask–answer relation takes the form, not of a discourse, but of a rigid code. The offer will be regulated in such a way as to reduce as far as possible the risk that some unexpected demand might appear. In these circumstances the child will also regulate, in his own way, his relation to his body image: if he presses this button and if that button works, the same result will always be obtained; if it is not, it is because the button has broken and the machine is not working. Hence the presence in these children of that sort of non-history, that obedience that tells the mother that her child was the perfect model of what should be, a picture that alternates with another in which is expressed the dramatic refusal to make the body the copy of a model that was not cathected and not chosen. This refusal will find expression in anorexia, sleep disturbance, frequent illness in early infancy.

It is in this kind of relation that the activity of thinking will be born and it is that pre-existing relation that it must make intelligible to the thinking agency. If we set aside those two extreme cases represented, on the one hand, by infantile autism and, on the other, by the ability of the I to employ an alternative discourse that allows it to structure itself in such a way as to preserve its relation to the project – and it is in this second case that *what the father's discourse may offer or refuse assumes its full value* – it will be through primary delusional thinking that the I will be able to work out a compromise between the dictates of the mother's discourse and an activity of thinking that allows the I to think about the I.

One becomes aware of the precariousness of such a compromise if one considers the heavy past inherited by the activity of thinking: as a successor of the part functions, it begins by assuming the same role of stake in the mother–child relation, but, as soon as it begins to function, all the mother's demands will be focused on it and she will expect a response from it: this new activity proves to her that her knowledge of what the child is thinking is well founded. This is a disguised form assumed by the prohibition to think and the attempt to compel her child to think only what has already been thought by her. What we have here is an excess of intolerable violence committed by the mother's discourse, an excess against which the I, if it wishes to continue to exist, will defend itself by delusional thinking; that is to say, by projecting into an elsewhere, and onto another support, the supposed cause of the prohibition or compulsion. Indeed the mother could preserve her grip on her child's thinking activity and on the thoughts produced by it only by reducing that activity, like its predecessors, to the equivalent of a function without project. But what is to some extent possible for the other bodily functions is not so for thinking: the activity of thinking demands the presence of a project. The eroticisation of this activity may 'in itself' be a source of pleasure, but only if that pleasure represents a mere moment, a truce, a recreation – and a temporary re-creation of thoughts – in an activity that is guaranteed to rediscover a certain unity and continuity. In the opposite case, there is no longer any 'thinking' in the proper sense of the term, but 'thoughts' that will be defined, by the subject himself, as echo, commentary, compulsion, and all those terms by which the psychotic tells us what 'comes into his head'. It should be noted that this statement implies that the I is still capable of thinking, somewhere else, that which is thought inside him. There is a splitting of space from agency, by which the subject may give back some meaning to 'thoughts' that will become comprehensible when he sees them as proof of the persecution, ordeal or enigma, imposed upon him by an Other's desire and intention.

It is clear that even in manifest forms of psychosis a last bastion may be defended by rediscovering a meaning concerning 'what is thought' that can make it intelligible, even if, as in the case of Schreber, it is by declaring that it is God's wish that you think only the non-intelligible. But the picture sketched out here no longer corresponds to psychotic potentiality: it demonstrates the effects of a victory of primary delusional thinking in the space of the psyche and the price that is paid by the I to preserve a last bastion and the few square centimetres needed if both feet are to be placed on solid ground.

If we go back to the moment when primary delusional thinking may be constituted, it might be said that the injunction, contradictory and unrealisable, to which it responds would imply that the child is able to appropriate an ability to speak that would not be accompanied by an 'ability to think' and a right of autonomy over thinking.

In the analysis of the basic language, we have seen how it reduplicated, and therefore gave a definitive form to the violence, necessary for the structure of the I, practised by discourse. This necessary violence is intended to substitute for the affect a feeling that can be expressed and known by the I: a substitution whose structuring role can operate only if the I finds, in naming the experience, that which comes back to him in the form of an identifying statement, a source of pleasure. The first condition for this pleasure to appear will be that this statement is actually what will allow the I to grasp itself as an autonomous existing being, as action, desire, project. It must be possible therefore for the statement to be questioned, to be rejected in favour of another: what comes back only in the repeated form of something compulsory could not offer the I the fundamental attribute represented by the possibility of choice. This choice is partly illusory, since, in fact, the range of statements is previously laid down by the basic language itself and by its law; but it is a choice nevertheless since it must remain within the power of the I to select certain of them, to resist others, to substitute one for another. For this choice to be made, a minimum of autonomy in thinking must be accorded the I from the outset; the first result of this autonomy will be the ability to think secretly. It is this 'thinking secretly' that allows the child to discover that this new activity, for which he has paid dear in the renunciation and the mourning that it requires, offers in exchange and for the first time forms of solitary activity and pleasure that are not subject to prohibition, but, on the contrary, are valorised by her who allows them. It is a pleasure that is reinforced by the unexpected discovery that, despite the little real power possessed at this stage in terms of bodily autonomy, despite one's state of dependence for the satisfaction of one's needs, despite the vital demand for love to which one is subjected, *in the register of thinking the Mother may be just as much at your mercy as you are at hers.* The discovery that others' ability to guess what one is thinking, which one attributed to the parental gaze, is an illusion is a step *as fundamental* for the psyche as the discovery of the difference between the sexes. But for this discovery to take place it must not come up against a fear of punishment that would cut one off from the guilty function. It is that punishment that the mother's attitude and discourse seemed to threaten and, in this case, it will appeal, and for very good reasons, to no third party as agent of that earlier, and just as traumatic, castration; it spells out that, if one transgresses, one will be deprived of speech, one will become an object rejected in total silence.

This excessive violence is all the more active in that it offers a threat that is carried out from time to time: one may never have one's penis cut off because it has become a source of pleasure, but one is certainly refused the right to speak, to hear, or to be listened to. That threat to the child does not invoke any law shared by the group, any shared, structuring trial; on the contrary, the child has to pretend that he does not recognise the abuse as such; here again is reduplicated the operation by which the aim of violence becomes that which the person undergoing it demands, desires and expects. This violence has every chance of succeeding, since to exist has as its condition that this first representative of the Other and of the world shows interest in you, that she offers one signs of love; it will be of no use to the I, except to hasten its death, to reject the violence and find itself face to face with a void, without desire and without speech. This demonstrates how excessive is the excessive violence practised by the mother's desire in her appropriation of the child's activity of thinking. It is true that if it fails, if the infantile I succeeds in its aim, the mother could discover herself as 'mother' only in a sense that does not conform to the generally accepted 'notion' of mother; she would see the child's I, her child's I, move away from her and seek possible substitutes elsewhere. Whenever, in spite of her, the child does succeed in conceiving of the concept 'maternal function', he discovers, in doing so, that the mother does not know its meaning and he therefore has no alternative but to find the necessary mediations elsewhere. It is not impossible to do this, but it is difficult; if the child succeeds, he will have avoided psychotic potentiality, the necessary conditions turning out to be insufficient. If the contrary is the case, the I, in order to survive, will have to be able to create primary delusional thinking. Unfortunately, it is possible that this creation cannot be achieved; and there will follow a withdrawal of the cathexis of the function and of the thinking agency, a quest for the silence of the I, of the world, of others, a shattering of thoughts into fragments that mark a path through psychical space, but which amount to little more than fragments of a jigsaw puzzle that one neither can nor wishes to reconstruct: this is the autism of the very young child. I shall not be dealing with this here, since, quite obviously, this is no longer a matter of schizophrenic potentiality but of its most exacerbated manifestation.

3 Forbidden knowledge and delusional theories concerning origins

The unrealisable aim of the mother's discourse would involve being able to split that which cannot be split; namely, the two constituent parts of the basic language:

- She apparently thinks and states the terms referring to the naming of feelings that she demands that the child make his.
- She forbids him to find elsewhere what her discourse cannot give him: the meaning of a term in the kinship system that conforms to the symbolic function that is hers.[7]

This prohibition, which she does not recognise but which, unknown to her, will find overt expression in the prohibition that affects any question from the child concerning the origin of his life, the reason for certain of his experiences, and in the 'secret' that is often present in her stories. This secret, jealously and shamefully hidden from the child, usually conceals a suicide, a lie as to the real father, a 'shameful', often mental illness, an abortion, etc. In all such cases, this secret, which the mother claims to hide, concerns the reason that *she gives herself* for the problems encountered by the child, or for the problems that he would encounter if he knew that secret, and therefore the problems that she may recognise as being present in her own family relations. It is because the father was mad that the child has certain problems, it is because her own mother killed herself that her child might do the same, it is because she had to abort one child that the child might believe that she does not love him: we see how the 'secret' takes the place of what she posits as the *original cause* of the problems created for her by her mother–child relation. But we also see how, by rationalising the motives for which that cause cannot be revealed to the child, she will be able to exclude any demand from him concerning origins and justify the need to be silent or to lie about it. The process operates in much the same way as free association in the analytical process: if the subject wishes to keep an idea, a memory, a fantasy secret, he will be gradually forced to set aside all the associations that may refer to it, with the result that, from exclusion to exclusion, he is obliged to keep silent about everything that may be said, or reduce it to the empty recital of the insignificant facts of everyday life. It is the same process that is set in train by the mother's anxiety: in every why spoken by the child she sees the risk of a 'why of the why' that might culminate in a final question that she does not wish to hear, because she will not be able to answer it.

Paradoxically, however, the acquisition of knowledge about language, the condition for the existence of the I, is usually something that the mother insists on. This confronts the child with a paradoxical situation:

- to appropriate that knowledge, to accept the order of meaning proper to discourse, to transform the representable into something nameable and intelligible, and therefore to have access to a reality that conforms to the definition that discourse gives of it;

- to lack that on which reality and language is founded, and can only be founded, not to possess the statement of foundations, or that foundation of statements, necessary for his own historical narrative to concern him, to lack that indispensable point of departure, the statement concerning his origin. Can we imagine a subject who is forced to recognise himself in an oriented space in which he would be forbidden to use one of the four cardinal points?

Psychotic potentiality is the result of a similar ordeal: the subject has been forced to order space, time, lineage – and to find his order in them – by resorting to others' cardinal points, when he has lost, indeed has never possessed, the North. The absence of a response to the statement concerning origins undermines from the inside the origin of statements, makes them rest on shifting sands that may always swallow up whatever is built on them.

Primary delusional thinking is the creation by the I of that missing statement: it is on the basis of such thinking that an 'infantile theory concerning origins' will be worked out, whose function and functional analogy with the role played, in neurosis, by the family romance I shall demonstrate by the following example.

4 The story of Mme B . . . and primary delusional theory concerning origins

Thanks to the presence of primary delusional thinking, conceived as a statement that fills a gap in discourse, a theory concerning origins will be worked out that might be called 'the primary delusional theory'.

Mme B . . . has just been to see me hoping to be cured of an impulse phobia that began two years ago: whenever she is in the street, she is afraid that she may feel compelled to take off all her clothes. This symptom does not seem to be accompanied by any manifestation of a psychotic order. A woman of thirty-two, married and the mother of two children, everything was fine, she tells me, until two years ago: then, one day, while waiting her turn at the chiropodist's, where she was going to have a corn removed that stopped her walking unless she supported herself on her husband's arm or on the shoulder of one of her children, there suddenly rose up inside her the terrifying idea that she might take all her clothes off. Appalled, she returned home; in six months the phobia forced her to give up work and to refuse to go out unless she was accompanied by her husband, one of her children or a member of her family. Only the presence of one of them made her phobia disappear. During the early sessions, the only thing that particularly struck me about her was a rather problematic relationship with her husband: she told me that she had no concerns about her married life, but, on the subject of her fourteen-year-old son, she expressed with some force her wish that he should become 'passionate in the search for solitude'. She and her husband were shopkeepers, sharing the worries and hopes of most people, but apparently content with their lot. Why did she hope that her son would become a 'solitary'? So that 'he won't be interested too much in anything else'. In the course of these sessions I learnt that she had an older sister; that her father, a pilot in a civil airways company, had been killed when she was five or six, which meant that there was 'no corpse, no burial'; that at the age of two she had an accident that nearly cost her her life, her mother having 'absent-mindedly' given her a tin containing medicine instead of one containing her sweets. Her mother was an authoritarian woman, forever shouting or having outbursts of violent tenderness that 'frightened me as much as her shouting'. She said all this quite calmly, usually with a touch of humour; as for her phobia, 'I can't understand it at all, but it can't go on like this.'

The relationship with her husband made me think that what she was looking for was a good maternal image rather than a virile image, but not once during these sessions did I have the feeling that I was in the presence of psychosis.

However, during the first weeks of her analysis, I was surprised to hear her say what she thought about women and procreation:

- In procreation, the man's sperm plays no part, except to excite 'the procreative apparatus' that only women carry inside them.
- Whenever sex takes place, the woman, like a praying mantis, is *forced* to take into her vagina part of the male substance, which is deposited in her apparatus. That's why men die younger and lose their hair.

It took a few sessions for me to realise that this was not some remnant of an infantile sexual theory, nor the formulation of a fantasy, but that she now firmly believed this to be the case.

It was a conscious delusional kernel, split off from her discourse as a whole, which functioned normally as soon as she spoke of something else. It should be noted, however, that the implications of this 'theorisation' certainly appeared in the manifest discourse that she had with others: thus, when she explained that she hoped that her son would not be interested in girls too soon; when she idealised and valorised such men as missionaries, explorers, navigators, who live alone and are passionate about 'ideas' rather than women; when she admitted that 'sex' did not interest her, that she was quite content that her husband wasn't particularly interested in it either; when she said that when she did have sexual relations she felt 'blown up and guilty', it became quite clear to me, once I had got used to her theorisation, how especially significant sex was for her. Nevertheless, that series of statements, as expressed by her, were perfectly understandable by others and by the group: at most one might regard her as prudish and her preferences for navigators and missionaries as rather strange. But, since it had not occurred to anybody to ask a married woman and mother if she knew how children were born and that, moreover, as she said, as soon as anyone around her spoke of such things 'either I go out, or I don't hear', she could participate in others' discourse without any apparent difficulty.

Psychotic potentiality probably does not often provide us with so typical an example of the encysted presence of a primary delusional theory, but in analysis it is rare not to find something very close to it whenever this potentiality exists.

Here is another example, much more mysterious and more concealed: in the course of a session in which Monsieur C . . . told me of a childhood memory concerning his grandmother, the following dialogue took place:

'Was she your father's mother or your mother's mother?'
'What was that?'
'I asked you if she was your paternal or maternal grandmother.'
'Yes . . . ' [then forcefully and with some irritation in his voice]. 'Yes, I never thought about it. It would have been quite absurd.'
'Why?'
'Because *I could never have thought of such a thing.*'

What we notice at once here is the radical difference between 'I never thought about it', a denial that confirms that it was definitely what 'it' (the id) was thinking about, and 'I could never have thought of such a thing', which amounts in effect to a missing statement concerning the father's origin, a 'declaration' that foreshadowed the presence of a primary delusional thought by which the subject made sense of a gap in the family history.

Usually primary delusional thinking assumes a form that is more difficult to unmask and above all to separate from what Freud rightly called 'the oddities' that can be found in anyone. What it amounts to, then, is a certainty that is in flagrant contradiction with the entire logical system according to which the subject functions, a certainty that concerns either the functioning of the body, or some physical law, or an event belonging to the subject's genealogical history. What characterises this type of false belief is not the unshakeable conviction with which it is held, or its apparent contradiction with the subject's knowledge of physiological, physical or temporal laws, but the fact that as soon as one listens carefully one realises that this conviction radically challenges the origin of the body, the origin of the world and the temporal order on which the genealogical order is based. This can be borne out by any analyst: if, on the basis of that apparently firm conviction, he tries to consider the logical implications that derive from it, he will see that they lead to a representation of reality that differs at every point from the model that discourse gives of the subject–world relation. In such cases, the 'oddness' has replaced the causal order, to which the group appeals in order to explain the origin of the subject and of the world, an interpretation that links origin to a cause incompatible with the models according to which the group functions. It is this characteristic that for me indicates the presence of primary delusional thinking.

I shall return to Mme B . . . 's discourse in an attempt to identify which statements and which absence of statements are replaced by her theorisation.

The discourse of Mme B . . . 's mother

It was difficult for me, even after three years of analysis, to decide whether my patient's mother merely shared a number of superstitions common in the particular part of Brittany where she had spent her childhood and adolescence, or whether her convictions were closer to delusion. She firmly believed in the divinatory gifts of an old peasant woman whom she had met up with again in the town and that the whole family called 'Lamère' – it was only in the course of the analysis that Mme B . . . came to realise that the woman in question, to whom she went to have her cards read once a month, and whose ability to cure people of their ills she claimed to be superior to that of doctors, was not known as 'La Mère' (The Mother), but that her surname happened to be Lamère. Her own mother, she said, had the power to speak to the dead; she had never spoken about her father – Mme B . . . even admitted that she had never asked her anything about the character who was so obviously absent from her discourse. This young peasant woman was to go to the town and marry a notary's son: she always referred to her husband as 'a bad lot', criticising him for 'running after the girls'. When he died, his name disappeared from her discourse except in a strange threat to her child: 'You'll end up just like your father.' To which the little girl asked 'How? And what does "father" mean?' At the time of his death, nothing was said to her about it; all that she learnt, from overheard bits of conversation between her mother and others, was a story of a 'blowing up' (that of the plane), which she interpreted to mean a 'blowing up of her father'.

The mother's secrets

Mme B . . . has always lived with a sister, who is eight years older than she, whom she found 'funny' without really being able to explain why: she had a funny way of speaking to her father, she had a funny relationship with her mother, there was something funny about that same mother's refusal to allow her to kiss her father and about the 'pocket money' that she always seemed to have. Much later, she was to learn from her own husband that this daughter was in fact her mother's illegitimate child, that she was leading 'a life of pleasure', apparently with her mother's silent complicity, and that people were saying that she was 'a bit crazy'.

As for her mother's father, it was during her analysis and at her insistence that she finally learnt that he had committed suicide, probably during a depression,

158

after trying to gas his wife and daughter. From then on the mother spoke of that father with hate and fear: he was the 'madman' and the 'murderer', doubly bad and doubly dangerous. It was following this confession that Mme B . . . learnt in what circumstances her mother had met the man she married: she came to the town in order to work with her illegitimate daughter, had been taken on by the notary to look after his son, who suffered from 'some nervous disease', married him, convinced that he was sexually impotent and that there would never be 'some kind of mad child who couldn't do anything'. To her astonishment and annoyance, the notary turned out to be very different and she never forgave him for 'misleading her'.

The secret kept by Mme B . . . 's mother concerned the father of the first child, whose name was never to be divulged, and the madness of her own father: reading between the lines one suspects that this madness was a way of expressing her question concerning the desire that nearly made that father a double murderer. 'Madness', which appears, on the one hand, as the only possible justification for that desire to murder, but which, on the other hand, makes it impossible to posit at its origin a paternal desire that one may assume, since it will be the desire of a madman and a desire for 'madness'. One may well wonder if the 'madness' was not also to be found on the side of the father of the older daughter, but I have no evidence on the matter. Certainly the 'madness' that fascinated her so much was also to be found as the pivot of her problematic: the daughter of a 'madman', she married another 'madman', who, it certainly seems, was driven by her to an accident–suicide that repeated the fate of her father. The mother of a first child without a father, this rigid woman concealed her daughter's shame, but did not know how to stop her being a prostitute, saying of her that 'she has always been mad'.[8] Potentially the murderer of that second daughter, she will claim quite improbably that the medicines were harmless, that the pumping of her daughter's stomach was pointless and that the doctors only performed it in order to make a big drama out of it, and that 'Lamère' would have sorted everything out 'without fuss'.

As soon she is able to understand, Mme B . . . 'hears':

- utter silence concerning a father, her mother's father, a silence that she rightly interprets as the mother's desire that his very existence should be denied, that one should pretend that she owes nothing to that father, that there never was a father;
- a stream of hateful abuse about the 'headstrong' man who is her father, who is driven out of the house, only to be criticised later for leaving;
- a 'funny' silence about the sister who was always so well dressed and in whom the mother always seemed to be looking for 'signs' of a mysterious oddness, a sister who is forbidden to kiss the man whom she nevertheless calls 'Daddy', as if the mother feared some transgression or some possible 'madness' in their relationship;

- the presence of 'Lamère', the old woman who reads fortunes and performs miraculous cures, and who challenges the knowledge of the men of science;
- lastly, during the few days spent in hospital following her intoxication, she remembers very well hearing the doctor criticising her mother and referring to '*poursuites*' (prosecutions), which she understood as '*suites*' (what will follow), i.e. that 'she will remain ill'. Back at home, the mother was to criticise her for 'being ill on purpose', for 'making a fuss about nothing'.

From the side of her father's voice, she will hear:

- violent shouting during rows;
- the accusation made to the mother that she 'got pregnant just to force me to marry you';
- that 'she would have preferred him to stay mad', that all she wanted was his name;
- his demand to be free and his criticism of 'what you let your daughter do' (words that make it impossible to know which daughter he was referring to);
- the accusation that she is exploiting him, taking his money;
- lastly, his *cri de cœur* that 'he was forced to have kids or to shoot himself, which amounts to the same thing'.

As we can see, these statements do not, any more than the mother's, make it possible to see oneself as the fulfilment of a desire: moreover, the couple makes two statements, neither of which can be assumed as defining the 'desire' responsible for the subject's existence, since each reproaches the other for imposing the child on the other partner, both saying quite overtly that it was not the child, but a name, money, power that were desired.

In this context, it is understandable that, when the little girl asks 'Why does Daddy have a strong head?', 'Why can't my sister kiss him?', 'Why does her mother always tell her that if her father hadn't been unfaithful, she [Mme B . . .] wouldn't have existed?', 'Why will she end up like her father?', she can find no answer. The mother either forbids her daughter to ask questions or replies with such astonishing aphorisms as 'A woman with a strong head should have it cut off', 'Men are never any good', 'Girls eat you from inside', the exact words spoken, which assume the form of insoluble enigmas: Which head ought to be cut off?, Why aren't men ever any good?, What is eaten from inside?

The delusional thinking that solves the enigma plays the same role here as that played by the family romance in neurosis, but for different reasons. The essential difference is that, unlike in the case of the family romance, delusional thinking takes no account of the cultural system and the kinship system (to dream that one's real parents are different from those who claim to be so, or that one is an adopted child, conforms to the kinship system proper to the culture), no attempt is made to ensure that the fantasies are worked out with greater or less effort to obtain verisimilitude and, above all, delusional thinking is never subjected to that particular restriction that has as its prerequisite that the child should have grasped that '*pater semper incertus est*', while the mother is '*certissima*' . . . The family romance is content to exalt the child's father, but no longer casts any doubt on his maternal origin, which is regarded as something unalterable.[9]

On another level, what distinguishes this thinking from an infantile sexual theory is that it is not repressed: if, like infantile sexual theory, it borrows its model from bits and pieces heard and seen, from models of bodily functions with which it will identify the function of procreation, there is not, in this instance, any abandonment of that first theorisation.

If we now consider Mme B . . . 's delusional theory concerning her origins, we see how, on the basis of a fundamental postulate: 'the woman is the sole procreator, the man is just swallowed bit by bit', an explanatory system is set up that explains why 'giving birth' is a disagreeable experience, since it requires that the woman take in, against her will, bits of the father, a law of nature from which she cannot escape, why man, by being swallowed, makes one run the risk of bursting like an empty windbag, which in turn accounts for the fact that one doesn't want to talk about it. But we also see how this thinking reshapes 'bits and pieces of knowledge' as to the danger of sudden death, and how it reconstructs in its own way a possible transcendence of the 'maternal function'.

The risk of death actually incurred, which provoked the doctor's accusation of the mother, obviously cannot be anything other than a mistake: an acceptable admission, whereas anything that showed the presence in the mother of a desire for death that would make her your murderer would not be.

'Lamère', endowed with a power of divination, ensures that the truth of what the strange mother declares concerning origins is supported by another discourse, which just about takes the place of the role that the discourse of the group ought to have played for the child and, to begin with, for the parental discourse itself.

I am not claiming that all primary delusional thinking will give rise to the same theorising, but I do believe that whenever it appears, in a situation in which it may be analysed, one will find:

- A statement that, for reasons different from those proper to the family romance, tries to reconstruct the origin of the subject's history (in this case, the purpose of that attempt was to demonstrate the truth of the postulate implicit in the mother's discourse and, by that fact, to ensure that this discourse does not lack meaning and that truth may have a place in it).
- On the basis of this statement concerning origins will be set up a theorisation that will try to give the concept of 'the maternal function' a meaning that, in its own way, transcends it by linking it to the representative of omnipotence, usually of the same lineage, the mother, the witch, the fairy, which offers the

161

subject some kind of order in the succession of the generations and therefore in time.

• The passage from the representable to the sayable, and therefore from affect to feeling, can now take place, except in the case of those affects associated with any experience for which the flaw present in the mother's desire and discourse is responsible. Whenever the I is confronted by any experience that is linked to that cause, it will be able to find no intelligible statement in the discourse of the 'word-bearer', for the very simple reason that the 'word-bearer' is unable to recognise that the non-transmission of a 'wish to have a child' is actually at the origin of these experiences; the best way to ignore it is to deny that these experiences exist or ever did exist. As a result, everything that concerns the origin of the subject, of desire, of pleasure and of unpleasure is banished from a discourse that cannot speak of origins when the subject who is speaking cannot answer the question of the origin of his own function. The delusional theory concerning origins is constituted around a statement that answers that question; it substitutes something said, which it has made up, for something that cannot be said in the mother's discourse.

Before confronting the analysis of the condition that seems to me to be necessary for psychotic potentiality to remain such, a question arises: on the basis of what I have just said about the problematic of the woman who will induce in the child the setting up of primary delusional thinking, must we conclude that we are already confronted, in her case, with primary delusional thinking? It is difficult to give a straightforward answer.

From what I have been able to understand in the discourse of those who spoke to me of their history, I have the impression that, in a large number of cases, the answer must be in the affirmative.

In other cases, however, these women seem to have been able to set up against the mother's non-transmission of a 'wish for a child' a well-adapted defence that enables them to lay down relatively stable identificatory markers. It is a defence that consisted in privileging activities modelled on the relational mode of a mother–child type, without however having to be a mother, and I am thinking of the variety of different vocations of a humanitarian type, or by hypercathecting intellectual activities, in which any desire for motherhood will not be recognised. But this reorganisation of the libidinal economy can be maintained only as long as these women remain protected from the experience of actual motherhood. When this occurs, they will be confronted by the problematic that I have just described. They will then have to do their best to avoid the child's discourse revealing to them what is untenable in their position whenever they address him *qua* Mother. This hypothesis was confirmed to me by what I actually heard, not reconstructed on the basis of their children's discourse, when I was able to have in analysis women whose children, or one of whose children, I knew to have disturbances of a schizophrenic type.

162

5 The necessary factor for psychotic potentiality to remain such

In this potentiality I saw the result of the encystment of an unrepressed theorisation concerning origins that may, as long as it remains in a state of cyst, allow to take place, parallel with it and contradictory to it, a discourse that, with the exception of the statement concerning origins, seems, and seems only, to conform to the discourse of others. Given this, the I may, more or less, speak a discourse, which does not conform to its own foundations, and allows to coexist contradictory conceptualisations of being, of desire, of the world.

If one listens carefully to Mme B . . . 's discourse, one sees, side by side, the presence of a certainty concerning *her* theory of origins and the presence of meanings apparently shared by the group. She thus succeeds in 'inhabiting' a discourse in which what she expresses about the 'feelings' that link her I to others conforms to the discourse of others, whereas the cause she gives for it is very odd, a cause that she is not unaware of, even if it is prudently passed over in silence, as if it 'went without saying'. For this split between explicit meaning and implicit cause to be possible, the first condition will be that the surrounding reality and, above all, the family reality is so arranged as to support this contradiction.

Mme B . . . 's family context reveals:

- a husband who agrees, indeed wishes, not to have, so to speak, any sexual life, who regards as childish what his wife has managed, from time to time, to say about her own theories;
- a mother – we shall return to this point – who hears enough to confirm her in her secret conviction that what she believes is right: 'making love is disgusting', 'you'd better watch your son, or he'll end up like his father', 'men are a feeble lot, they easily go off their heads'. (It is striking that Mme B . . . 's mother uses the term '*le père*', 'the father', to denote husbands, which irresistibly reminds us of the woman she called 'Lamère', as if she had created for herself the image of a mythical couple represented by 'Lamère', who sees the future, cures illnesses and is possessed of supernatural powers, and the '*le père*', the seat of madness and evil).

When Mme B . . . speaks to her mother, whom she sees very often, she is convinced, quite rightly, that her mother understands perfectly well what she means and agrees with her; moreover, her mother's discourse, in the aphoristic form so peculiar to it, has taken over a series of statements, heard long ago, that confirm the interpretation that the child had once given herself of her mother's thoughts and instructions, such as: 'never love a man', 'don't tell your son that you want a child', 'the father's a weak, dangerous thing'.

Thus, on the stage of the real, there persists a voice embodying the representative of the Other, which guarantees the truth of the theory concerning origins, that the subject's discourse is therefore the place in which truth is possible, that the existence, in the same discourse, of contradictory postulates is a 'normal' paradox:

- Two children who, for all these years, have agreed to play a strange game of questions and answers. With little affection for their father, very close to their mother, they and their mother have invented a language, in play of course, but not just any language: 'when we talk among ourselves in "ourlanguage" [a strange reinvention of a metalanguage of their own devising], one word can just as well mean another, you have to guess the answer'; I would add that 'ourlanguage' makes it possible for any answer to be interpreted at the whim of the listener, for any demand to demand everything or nothing.
- A social life that, while seeming normal, is extremely poor in terms of circulating ideas: they are shopkeepers and talk to their customers or suppliers only of prices, credit, quality of merchandise, etc.
- So far, Mme B . . . 's life has not been a particularly difficult one.

(It is not my intention to analyse here how the phobia began. However, I should like to make one point: it began a few days after Mme B . . . discovered sperm stains on her son's bedclothes. This event posed a threat to her relations with her son, whom she continued to treat as a little boy, about whom one could ignore that he had a sex and that one day he might use it.)

In the context thus described, three elements merit particular attention:

- the role of the voice and of what the mother hears;
- the family's complicity in Mme B . . . 's 'strange thoughts';
- the absence of traumatic events, illnesses, bereavements, which might trigger off the return of earlier experiences.

The organisation of an everyday reality that explains why one sometimes finds in such cases a feature similar to one to be found in perversion: if the pervert is certain that he knows the truth about his partner's desires and tastes, these subjects are convinced that others are privy to their theories, that they are 'thinking' similar thoughts and that, for reasons best known to themselves, they defend other theories that they know to be erroneous. These subjects preserve their fragile belief by prudently arranging matters so as not to hear and not to say 'certain things'. But for this conviction to be preserved, two major conditions are indispensable:

1 The presence, on the stage of the real, of at least *one* voice and *one* person listening, which provides them, whenever there seems to be a risk of a radical challenge to their discourse, with the assurance that it conveys a truth communicable to that voice and to the person listening.

2   The frequent non-repetition of situations in which frustration, pain, bereavement would reach a certain threshold, which most people can bear, but which these subjects find unbearable, since they are accompanied by a return of the affect proper to the first experiences out of which they were made.

I shall analyse these two conditions separately; the second will enable me to explain the function that I attribute to 'historical reality'.

The embodied voice and listener

The specific feature of the temporal experience of psychosis is the sameness of a life always-already-lived, which the subject rediscovers and repeats whenever experience and an encounter with someone else confront him with a situation that I shall call 'traumatic': a description that depends not on the objectivity of the situation, but on what it reactivates, by way of response, in the subjects concerned.

In the register of his significant cathexes, the subject repeats the same: the same demand, the same response, the same anxiety, the same idealisation of the object. That is why any object selected by his libido arouses in a direct, inverted, reflexive mode the same form of cathexis present between the subject and the first libidinal supports encountered in the external world. As a result, in the space of the world, either there exist only objects that are 'neutral', indifferent and, in a sense, undifferentiated from an affective point of view, which pose neither problems nor questions, or only the same can appear, whatever form it disguises itself in. This situation is reproduced unchanged in the I's encounter with discourse: either all that is heard, in the almost mechanical sense of the term, are 'indifferent' discourses that speak of a flat, everyday life, for which the question of a secondary connotation does not arise; if one hears 'the cost of living is high', 'it's raining', 'you must go to school', 'X has died', these statements will be taken literally, as a descriptive statement of what is self-evident, a reality emptied of the implicit. Or, on the contrary, *the speaker*, independently of what he says, is the embodiment of a primary voice and, in this case, the subject re-experiences the situation of encounter that had been present between the listener and the 'word-bearer'. From now on every statement becomes an enigmatic meaning, the support of meanings that forbid any doubt, any truth testing, any reference to others' discourse; it is denied that the statement can lie. This negation dispossesses the subject of any right to claim any truth for what he says when it is not a faithful repetition of what his mother says.

That is why he must endow, a priori, the voice making the statement with a power of certainty: the voice must say what is true, even if it is expressed in the form of riddles, a necessary postulate if the meanings that the child had made his so that 'a power to speak' is preserved may in turn claim the attribute of truth.

In these subjects it has never been possible, except in appearance, for the indispensable separation between the voice and the meaning of the statement to take place: the voice making the statement remains the support of an extreme idealisation, it preserves the attribute of an 'omniscient omnipotence' and is posited as sole possible dispenser of a guarantee of truth required by the I. The meaning of statements ensures its truth and maintains its identifying role only thanks to the libidinal cathexis enjoyed by the voice speaking them; they cannot be referred to a foundation of statements shared by the group. The first point, indispensable if we are to be able to appeal to that reference, would have implied that one assumes a certain distance towards the first things one hears, that one sets out on a 'solitary quest' for self-knowledge, that one may think on one's own that which is not thought by the Other and, lastly, that one may give oneself the right to find outside the family a discourse that will allow one to contradict, without losing, in doing so, all right to speak. Forced to create the theoretical foundations of one's own peculiar discourse, thanks to a theory that is just as peculiar, the subject can no longer expect any support from the discourse of the group. If psychotic potentiality is not to lead to manifest delusion, the discourse and the I must find a possible point of anchorage in the voice of an Other, rather than of others, and this voice should play the same role as that played, for others, by the text. This subjection is the flaw, hidden behind the form, and the apparently discordant formalisation, of discourse: an I that can do something only 'as if' he possessed autonomous, internalised identificatory markers, 'as if' he were not still dependent on the voice of an Other who alone may assure him that the discourse that establishes him is the bearer of truth. If the voice of a living person is generally chosen to play this role it is because the same, single support must be at one and the same time the point that draws the narcissistic libido towards the outside-self, thus preventing it from reversing the meaning of its vector and setting up a closed circuit, and the source that ensures the I of its identificatory statements. By this reappropriation of part of the narcissism projected onto the idealised voice, the I will be able to preserve that minimum of self-cathexis indispensable to its existence. It might be added that, if the voice should preferably be one voice, that is to say, that of a living being, it is also because its role as exclusive identificatory marker requires that it coexist throughout the discourse and can confirm to the subject that it is speaking the truth whenever another discourse, that of others, may show that it is doing nothing of the kind. The subject cannot accommodate himself, or cannot do so successfully, to a demonstration given once and for all; the subject must be able to find it again whenever his discourse is threatened by a verdict of untrue. One can see the trap in which the subject is caught: in effect the 'word-bearer' has been responsible for an unsustainable lack in the texture of discourse; the child has concealed, filled in this lack, by constructing an inter-pretation that, by inventing some supposed cause for the presence of this 'hole', has filled in the void. This interpretation in turn can claim a power of meaning, and therefore a power of communication, only by seeking and finding in the same 'word-bearer', *or in some substitute*, an answer that will show him that the meaning can be heard, that it can be assured of being acknowledged by him. His discourse is what it is because of the 'word-bearer'; as a result this 'word-bearer' alone holds the power to guarantee the truth to what he states.

The discourse and the I remain dependent on the presence in the outside-the-psyche of a judging agency that has failed to become internalised and autonomised. It should also be remembered that 'primary delusional thinking and theory' have a very precise aim: to give meaning to a senseless signification transmitted by the mother's discourse, to make unintelligible instructions reasonable, to reply to the enigmas of a discourse in which the enigma covers not some hidden knowledge to be guessed at but an unknown lack for which he must invent and create an interpretation.

Delusional theorisation makes it possible for this 'lack' never to reveal to the subject that the cause of his theoretical construction is to be found in this non-desire of a 'wish for a child' present in the mother, itself the consequence of a flaw in the symbolic register. One will thus be able, as Mme B . . . demonstrates, to convince oneself that if the father 'blew up' it was because of a law of nature for which nobody is responsible, that if a catheter has been violently inserted in your oesophagus, if one nearly died, it is because of some mistake: such formulations are far more acceptable than those that demonstrate that the mother wishes your death, that maternal hate was responsible for the blowing up of the father.

The over-determined relation that these 'theorisations' and these 'meanings' maintain with the desire of the 'word-bearer' appears quite clearly here:

- They are induced by the intuition of a truth concerning the desire of the Other, the mother, which is perfectly understood.
- They transform this 'intuition' in such a way that it becomes acceptable for the child's psyche: 'she didn't want to kill me, I just picked up the wrong tin'.
- They continue to conform to what the mother demands that the child think: 'men are bad by nature' and 'blow up', 'to give birth is a mistake since it is the effect of swallowing part of the father', 'if you take after your father, you'll either go mad or fly off and get blown up'.

But this 'theorisation' can assume its function only if it can claim to be true: it can find this attribute of truth only in the confirmation implicitly guaranteed it by the listening and discourse of her on whom the I is still dependent. As far as 'others' are concerned, not only is this theorisation in contradiction with theirs, but it can be received by the group only as a radical questioning of the foundations of its discourse, proof of the non-evidence of the evident, as 'mad' speech that upsets all order, that threatens the definition of reality and of truth that one thought had been accepted once and for all by every member of the group. The group of others will now violently refute such a discourse, deny it any possibility of compromise, silence it by refusing to hear it or do whatever is necessary to exclude the speaker from anywhere he might be heard. Confronted by this threat, psychotic potentiality allows one to avoid contradicting that discourse by speaking *truly* only to a single Other, into whose answers the subject may project, without evident contradiction, the truths once laid down by the 'word-bearer'. The first condition for the potentiality to remain such is the guaranteed presence on the stage of the world of an Other – whether it be the first who maintained one's life or some substitute who possesses attributes favourable to this transference – who gives proof of a certain complicity and closeness with the subject's thoughts and theories. A husband, a wife, a friend, a boss, a child: *at least one subject on the stage of the real* must agree to take over the function and attributes of the 'word-bearer', providing the I with that point of anchorage and cathexis indispensable for an 'outside' to continue to exist and for the I to find there an image acceptable to him. The first condition that gave birth to psychotic potentiality becomes the necessary condition for it not to go beyond this stage, for the I to appear 'as if' nothing differentiated it in the eyes of others.

It is not my intention to say very much here about the psychoanalysis of a subject in whom the psychotic potentiality as well as its manifest forms is present: nevertheless what I have just said shows the role that the analyst will be expected to play in such cases from the outset. From the moment when an analytical relation is established, it is the analyst who, on the stage of the real, will have to take over the function of that sole voice that guaranteed the subject the truth of his statement concerning origins. It is a function that, on one level, is no different from the one that the transference relation always projects onto us, but it is a function that, in this case, makes us the person who ought to guarantee the truth of 'delusional thinking', whereas we can only assure the subject that this thinking actually has a meaning, but a meaning that we can find only by appealing to an order of causality that is not his own. The difficulty posed by the analytical relation to both partners results from the ambiguous relationship maintained by the analyst with his interlocutor's delusional thinking: thinking for which he claims a meaning but cannot share the causal order invoked. It is a difficult position and one that runs the risk of leading either to a break in the relation or to excessive violence, this time committed by the analyst himself, trying to force the other to share a truth that is not his, and one that *he cannot be expected* to recognise as his own, which amounts to saying that the only choice left to the psychotic, in this case, is to choose between two possible forms of alienation.

I have said that for psychotic potentiality to remain such two conditions are necessary: the presence on the stage of the real of another voice that guarantees the truth of the subject's statement and the non-repetition of situations too close to those responsible for the first experiences. It is the second condition that I shall now analyse.

6 The historical reality and the effect of reduplication

This second condition confronts us with a concept that, for me, holds an essential place in the human problematic and more particularly in the psychotic problematic: historical reality conceived as that set of events that actually took place in the subject's childhood and that, for reasons already analysed, affected the destiny of the psyche in a specific way. The essential reason for this is that, on the stage of reality, once that stage has been recognised as an external, separate space, there rises up in a way that is either too intense or too repeated an event that *acts out* a fantasy representation; a telescoping will take place between the two, with the result that it will be impossible to repress and re-elaborate the fantasy whose legend has been confirmed by reality. I have emphasised that this reality, which is acted out on the stage of the outside-self, assumes its pathogenic value only thanks to the particular character of the commentary that the discourse of the Other gives of it, or of the absence of any commentary capable of relativising its effects. If we remain at the schizophrenic potentiality, we know that some event or series of events, belonging to reality, has had an inductive role in its constitution; whether the potentiality remains such will still depend on the way in which this same reality is organised throughout the subject's existence.

To explain what I mean, let us leave the potentiality to one side for a moment and turn to the most complete form of psychosis, psychosis in early childhood – it does not matter whether it takes the form of autism or profound mental deficiency.

On the subject of the narcissistic contract, I have already referred to the frequency with which one finds in autistic children, or in children labelled mentally deficient, a similar real drama: abandonment, rejection from nurse to nurse, openly rejecting parents, the intervention of the law that deprives them of their rights, some somatic catastrophe, etc. There is one mistake that should not be made: to extrapolate from these cases justification for the view that if the majority of the population of psychiatric hospitals belongs to the unfavoured class,[10] it is because the rich keep their mad at home or in luxury clinics. Infantile madness is neither a characteristic of a sub-proletariat nor the direct effect of belonging to that class, but the fact of belonging to it does encourage the telescoping of which I spoke. On the subject of the narcissistic contract I also stressed that, if the child, observing the space outside the family, perceives in the relation of others towards the parental couple a repetition of the one that he fantasised as existing between him and the couple, there will be a reduplication, on the stage of reality, of a previous identificatory statement, with the risk of a fixation on that same double statement.

When we read the life stories of these children and learn that the father had been in prison, interned or was unknown, that the mother had had ten or twelve children (she wasn't quite sure), that being left alone was an everyday occurrence and sometimes necessary; or, in other cases, that the child, suffering from third-degree burns, was left uncared for in the corner of a dark room, where she was found quite by chance by a social worker; or, again, in another case, that a malformation of the oesophagus had meant that between the ages of six and ten the child had to go to hospital once a fortnight to have a catheter adjusted and that these were the only times when the mother, a nurse, showed any tenderness towards her; or that another child, after a series of operations, had to have a leg amputated, after which he was sent away for three years of 're-education', without being visited once by his parents; when these facts no longer seem to be exceptional, but occur quite frequently in such stories, one cannot help wondering what their role was.[11]

Side by side with such 'extreme' cases, clinical practice provides another series which seems to provide 'fruitful experience' of a different kind:

- Mme D . . . was breast-fed up to the age of twenty months and clearly remembered the particular circumstances of her weaning. One fine day, noticing that her daughter was refusing to eat solid food, the mother decided to force her to *desire the rejection* of milk. When the child insistently demanded 'milk', the mother picked her up, took out a spray bulb that she had previously hidden inside her dress and violently squeezed a blackish, bitter liquid over the child's face. The terrified child began to scream and, indeed, rejected the breast from then on: unfortunately, contrary to her mother's expectations, she also refused to eat and came close to dying.
- Mme R . . . is the third daughter of a woman, probably of a paranoid character, who had decided that her children would be potty trained by the age of twelve months. She succeeded with the first two, but not with the last. This child was eighteen months old when the mother, discovering that the child had soiled herself again, went into an uncontrollable rage, scraped up the excrement, wiped it over the child's face, then locked the child in the cellar for two days.
- M. L . . . 's childhood was marked by a succession of deaths. Between the ages of twelve months and five years he was to lose, one after the other, a brother, an uncle, a sister and finally his father. All this in the particular context of real persecution, experienced by his Jewish family, living in occupied France.

No purpose would be served by adding further examples; it would be illusory to believe that we would learn anything more from them, that the event is sufficient to explain the psychical sequelae or, on the other hand, that the event is merely a secondary justification and that, in any case, these children's experiences of weaning, potty training or death are sufficient conditions and alone responsible: and for what? Of the three examples quoted, taken from three clinical histories, the first never passed over into overt psychosis, but from the beginning of the analysis it became clear that the patient was suffering from an extreme fragility of the I's markers, disturbing phenomena of depersonalisation, a tendency to anorexia alternating with periods of deep depression and, lastly, the absence up to the age of thirty, when the analysis began, of any sexual life.

In the second case, there were repetitions of delusional episodes, involving themes of persecution, in which poisoning played a central role. They were preceded at the age of sixteen by an agoraphobic episode, which meant that the subject had to give up going to school, and followed later by a homicidal phobia towards an illegitimate girl whom the young woman had adopted as a two-year-old baby.

M. L . . . presents what we call a characteral structure, which amounts to saying that we are not quite sure what to say about it. It is not simply a neurosis, but we observe in it elements that remind us in turn of sensitive paranoia, hypochondria and perverse tendencies.

On the other hand, in all three cases the 'symptoms' showed *a direct relation*, in their manifestations, with the event whose scenario they repeat, in positive and negative.[12]

Before continuing I would like to sum up what seems to me the place accorded by Freud, in the triggering off of delusion, to what he defines as material reality, a term that covers my concept of historical reality. There is no question here of considering what Freud meant by reality or by the reality principle: to do so would involve a consideration of the whole oeuvre, which would not be what it is if Freud had not redefined what should be understood when human beings speak of reality. On the other hand, what does authorise a succinct summary that, despite the simplifications involved, does not betray the spirit of the author is the relation posited by Freud between the frustration imposed on the impulse by the reality test that *ananke* imposes and the rejection with which *das Es* (the id), as Freud calls it, opposes frustration and the reality test. Two texts are particularly enlightening in this regard: 'Neurosis and Psychosis' and 'The Loss of Reality in Neurosis and Psychosis', both written in 1924; that is, ten years after *The Schreber Case*. I shall begin by quoting three passages:

> Normally, the external world governs the ego in two ways: firstly, by current, present perceptions which are always renewable, and secondly, by the store of memories of earlier perceptions which, in the shape of an 'internal world', form a possession of the ego and a constituent part of it. In amentia, not only is the acceptance of new perceptions refused, but the internal world, too, which, as a copy of the external world, has up till now represented it, loses its significance (its cathexis). The ego creates, autocratically, a new external and internal world; and there can be no doubt of two facts – that this new world is constructed in accordance with the id's wishful impulses, and that the motive of this dissociation from the external world is some very serious frustration by reality of a wish – a frustration which seems intolerable.[13]

171

The aetiology common to the onset of a psychoneurosis and of a psychosis always remains the same. It consists in a frustration, a non-fulfilment, of one of those childhood wishes which are for ever undefeated and which are so deeply rooted in our phylogenetically determined organisation. This frustration is in the last resort always an external one . . . [14]

And, in fact, some analogy of the sort can be observed in a psychosis. Here, too, there are two steps, the second of which has the character of a reparation. But beyond that the analogy gives way to a far more extensive similarity between the two processes. The second step of the psychosis is indeed intended to make good the loss of reality, not, however, at the expense of a restriction of the id – as happens in neurosis at the expense of the relation to reality – but in another, more autocratic manner, by the creation of a new reality which no longer raises the same objections as the old one that has been given up. The second step, therefore, both in neurosis and psychosis, is supported by the same trends. In both cases it serves the desire for power of the id, which will not allow itself to be dictated to by reality. Both neurosis and psychosis are thus the expression of a rebellion on the part of the id against the external world, of its unwillingness – or, if one prefers, its incapacity – to adapt itself to the exigencies of reality, to Necessity. Neurosis and psychosis differ from each other far more in their first, introductory, reaction than in the attempt at reparation which follows it. [15]

These quotations, however succinct, show that from the very beginning of that attempt to reconstruct and 'cure' delusion Freud posits a test that one owes to reality, a term understood here as equivalent to the reality principle, which sets itself up in opposition to an impulse of the id: the impulse wins the struggle and refuses to comply with the verdict of forbidden or impossible; all the ego can now do is obey this order and decathect those fragments of reality, replacing them with a delusional construction that conforms to the impulses of the id and brings the illusion of a possible fulfilment.

Although he does not say as much explicitly, everything leads one to believe that when Freud defined frustration as 'the common aetiology' for the onset of a neuropsychosis or a psychosis, he sees this frustration as the normal result of an *ananke* that is just as normal and normalising. What makes it intolerable is demanding the 'non-fulfilment of one of those infantile wishes that remain for ever untamed'. One certainly has the impression, confirmed indeed by other texts, that just as 'those wishes' are universal, it is 'something' in the subject's constitution that makes them particularly intense and has made their repression or sublimation impossible. That this 'something', whether or not it is constitutional, exists, even though we can say nothing about it, is certain. It is because of this 'something' that the necessary conditions are not sufficient. But this unknown thing must not conjure away the actual role of an experienced reality, a role that indeed can never be enough to ensure that a psychotic response will result from it, but it is a role that is unquestionably responsible for its possible appearance. If we return to the passages quoted from Freud, we see that nothing is said about the reality that would bring with it additional frustration. Moreover, already in *The Schreber Case*, the wife's abortions, to which Freud accords a role, were certainly painful events, but they did not go beyond the trials that any man may undergo.

One may indeed take advantage of the reference to Schreber to confirm how little place is held in the Freudian analysis of psychosis by the idea of a complicity on the part of reality that no *ananke* justifies. The writings of Schreber's father were known to Freud and, in every case, perfectly knowable. Astonishingly, Freud says no more about them than to remark that the glow of success that surrounded the father for his contemporaries must have facilitated the projection onto his person of a divine power. When we examine the writings of that father, we see to what unbearable reality the father's discourse subjected the young Schreber, to what control, in the form of a sadism so subtle as not to appear such, but not enough for it not to be manifested as such, he wanted to subject the child's body, deprived of the slightest autonomous movement and programmed like a computer. A total deprivation of thinking, acting, saying, doing is required by the paternal power, which must:

> *Suppress everything* in the child, keep everything away from him that he should not make his own, and guide him perseveringly towards everything to which he should habituate himself . . . The most generally necessary condition for the attainment of this goal is the *unconditional obedience* of the child . . . The child must gradually learn to recognise more and more that he has the *physical possibility* of wishing and acting otherwise, but that he *elevates himself through his own independence* to the *moral impossibility* of wishing or acting otherwise . . . the most important thing is that the disobedience should be *crushed* to the point of regaining complete submission, using corporal punishment if necessary.[16]

When we read the books of this father and when we know something of the influence they had in Germany, which makes it unlikely that Freud would have been unaware of them, we have to recognise that the omission is not forgetfulness on Freud's part: it is just that he is not particularly concerned with something that appears to him to be of little significance in the constitution of a psychosis. 'Furthermore' frustration hardly interests him. This does not in any way diminish the fundamental discoveries to be found in his analysis of the Schreber case, or in the two texts quoted above on the ego–reality conflict in psychosis. The point on which I part company with Freud concerns the importance given to what *actually* appears in the reality of the subject who may become psychotic and to the link that this event may forge between what is inscribed on that stage and what has been represented by the primary process.

173

It is this link, which we have already encountered, that I wish to examine for the last time.

Taking up again, but in a different way, the approach suggested by Freud, I should say that what is at the origin of the schizophrenic response and its delusional construction corresponds to three conditions:

- The subject is 'intolerably' deprived of meaning.
- Untamed and untameable desire, which refuses to be silenced, also concerns the demands of interpretation and the identificatory need that constitute the I.
- Primary delusional thinking tries to reconstruct a missing fragment in the discourse of the Other, which, from now on, will reappear apparently in conformity to the identificatory demands of the I.

If this lack of meaning and this refusal of signification were not made up for by primary delusional thinking, the psychosis would be anything but potential.

The ambient psychical milieu, as encountered and perceived by the infant, that space in which the primal contemplates its own reflection, confronts infant and primal with a reality that 'resists' reflecting a state of fusion, a self–world identity as realisation of a reunification.[17]

The pictogram of the taking-into-self, of a unifying and totalising joining, will be denied by the unpleasure, the refusal, the rejection and, at least, the ambivalence actually shown by the mother when she encounters the infant's body.

In its quest for a shaping of a primal scene and a meaning concerning the origin of desire, the primary, in turn, no longer finds in the seen, the heard, the perceived, fragments that allow it to fantasise a primary couple, linked by a mutual desire for joining, totalisation, integration, by a pleasure that is shared and which the various parties wish to share.

The secondary comes up against the absence of any meaning that might reintroduce, in and by what is heard, the absent pleasure of the seen.

A first lack inscribed in the psychical reality of the woman whom the child encounters on entering the world will be inscribed in his bodily reality, an inscription that may transform into an experience of pain the act of swallowing – air or milk – excreting, seeing, or any other function of a body that ought to have been able to represent itself to itself as a space experiencing pleasure.

To this 'reality' of physical experience will be added *the reality of something heard* that 'speaks' it and which is addressed to him who inhabits that body.

The reality of a lack in the 'word-bearer', the reality of an inscription in the body, the reality of something heard from the voice of a parent: these three realities, reduplicating the earlier reality, will be superimposed and inscribe in indelible letters the same, single verdict that will confirm 'from the inside' the representation of a psyche–world relation in which the desire for unpleasure reigns.

The response to this verdict will be primary delusional thinking, which will try to reshape what is heard and, therefore, him who perceived it. But once this 'thinking' is constructed and returned to sender, a certain equilibrium, obtained at this cost, will still have to be able to be preserved.

If the first condition for schizophrenic potentiality to remain such concerns a presence on the stage of reality, the second requires that the experiences that reality continues to impose on any subject, throughout his life, should not, as they come close to those experienced at the moment of the constitution of primary delusional thinking, reveal that the reshaping carried out by that thinking was illusory.

Otherwise that glimpsed truth will resume its unsustainable brilliance: nobody desires your pleasure and the truth of your desire. Although it is true that any desire fantasy comes up against a reality that resists it, in this case that resistance goes well beyond anything that *ananke* could be responsible for, to begin with, a 'lack' in the discourse of the representative of the Other: a lack of desire for the child, a lack of desire for the pleasure in giving birth, the lack of a meaning that would make their encounter a source of pleasure that could be conveyed by word and deed.

Too near and too far, demanding too much and not enough, the mother's body and discourse fall short, the too much confronting the other with the impossibility of satisfying demand, the not enough with the non-value of any response. In this state of repetitive unsatisfaction, the psyche may respond by closing in upon itself, by losing any cathexis of its instruments of response – the sensory supports, by the decathexis of any pleasure as soon as one expects it and hopes for it from the outside-self. Hence the ease with which 'functional silences', which reduplicate the vicious circle, may arise. De-eroticising the pleasure of swallowing, excreting, seeing and the pleasure of living in general will be expressed in and take the form of a disturbance of the corresponding functions. But just as the body exists 'in itself', there will follow physical pain, the experience of hospital and, by way of response, an exaggeration of the mother's feelings of anxiety, rejection, disappointment and, as a consequence, an exacerbation of the infant's feeling of anxiety, in a circle that may be endless. If none of all this is apparent, one will usually learn by anamnesis, recounted by the subject or by someone known to him, that its equivalent has been manifested in an inverse form: the calm of a sea in which no wind ruffles the water, the wisdom and good functioning that conceal the renunciation of any intentionality of which one might be the active agent, silence or a response that is merely an echo, revealing the loss of any pleasure in hearing or any desire to be heard. Such an alternative is quite as disastrous. It may pass unperceived by others, but it will leave a profound scar: the experience of an empty life, a space without relief, a time in which the sameness of each moment is endlessly repeated, endlessly interchangeable.

I have said that it is in such a situation that the activity of thinking must be capable of being reshaped if it is to be sayable and intelligible. Only if this is done will infantile autism be avoided: hence the appeal to primary delusional thinking.

Such delusional thinking may either be encysted and form a psychotic potentiality, or give rise, without any solution of continuity, to schizophrenia or infantile paranoia.

I have now come to the end of what I proposed to say about primary delusional thinking and psychotic potentiality in the register of schizophrenia. The place given to the interpretation that the I makes of excessive violence experienced, an exploit that enables it to regard as conforming to 'reason' what was intended to exclude him from that register, is justified if one accepts my hypothesis that 'thinking' becomes the pivot on which the delusional discourse and schizophrenic construction will be elaborated.[18]

6

Concerning paranoia: primal scene and primary delusional thinking

On the horizon of paranoiac potentiality there rises what others see and hear as delusion. These considerations on paranoia, with which this book ends, will allow me to extend my reflection on the role of historical reality and on its action in the 'sense-making' that will be privileged by primary delusional thinking. I am not proposing a theory of paranoia, but showing how a 'perceived hate' marks the destiny of these subjects and becomes the pivot around which their theory concerning origins is developed. Like a wicked witch, this hate leans over their cradle from their entry into the world: the rest of their lives will be simply an unequal struggle against this evil spell that inexorably persecutes them.

In this chapter I shall confine myself to isolating the characteristics that mark the familial organisation that the subject encounters and the discourse that he hears; it is this organisation that makes the space in which the I comes about the space in which paranoia may come about. I shall not go further: paranoia and schizophrenia, like psychosis in general, offer no short cut to theory; a 'summary' of such cases invariably turns out to be impossible or amounts to little more than the monotonous repetition of a few only too familiar theoretical slogans.

At the moment when psychosis becomes manifest, one encounters the same question: what has transformed the necessary conditions into sufficient conditions for psychotic potentiality to be expressed in sound and fury, if only in the sound and fury of a silence that may be even more terrifying? An excess of one of these conditions, already in itself excessive? The particular moment in time when it takes place? I have no satisfactory answer to these questions. What I have said about the necessary presence of a referent on the stage of the real and what comes about if the subject finds himself dispossessed of it may offer an explanation of what triggers it off, but certainly not an exhaustive explanation. I am abandoning any attempt to answer this question until I have learned a little more of what psychotic discourse may have to teach me.

1 The fantasy of the primal scene and infantile sexual theories

Let us return for a moment to those 'primary sexual thoughts' or those 'infantile sexual theories' that every subject has experienced. These are the 'thoughts' by which the child's I is able to give itself initial answers to its questions concerning the place in which its body originated, the desire of that place with regard to that same body, the pleasure or unpleasure that this body experienced of the Other at the moment when it gave birth to yours and the reasons that account for that experience. Every infantile sexual theory is a theory concerning birth, which, while answering the question concerning the origin of the body, in fact answers the question concerning origins in general, by constructing what I have already analysed under the term 'primal cause'. I said little about the relation between this making sense of origins and the representation of these same origins: a representation, or a fantasy, in which the relation present between the elements occupying the stage come to represent, in the literal sense of the term, what it is the task of 'infantile sexual thinking' to make sayable. Primal *scene* and infantile sexual *thought* are the two psychical productions by which primary process and secondary process answer a question concerning origins that can neither be silenced nor ignored. The reshapings undergone by this fantasy in the course of psychical evolution are concomitant with the successive changes that the I will or will not be able to bring to one's infantile theory concerning one's origin and origins in general. The presentable and sayable follow, for a time, parallel paths: scenic representations of origin show how what is represented will be reshaped in order to become capable of a representation, in which there will be room for what I shall now call the 'infantile theory on the Oedipus complex'.

The reshaping of fantasy will not go beyond this stage, but there is nothing to guarantee that it will be able to reach it. It is clear that this representation will continue to respect the double demand imposed by the primary process: to conform to its postulate and to link images of things to images of words in such a way as to allow anything represented to be also a representation of the image that the psyche makes of one's own body. I have used the term 'reshaping'; a better term might have been 'successive representations'. Indeed, the psyche's ability to set up a representation of desire capable of representing the Oedipal problematic never annuls, for all that, the representations that preceded it: nevertheless they will be able, from that moment, to remain in the shadows and to leave the front of the stage to the representation that conforms most to what is *actually* experienced by the fantasising subject.

It is clear that the 'Oedipal' fantasy presupposes an 'Oedipal' theory. Neither is there from the outset: they are both consequences of the elaboration imposed on the psyche by the elements that inform it of the 'qualities' proper to objects, qualities that it will have to consider in its representation of the desire of those who move on the stage of the outside-self and of the relation that links it to them. This interaction between the scenic and the sayable, between fantasy of the primal scene and infantile sexual theory, is the manifestation of a more fundamental law: access to the unified image of the body goes hand in hand with access to the unified image of language. This law may become clearer if we analyse the relation between the image of the body and the discourse that speaks of the body. It will then be seen that the psyche's cathexis of the names that discourse gives a subject of a part and a function of the body is a decisive factor in the place that will be given to that part and to that function in the image of the body, an image by which the psyche represents to itself the space inhabited by the I and *also* the I that inhabits it. What I have just said concerns the universals of psychical functioning; I spoke of this at length in the first part of this book. Before approaching the image that paranoia will impose on its representation of the primal scene, it is important, I believe, to stress why this fantasy, in every subject, corresponds to a discourse on the body spoken by the representative, and the function that is played in this discourse by the presence or absence of pleasure.

The spoken body and the pleasure of the woman who speaks it

On a number of occasions, I have stressed the task that falls to language: to enable the I to become acquainted with the forces at work in its space. This knowledge becomes the object of its quest only if it promises the I a bonus of pleasure; the ability to 'think' the term 'pleasure', the wish 'to think' it, implies that this action is in itself a source of pleasure. 'To speak without pleasure' is accompanied, in the present of the said, by a 'to think without pleasure', which contradicts the truth of the 'said' whenever the latter claims to 'speak' of a pleasure of the I. As a result, if this contradiction is constant or too frequent, the discourse becomes the locus in which no statement concerning pleasure can make claim to an attribute of truth; it may well become the locus in which no truth is expected any more. We saw what the result of this may be in my analysis of the basic language.

I should now like to be more specific about the action of the 'word-bearer' when, for the benefit of the child, he or she names his body, his functions, his productions, and the consequences of this naming on the representation of a fantasy that is, by definition, a representation of the subject's relation to desire and to pleasure.

Among the names that the 'word-bearer' has the task of communicating, those that refer to functions and zones as a source of erogenous pleasure will enjoy a privileged cathexis: the naming of the erogenous zones and the appropriation of this naming will be accompanied and must be accompanied by 'erogenous' speech, speech that can only be such if it is a source and promise of pleasure. Whether the 'word-bearer' names the parts of the body by neologisms, periphrases or by their canonical names, the voice that names inevitably communicates to the listener the pleasure, unpleasure or indifference that it experiences in the naming of those functions, organs, parts. As he learns these names, the child also receives

179

a message concerning the emotion aroused in the mother by what is being named and its function. It is of little importance whether one calls the little boy's sex a 'willy', a 'little beast' or a 'penis', though the choice of term is seldom without significance; what is important is that the voice is able to communicate that it experiences pleasure in recognising its existence and in communicating it to the child. What is exemplified by the sexual zone remains true, if in a more subtle way, for the total set of terms used for the body's part-functions. This pleasure that the naming by the 'word-bearer' ought to communicate has an essential role in the irradiating and totalising effect that we encountered in the analysis of instinctual pleasure, and whose importance I stressed. But, for this effect to be produced, the child must be convinced of the mother's pleasure concerning all the part-functions and their production, including the thinking function. Otherwise one would have to be able to see without thinking that one sees, denying that one hears or touches: the pleasure of seeing that would accompany the fear of being discovered listening and thinking would have soon disappeared.[1] To this is added another requirement: the integration of the erogenous pleasures necessary to the setting up of a unified image of the body is accompanied by the appro- priation by the child of the series of statements naming the various parts and functions of his body. I have said that this series must offer a unifying meaning from the outset, even if it is discovered by the psyche only in stages, a meaning that integrates the part under the aegis of a whole, which anticipates the presence of the project of the I in the child.

It is therefore by what the child hears in the mother's discourse concerning his body that he will gain access to a unified image of the body. This unification of the body image has as a consequence the ability to integrate the part-pleasures and so put them at the service of the 'unified' aim that we call sexual pleasure (*jouissance*). The *jouissance* of a unified body will have to take the place of the pleasure of an erogenous zone: the promise of a deferred pleasure that makes it possible, later on, to give a new meaning to the ordeals undergone, to the delay accepted, to the unpleasure that is more frequent than pleasure. This is the future experience of a possibility of the body and of a power of the I that must remain the loci in which sexual pleasure is possible. Only in this way can discourse in turn be posited as a locus in which truth is possible: the renunciations that the 'word-bearer' and the law of the father have demanded, the promises that they have made, the projects that they have initiated may be acceptable only as long as, in however intermittent and fleeting a way, proof is offered to the I that they were not lying, that the deferred pleasure that they promised was not a lure by which they were tricked.

That is why, if there is lacking in the 'spoken body' a word that names a function and an erogenous zone and, moreover, if that word exists, but one refuses to recognise that for the child and for the 'word-bearer' it is a source of pleasure, that function and that pleasure may be lacking in the body itself. To name the arm is to possess, of course, the idea of a limb that continues from a shoulder and extends through to a hand, but it is also to know that this limb is the seat of prehension and that the *essential meaning* of prehensibility, a meaning that runs through everything one will discover and which one will place in the category of taking, doing, letting go or gesturing a goodbye, is to be found in the first discovery of the power of the hand to touch a breast, to take the Other's hand, to stroke a face and to 'know' that those actions are a source of pleasure for the Other's body. For there to be an image of the structuring and structured body, the 'word-bearer', who names what the sensory power discovers, must accompany that naming with a sign expressive of the pleasure that he or she experiences in recognising what the child's part-functions produce. The mother's pleasure in naming the body and giving the child a knowledge of it is a necessary condition for the child to conceive of his body as a unified space and, in a second stage, for the part-pleasures to be able to be reduced to preliminaries in the service of sexual pleasure.

Although sexual pleasure is an experience that is lacking in the child, nevertheless the pleasure that the mother demonstrates in her relation to the father must show that it is of a different 'quality', that it cannot be reduced to the pleasure of seeing, hearing, saying, that it entails some enigmatic 'plus' which one is assured of experiencing in the future. For that promise to be heard, and for the child to appropriate it as a future aim of his own search for pleasure, it must appear to him as the experience of a body and not as the experience of a zone of that body. So far I have stressed the fantasy representation that the subject gives himself of himself and of his relation to pleasure, through his presentation of the body image: clearly the possibility of representing a unified image of one's own body and an integrating representation of the part-pleasures is a necessary condition for the psyche to be able to represent to himself a unified image of the body of the Other and an integrating image of what may be a source of sexual pleasure for that body.

The fantasy of the primal scene in psychosis shows what happens when the subject cannot have access to that unified image and when any fantasy of pleasure may represent only fragmented bodies, with, as a consequence, the risk of making a 'desire for fragmentation' the omnipotent cause of the pleasure that the Other may experience. The fantasy of the primal scene merely exemplifies the characteristics that will be shared, in the register of psychosis, by the fantasisations of a desire of which the body is the object: it is at the stage of body parts seeking and rejecting one another that the reshaping of the scene and the elaboration of statements referring to the pleasures of the body come to a stop. Before analysing the reasons for this stop, I shall consider the necessary conditions for the successive representations of the fantasy to be elaborated.

2 The conditions necessary for fantasy re-elaboration

I have shown how the passage from the complementary couple to the primary couple is coextensive with the recognition by the psyche of an outside-self, an observation from which no subject, beyond the infant stage, escapes – the outside-self, which entails the recognition of the mother's body as a separate entity from one's own body, possessing a 'breast' that is at first the representative of every object of pleasure. This first representation of the outside-self will occur in an identical way in every subject; that is why it is quite incorrect to say that the schizophrenic does not recognise the separation between his own and his mother's body. The schizophrenic *knows* of the existence of an outside-self; what he can no longer 'know' concerns the autonomy of a 'self'. That a heterogeneous desire exists and annuls his own desire, that an Other decides in all sovereignty the order of the world and the laws according to which his own psyche ought to function, are for him propositions that possess the attribute of certainty. What he cannot posit, in any imaginable place or time, is a himself that might continue to be while showing itself to be different from the form and speech imposed upon him. He can perceive of himself only as a marionette whose strings are being pulled by another, or as an 'extra', an 'additional bit of flesh', which agrees to offer itself to another body, to become the proof that the earth mother possesses colonies, that in those strange lands her law, her language, her institutions are alone recognised. In his fantasisation it is clear that the schizophrenic can also project himself into the place of that Other; it is he alone who assumes the place of the earth mother and the Other that of the colonies; but in the first case, as in the second, the earth mother and the colonies are not one and the same thing. The so-called fantasy of fusion expresses the desire that frontiers should come down, the desire for a universal earth that would no longer allow a distinction between colonising state and colonised state: but this fantasy is just a 'dream' that the schizophrenic, like anyone else, may indulge in. If one tries to define, not the schizophrenic's dream (it is not very different from our own), but the fantasy that represents the world for him, what emerges is not a world of fusion but the image of a world divided by a bloody struggle, a struggle all the more desperate in that it has been known from the very beginning who the conqueror is.

Like every subject, the schizophrenic has encountered an outside-self under the aegis of the desire of the Other. The first occupant of that outside-self was for him, too, the breast, a moment of coincidence between the space of the world and the maternal space, which projects onto the desire of that occupant the power to engender the 'all' that was pictographed by the primal in an act of self-procreation.

From that moment on a screen will be set up outside the 'presenter' on which the images of a film will be projected that seem to him to conform to what is being acted out on the stage of the real: he does not know that they are merely the result of the projection angle that he has himself chosen. As the credits appear the observer discovers first a single star, a leading lady – the imago of the *primary woman* – followed by lesser figures whose names he does not know and who seem to have no other function but to assist the star in whatever she wishes to impose, do, say, refuse.

The first scene, then, represents for every subject the relation that the maternal imago has with the objects of her pleasure, the term 'object' being understood here in the sense given it by ordinary language; that is to say, a thing, some inanimate fragment, an instrument in the service of whoever uses it.

This relation between the mother and everything that appears as a source or instrument of pleasure (the breast, one's own mouth for hers, the presence of another without a breast, her own elsewhere) will be represented by a fantasy in which the power of taking into oneself or rejecting outside oneself any object present in space is attributed to the mother's desire alone. It should be remembered that normally there ought to be in the psyche a balance between the two representations: that in which the relation between the mother and the object, and between the mother and the father, gives evidence of a pleasure shared by both parties, and that in which the relation represents the mother's desire to reject one and the 'unpleasure' that results from this for the 'rejected' party.

What is true for this first fantasisation of the omnipotence of the mother's desire is also valid for the representation of the primal scene once the presence of the father has been recognised: for a double representation of the relation of the couple to exist, and for it to operate in the two equally necessary directions, the relation between that couple must not only be perceived but also be perceived as an action that may give them pleasure, even if at other moments it is a source of unpleasure. It is because in this way the subject who contemplates the scene may at the same time recognise that there exists a couple linked by a privileged relationship and that what he sees may become for him a source of pleasure. Although it is true that the relation of rejection that he may fantasise as existing between the two elements of the couple is a projection of his own unpleasure at recognising that there is a couple and of his wish that one reject the other, it is equally true that if what appears on the stage of the real is always accompanied by a sign that shows that he is a source of unpleasure for the actors, the observer, contemplating this relation, finds it difficult to make what he sees a source of pleasure. There is a limit to the power of projection; the excess of reality, the excess of denial, the permanence of the same single sign cut through the primary itself and leave their mark there. The observer begins by fantasising that he is the effect of a *cause* projected onto the desire of the Other, a prototype of the representations that the primary process creates of what lies at the origin of his pleasure or unpleasure, and therefore of what is the *primal cause* and *origin of himself*. This first fantasisation, which is a universal of the psychical structure, will undergo a first reshaping at the moment when the observer perceives *him* who occupies the elsewhere of the maternal space. As we have seen, it is in this elsewhere, and from that elsewhere, that the paternal attributes emerge: at an early and usually short phase, he will conceive of these 'attributes' as 'extras' that have no other function but to allow the 'star' to play her role, to play scenes that she alone has chosen. Although the father appears from the outset as proof of the existence of a maternal elsewhere, this elsewhere remains dependent on the mother's desire. How short this phase will be will normally depend on the signs of dependence that the mother's desire may or may not be able to manifest. Her waiting for a presence that is not that of the child, her pleasure in listening to or looking at a third party, her sadness during an absence when he himself is present, all these signs of a pleasure and an unpleasure that no longer concern him and about which he can do nothing mean that the observing subject is displaced, seeks the locus of that heterogeneous and unknown cause and discovers that 'the Other-without-breast', to which one already owes experiences of pleasure and unpleasure, is party to it and a power in the mother's experience. Once again I must repeat the same observation: for this 'third cause' to be acceptable and accepted, its discovery must, in turn, be a source of pleasure as well as of unpleasure. The inevitable unpleasure caused by the existence of a third party, desiring and desired by the mother, a third party that offers her a pleasure from which he is excluded, must be compensated for by the pleasure expressed in a look at their meeting, their presence together, and their reciprocal cathexis, thus expressing a situation in which pleasure reigns, in which to be together gives pleasure, a 'seen' that is offered to the observer, authorising him to see and to experience pleasure in it. In this way a transference onto the cause of the origin can take place: if the experience of maternal pleasure requires the experience of paternal pleasure, if what they both desire is their joint pleasure, then the subject will be able to represent himself as the effect of that double desire, and therefore as the fulfilment of parental pleasure. A double origin that, by mediating and relativising the omnipotence imputed to the desire of the Other, will allow the fantasy of the primal scene to be reshaped and so become that by which, and in which, will be represented a subject–desire relation, created by the Oedipal problematic, by the knowledge of the difference of the sexes and by the primacy accorded the genital zone in the hierarchy of pleasure. This last model, occupying centre stage, will now throw its predecessors into the shadows, aided in doing so by its temporal, but also textual proximity to a secondary process that recognises in it the familiar, to which it can accord a right of residence without taking too serious a risk. This summary of the successive representations of the fantasy of the primal scene shows what conditions they require:

1 In the first place, the 'presenter' must, from the outset, have at his disposal a double representation of the experience: the outside-self must be able to be represented as a space whose encounter makes unpleasure and pleasure possible.
2 He must be able to represent to himself that she who at first occupies the

whole of the stage allows observation of her to be a source of pleasure and that she shows that she wants it to give pleasure.

3 He must encounter an elsewhere, of which the attributes imputed to it will testify to the existence of a father and a desire that are not subject to the power of maternal jurisdiction.

4 He must see that father as he who desires the pleasure of the mother and as he who causes it, and to see that the mother's pleasure finds its source in that desire that she desires.

5 He must be able to represent the relation of the couple as an encounter that may give them pleasure, a representation that will be responsible for pleasure experienced by him who is unaware that he is the 'presenter' of the scene.

It is on the basis of this representation of the couple, as source and locus of pleasure, that the representation that the psyche gave itself of its own origin will be reshaped: a double desire and a shared pleasure will now give a new representation of it.

It will be noted that the passage from one representation to the other has as its condition that the new one should allow the representation of a pleasure, experienced by those who occupy the stage, that may for the fantasiser be the cause of a pleasure that he shares. This is a necessary condition if the unpleasure resulting from an encounter with separation, with the outside-self, with the heterogeneity of desires – an unpleasure that is inevitable, for it always entails the renunciation of a first representation and of a first model of the self–world relation – is not to lead to a break between the look and the seen, between the activity of fantasisation and that which in terms of reality inevitably amounts to a proof of non-conformity to the fantasy.

When this condition is not respected we shall have a persistence of the fantasy of the primal scene, and of a fantasisation of wish fulfilment, which will reveal the function that the psyche accords to that 'elsewhere' of maternal space. The construction operated by the schizophrenic shows that the attributes that prove to him the existence of that elsewhere are little more than 'extras': the leading lady continues to occupy the front of the stage, to dictate the roles. Any relation of desire will be represented as a relation between the agent of absolute rejection, or the agent of swallowing, of the taking-into-self, and fragments of bodies, fragments of things, tools that he draws towards himself or rejects depending on his whim. In either case, the spectator is present at a violent action that *ignores what the 'fragment' may or may not desire*: he is left with the choice of identifying with either the agent or the victim of violence, but between the two there will remain a relation of non-reciprocity, the presence of a non-desire and an unpleasure for one of the two. Things will be quite different for the paranoiac.

3 The 'heard' scene and its representation in paranoia²

I have often suggested, half seriously and half in jest, that the 'mother-of-the-schizophrenic' was the only clinical entity created by psychoanalysis whose correctness can be proved. It is true that when one meets these mothers, most of them confirm the clinical picture that we have made of them. Things are very different when we are dealing with the mothers of paranoiacs: not only is it impossible to generalise about them, but what strikes one from the first meeting, at least in my own experience, is the sense of unease given by a clinical picture characterised by its ambiguity. In my opinion it is a feeling very close to the one felt by the child himself: everything that the mother says about her relation to her child, a relation that she often finds difficult, an account that is intended to convey the courage that she has shown, the sacrifices that she has endured, ought to arouse understanding and sympathy, and yet . . . 'something' sounds false and arouses the same feeling of irritation experienced when confronted by a lie that one cannot quite put one's finger on, but which one is sure is there. In view of this, one can but advance with great prudence when trying to pass from what is said to what might lie behind it, and when trying to find precise features common to these mothers. In contrast to this vagueness is a style of relationship between the couple that seems to be repeated faithfully and, on the part of the fathers, the very frequent presence of specific features, features that are already paranoiac. That is why it is easier and more justified to refer to the particular features of a problematic proper to the couple than to privilege a purely maternal problematic. Whether they were subjects that I have had in analysis or subjects that I have merely interviewed in hospital, I have observed an astonishing similarity in their relationship to their parents. Before confronting such case histories, it might be useful to say what questions touch on the delusional problematic for which I expected to find an answer at the beginning of my researches. When faced with paranoiac delusion, I was struck by three specific characteristics:

1 The need not to leave room in the system for the slightest opening, for the slightest possibility of doubt in one's interlocutor. In that unquestionable nature of the logic proper to the paranoiac system, once the delusional postulate has been posited, I have seen proof that the subject cannot tolerate, and rightly so, the slightest flaw in its system; such a flaw would open the way to an avalanche that would carry everything into a bottomless precipice.
2 The place accorded in their theorisation of the world to the concept of 'hate': a nodal concept around which they will cause to gravitate all their feelings, actions and reactions. Here again I had the impression of an absolute necessity, a cement without which the whole construction would collapse, like a house of cards.
3 The ability to keep, in their discourse and in their fantasisation of the primal scene, a place for *two* representatives of the couple, on condition that between

the two a conflictual relationship, and often a relationship of hate, may be represented. It soon struck me that this relationship could not be reduced to a mere projection, but was the response, amplified of course, given to things heard and seen that made the scene, played out in the external world, susceptible to the fantasy of rejection and not at all to the fantasy of the desire for reunification.

That the paranoiac should retain a privileged relation to hate is not a new discovery; any delusion of interpretation, in the register of paranoia, shows the place accorded others' hate of you: if the persecuting object cannot leave you a moment's respite, nor allow you to keep some distance, it is surely because it can exist only as long as it can direct against you its desire for persecution, which is almost always experienced by these subjects as a desire for destruction. It should be added that, in the case of the paranoiac, the reason for the persecution takes on a special meaning: he is being persecuted because he is envied for something that he possesses (material, sexual, ideological), and someone wishes to eliminate him because he therefore represents a real danger for the intentions of others, who impute to him some power that can do them harm. The paranoiac may claim that he does indeed possess this power, make it his standard-bearer and be ready to sacrifice himself for it. So the notion of sacrifice returns: however, this sacrifice is aimed not at happiness, but at an order and a law that will be imposed, not offered.

'Hate of hate', wrote André Green,[3] on the relation between the paranoiac and his objects. But before everything else, and above all, there is the need for hate and, still more, *the need to make hate intelligible and reasonable*.

To the question posed by the constant presence of these three characteristics, clinical practice provided me with an initial answer as soon as I began to lend a more attentive ear to what was being said about the relations between the father and mother. The first result of this was to remind me of other, earlier accounts and to note the relationship present in all these case histories.

This relationship may be characterised by the intensity and eroticisation of conflict, and by the evident expression of an animosity that sometimes goes as far as hate, which, in a number of cases, extended to the two nations to which the parents belonged. There would be little point in going through all these cases: I shall simply summarise two that seem to me to be particularly illuminating, even though they refer to extreme situations.

4 Accounts heard

1   Mlle A . . . is the daughter of a Frenchwoman and a 'Bosch'. Of this father, who disappeared from her horizon when she was three years old, she knows nothing except that she bears his German name, which for a long time her

mother forced her to pronounce in the French manner, claiming that one should be ashamed to belong to that nationality and that she did not want people to know that she had had a 'Bosch' for a husband. However, she has a vivid memory of one scene: six months after the separation (she was therefore about four) the father came to collect her from school; she went off with him, holding his hand; suddenly the mother appeared and took her other hand, trying to pull her towards her. The little girl saw herself torn apart between these two hands, neither of which would let go. She was seized with fright and was actually afraid that 'I would be torn in two, that my body would break and that each of them would carry off a piece of it'. Not a word was said as these two antagonistic forces fought over her in silence, neither wishing to give in, at the risk, apparently unconsidered by them, of destroying the very object over which they were fighting. Nevertheless, in the end, it was the father who let go; the mother took the little girl off with her and violently criticised her for giving her hand to the 'Bosch', for disobeying her order to run away if ever she saw him. On the few occasions when she heard her mother refer to her father it was always with obvious hatred, the mother ending up by saying that she hoped that he would die and never come back. Her wish was granted and Mlle A . . . never saw her father again. He came back to life only in her delusional phases, when he became the cause of the persecution directed against her, as punishment for crimes committed by the father or, at other times, because her mother feared that she might share some secret power possessed by the father, who was variously described as the guardian of Hitler's treasure, boss of an all-powerful gang or *éminence grise* of the Arab powers. This was the only case in which the hate of the couple was described without any compensatory factors and in which there was an early break-up in the marriage. In other cases, conflict and aggression persisted in a relationship that was clearly very strongly cathected by both partners, and which ceased only with the death of one of them or with a divorce that occurred only after many years of married life.

2   In the parental history of Mlle C . . . there was no ideological conflict: everything took place 'within the family'. From the first months of her marriage, the mother discovered her husband's 'vices': he was an inveterate speculator who had already been in trouble with the law, and she was certain that he would ruin the family, which, with a certain unconscious complicity on her part, is what happened. From her first pregnancy, he advised her to have medical examinations and admitted that he was having treatment for syphilis. From then on she was afraid that the child would be born 'tainted'. From her earliest childhood, Mlle C . . . had witnessed violent, stereotyped rows, the mother blaming the father for ruining them, threatening that she would go to the police, the father in turn demanding that she give him all the available money, while secretly selling whatever he could find in the house. Twenty years were to go by before they divorced: when the father finally left, the mother's reaction was a serious depression requiring hospitalisation.

★ ★ ★

Were I to add up the analyses and interviews that I have had with subjects corresponding to my definition of paranoia, the sum total would be quite small: the results that I have tried to extrapolate from them should therefore be treated with some caution. But, given the shortness of human life and the relative discretion shown by paranoiacs to psychoanalysis, which is usually matched by an even greater discretion on the part of analysts towards them, I feel sufficiently justified in adding the following considerations to the reflections of other analysts.

The one that strikes me as most firmly rooted in clinical experience concerns the common kernel to be found in the organisation of these subjects' familial situations. This consists of 'fragments' of a shared historical reality to which will correspond the setting up of a similar delusional theory concerning origins. What I have to say is centred on an analysis of these 'fragments' and of that 'theory', which, it seems to me, they share.

5 The 'family portrait': failed idealisation and the appeal to the persecutor

On the basis of the memories that these subjects retain of their childhood, there emerges a particular image not only of the mother's discourse but also of the father's. In the case of the mother, what is said is strongly reminiscent of the portrait of the alcoholic's wife, with, however, a more active, more combative attitude towards her partner. As for the others, they make themselves the standard-bearer of an ethic based on duty, work, self-denial. Often the 'perfect' mother, she actually leaves little room for any possible criticism on the part of the child: not that she violently forbids such criticism, but she so arranges matters that, on the level of behaviour, the child, who has the intuition that something is wrong, false, ambiguous, cannot discover what it is or, if he does think he knows what it is, cannot be sure that it is true.

Hence the climate of silent mistrust, and often, at an early stage, he has strong feelings of guilt; paranoiac mistrust, defined as a sort of character trait, finds its source in that presence on the stage of the world of a maternal image that bears little relation to the truth as he sees it, but which he cannot, by justified arguments, demonstrate to be untrue. Unlike the mother of the schizophrenic, one does not observe, in the case of the child, the same attitude of rejection or the same violent appropriation of the subject's autonomy: everything takes place in a chiaroscuro that is tiring to the eyes, in a padded space that makes any sound disturbing. Whereas in the case of the schizophrenic one might encounter threats, what one hears here is the *warning*, the 'reasonable' warning spoken in a tone of voice that is intended to be caring towards the child, and which claims that nothing is being forced upon him, but on the contrary everything is being explained: in a word, what the child encounters in the mother's voice is a so-called reasonableness that contrasts with and therefore serves as an accusation of the unreasonable excess of the father's voice. In reality, the screen that claims to protect the child against the excess of the father's voice reinforces, for the child, all the fears that the father's voice may arouse: if you are being protected by your mother and if she never stops warning you of this and that, you can only conclude that the dangers out there must be very great indeed! Now, the child who hears these 'warnings', a source of anxiety, has a certain intuition that they have some effect on the fears that he experiences and on the reactions that that these fears provoke: but how could he demonstrate this truth when he is being 'shouted at' on the one hand and 'protected' on the other? There remains the solution of mistrust, mistrust of both the shouting and the protection. What the mother says about herself and about what she feels may be subsumed under the image of the dutiful wife, who stoically puts up with the ordeals inflicted on her, who loses her temper only when it is a question of defending the innocent, who might in turn become victims, beginning with her own children, and who, like Cassandra, has always known that things would end up badly. The paranoiac is willing to accept that his mother loved him, but when he speaks of the reasons for that love he can only recite the mother's own values: duty, morality, what is 'right'. It should be added that usually boys or girls, before the delusion begins and becomes systematised, have gone over to the mother's side to defend her rights and to protect her from possible demands: but they do this, too, *out of duty*, because justice must be maintained and victims defended. There is therefore a recognition that a relation of love between them exists side by side with a secret negation, since the formula 'to love out of a sense of duty' is a contradiction in terms. Another expression that is found in certain cases is that of 'perfect wife': 'she was a perfect wife', who, confronted by the father's shortcomings and moral weaknesses, took it upon herself to keep the family together, to earn money and to appeal to the law of judges, police or psychiatrists. It is an exercise of power that always tries to be based on law, to prove that one is upholding it *despite one's gentler feelings*, because of a reality that was becoming more unbearable, in a word, out of duty and without pleasure. Hence what I said above: there is no obvious abuse of power (which, on the other hand, is often the case with the father), every judgement of this type can only appear to be itself abusive, unjust, guilty.

But this measured discourse is opposed by the excessive accusations and claims made against the father. Beneath the apparent good sense of a warning, what the mother's voice is actually conveying is the threat that '*your desire can never conform to the father's desire, unless . . .* ', the absence of something merely reinforcing the fear of some danger lying in wait for you. The excessive caution opposed to that excess explains the feeling of mistrust that the child experiences, a mistrust whose only obvious cause would seem to be the father, even though, while having nothing to prove this to be the case, he has a strong sense that it is in fact the mother. This is a feature that characterises the maternal discourse in its manifest side. Another feature particular to this discourse is that there is generally a term

190

missing; namely, *jouissance*, the pleasure experienced by both partners of the couple when they and their two desires meet.

We shall see how this absence is necessary to the preservation in the mother and in the couple of 'the desire for a *bad* desire', a desire that cannot therefore be a source of *jouissance* but a desire that must be present nevertheless.

Nothing in the mother's relationship to the father and in the 'relations' between the parents, nothing in what is said about motherhood, about the relationship with the young child, or indeed about the mother's own childhood (an important element if the subject is to be able to write his own history), nothing is linked to an effect of pleasure that would simply refer to a desire for pleasure. If one speaks of the pleasure of having had parents, or of becoming a parent, it is a pleasure whose fulfilment leads to a son and a father. Everything covered by this concept must conform to a legislation in which the idea of a *jouissance* deriving from pleasure is absent, and in which one attains sexual pleasure (*on 'jouit'*, one 'comes') only out of a sense of duty. There is no question here either of sublimation or of the appearance of the law of the father, whether the child's father or the father's own father, but rather, it might be said, of *a duty that becomes pleasure* by virtue of the fact that one would be imposing it on oneself: duty here is self-imposed, self-expressed, self-experienced. The pleasure that results from it, and the only pleasure that can be given value by the mother, finds its reason in 'excess' of which one shows oneself to be capable in what one has to put up with and what one has to face. It would be risky to speak of the primacy of the masochistic drive or of the presence, in the mother, of a paranoiac feature. That 'excess' is necessary in order for a '*state of justified conflict*' with the father's desire to be preserved; it alone can ensure that the accounts will never be closed, since it will always be possible to appeal to some outstanding debt. If the term '*jouissance*' is missing, and I shall not analyse here what it is in the mother's infantile history that would account for this, it is because the essential meaning, carried by this concept, is that of a reciprocal experience that precludes any calculation of more or less between what is experienced and what one makes others experience. This absence in the discourse of the 'word-bearer' leads to an incorrect transmission of the 'wish for a child', whose analysis has shown us that it presupposes the participation, on an equal footing, of the two desires of which the child is the result. This incorrect transmission is not equivalent to the non-transmission present in the mother of the schizophrenic. At the origin of the child, the mother may acknowledge her desire for creation *and* the father's desire, but only on condition that the latter desire remains that *against* which mother and child will have to fight. It is for the same reason that in the mother's 'wish for a child' an ethical pleasure must be substituted for sexual pleasure: otherwise it would have to be recognised that the father's desire may be a dispenser of pleasure, which is incompatible with the situation of 'permanent conflict' necessary to *both* partners. The consequence of this problematic will be that the discourse of the 'word-bearer' lacks the necessary term for the acquisition of language and the acquisition of the body image to produce in the child two unified spaces. The 'wish for a child' in turn comes up against a paradox when it is accompanied by an explicit order not to allow oneself to fulfil the father's desire. Such a wish is paradoxical, since it involves assuming or transmitting the paternal function, while telling oneself that the desire that sustains it is forbidden. This paradox may be illustrated by the two formulae that coexist in the mother's statement of the wish: 'that the child would inherit a wish for a child' and 'that the child should show "the fathers" that their wish for a child is unacceptable'.

One cannot but notice that, in such cases, the father's desire is acknowledged, the Name-of-the-Father spoken, the power that he is supposed to exercise, and that he seems to exercise, is present and recognised. But the acknowledgement, naming and recognition designate the father as the agent of a harmful desire, a dangerous desire whose realisation could only lead to 'evil'. (Personally I believe that it is likely that the mother transfers onto the father a parental imago, reduced to the dimensions of a mere 'other', with whom conflict is possible, which also explains why the conflict cannot cease. Were it to cease, it would be shown either, in the case of defeat, that the imago really did possess the power imputed to it, that fear was justified, or, in the case of victory, that the other had nothing to do with an image that your projection alone imputed to it. In the second case, the object that one had thought one had found again is lost once more, the mourning is repeated and depression may occur.)

It will be proved and demanded that the father have a desire, but only on condition that he provide his own proof, thus justifying the mother's conviction that this 'desire' is harmful, and on condition that he promise that this proof *will never be lacking*; that the mother will always encounter a desire to fight, a desire that will be opposed, a desire that one has the right to declare unlawful. What persists, in her relation to the man, seems to repeat her resentment about a desire whose first addressee was one of his parents; they have not been forgiven either for refusing it or for making him experience that rejection.

If we now come to the historical reality of what the child 'hears', one notes that the mother knows and says that she cannot desire the realisation of the father's desire; the justifications that she gives for this and the 'paternal reality' that she 'chooses' allow this formulation to occupy a place in the secondary without dismantling its logical order. This verdict, passed by the mother on the father's desire, cannot therefore remain hidden from the child, who is confronted with a discourse that gives expression to pain, demands, threats and the right to retaliate that the father's desire arouses. I shall now conclude this portrait of the mother and turn to her partner.

On the father's side

The frequency with which one encounters the following features is striking:

- in relation to the wife's desire, the same verdict that declares it to be 'bad' and 'dangerous' for the child;
- the exercise of a power that is used in such a way as to transform it into a manifest abuse that often takes a violent form;
- at the same time, or at a later stage, the child discovers the signs of a social decline or the appearance of charactereal features whose pathological aspect is obvious for the child;
- the claim to a 'knowledge' that would make him the unchallenged and unchallengeable possessor of an educational system imposed by violence and for the good of the child;
- lastly, in a number of cases, a feature that I have often encountered in the father of schizophrenics and that I shall define as a 'desire for procreation', which they realise in a fantasised way by positing an *equivalence* between 'feeding' and 'feeding the mind'. In the place of the breast, which has never been able to be given, the father will posit himself as the sole dispenser of 'knowledge' and try to create by this 'gift' a relation of absolute dependence that is just as dangerous, in its possible consequences, as the one that the mother may establish with her baby.

On the subject of the Schreber case, Lacan stresses the role of accomplice played by a reality that confirms that those fathers may impose rigid rules and regulations, but that they are incapable of positing themselves as agents of a law to which they ought first to recognise themselves as subject.

> whether in fact he is one of those fathers who make the laws or whether he poses as the pillar of the faith, as a paragon of integrity and devotion, as virtuous or as a virtuoso, by serving a work of salvation, of whatever object or lack of object, of nation or of birth, of safeguard or salubrity, of legacy or legality, of the pure, the impure or of empire, *all ideals that provide him with all too many opportunities of being in a posture of undeserving, inadequacy, even of fraud, and, in short, of excluding the Name-of-the-Father from its position in the signifier* (my italics).[4]

It is hardly surprising that Schreber's father, that 'rectifier of bodies', that 'righter of wrongs', who practised his violence in the name of an ethics that concealed his sadistic drive, could appear to his son only as the embodiment of some elementary force, to which any resistance would be pitiful and pointless, a devastating spectacle that could lead only to one of two conclusions: either that all Law is bad or that the Law imposed by the father is simply an illegitimate and unforgivable abuse of power, proof that God is bad, that nothing really justifies the renunciations imposed on you and which you cannot oppose, that the only thing to hope for is that the day will come when God will actually have dealings only with corpses, that he will thus be deprived of the victims that he seeks to satisfy his own purposes. The writings of Schreber's father exemplify in a caricatural way certain features often present in the fathers of paranoiacs: the fact that unlawful force is exerted in the name of morality, law, alcoholism, psycho-pathology, the violence that society exerts on you, in no way diminishes the possibly devastating effects on the child subjected to it, and who observes the excesses of which that force is capable.

To conclude this section, I would say that what characterises the discourse in which each parent 'speaks' of his or her relation to the partner is the presence of feelings in which conflict is constantly expressed and hate is often present. I am not saying that there is nothing else that cements such relationships: what matters is the excess that the discourse reveals and the endless repetition of the same themes, stated with the same violence.

6 What the child 'hears' and the 'delusional theory concerning origins'

In 'The Economic Problem of Masochism', Freud writes:

> in the case of a great number of internal processes sexual excitation arises as a concomitant effect, as soon as the intensity of those processes passes beyond certain quantitative limits. Indeed, it may well be that nothing of considerable importance can occur in the organism without contributing some component to the excitation of the sexual instinct. In accordance with this, the excitation of pain and unpleasure would be bound to have the same result, too. The occurrence of such a libidinal sympathetic excitation when there is tension due to pain and unpleasure would be an infantile physiological mechanism which ceases to operate later on.[5]

This hypothesis may, *mutatis mutandis*, be extrapolated to the scenic inter-pretation that the psyche makes of any event taking place on the external stage that is a source of intense emotion for the psyche, either because it is reminiscent of an experience shared by the actors with the same degree of emotion, or because the interpreter projects this interpretation onto the signs perceived. It will follow that, for the 'presenter', any representation of external space charged with 'sound and fury' is, whether it be the sound of mourning, of conflict, of pain, of hate, or of love, is presented, at an early stage of psychical activity, as the equivalent of a primal scene in the strict sense of the term: no distinction will be made by the observer between parental coitus, the sight of which is actually a source of intense emotion, and some other sight involving the same emotive reaction. In the situations recounted here three special factors recur:

- The couple actually eroticises conflictual confrontation, experiencing it with great affective intensity, which shows that for them it is primarily a substitute for sexual relations.
- The intensity of what is played out during such encounters is matched by their frequency.
- The exclusion of the observer takes on a different meaning: his gaze is not excluded; what is excluded is any consideration for the emotion that seeing and hearing might arouse in him. It often seems to me that the 'actors' like the fact that their child is there, seeing and hearing what they are doing: a witness is welcome; they make the best of the fact that he is only a child, knowing that they have only to wait for the child to become a witness worthy of trust, to whom each will demonstrate, without so much as a word, that the cries, the threats and the demands, made by one or the other, have all the 'legality' of a norm.

The eroticisation by the child of what he hears of a scene that acts out conflict is induced and strengthened by the sexualisation with which the couple has previously endowed it and by the evident pleasure experienced by the couple in the exhibitionism involved in 'showing it'.

A final reflection is necessary here: although knowledge of the term '*jouissance*', in its canonical sense, is absent from the child's 'knowledge', things are very different where 'hate' is concerned; never will he have a deeper or more glaring internal knowledge of it than in the first phase of his existence, hence his natural tendency to magnify, to the same dimensions, emotions that, later, he will be able to relativise and transform into anger, irritation, resentment. The more the feelings that are close to hate appear on the external stage, the more important and unquestionable will seem their equivalence and identity with an experience that he knows only too well.

This situation sends a message to the child that he will have to try to make intelligible and meaningful. The creation of a meaning, compatible with what he hears *and* with the identificatory demands of the I, will be the task of 'primary delusional thinking' and the 'infantile delusional theory concerning origins', making such pairs as *conflict* and *desire*, *couple* and *hate* synonymous, and positing the conflict of desires as the cause of origins and of his own origin. For the paranoiac, unlike the schizophrenic, it is this that enables him to posit two desires as his origin, to give them both a place in his representation of the primal scene. This 'first thought' concerning origin enables him to avoid the risk of being able to represent himself only as a fragment colonised by the desire of the Absolute Other and to confront psychical activity with an elaboration that

195

will irremediably mark and deviate the rest of the journey that ought to have been his. Procreated by conflict, the effect of hate, the result of the fulfilment of two desires, one of which must always be the one that one fights against, the subject runs the risk of 'discovering himself' as having a contradictory purpose, being the space fought over by two opposing desires. From the moment when conflict and desire become synonymous, 'desiring' and 'being in a state of conflict', to desire desire *and* to desire conflict, and more succinctly 'to experience desire, to experience conflict, to experience hate' also become synonymous. If the origin of existence, of oneself as well as of the world, which can never be separated, refers to a state of hate, one will be able to preserve oneself as a living being, and preserve the world as existing in its own right, only as long as there is something left to 'hate' and someone whom you 'hate'.

This is the logic on which the paranoiac relation to the world is based, once delusion is established; that is to say when the defences that the subject had been able to construct collapse.

The defensive system

On the basis of what these subjects tell us about their childhood and adolescence, one has the impression that they have tried to face up to the ordeals that the reality of the parental discourse has imposed on them by choosing one of the parents and becoming an ally against the other, who is regarded as solely responsible for the misdeeds of which they will bear the indelible scar. In cases that I have followed the choice has gone, after an initial phase of which the patient has no memory, to the father. Beyond the oral phase, during which the mother has had the absolute precedence, as for every subject, the child seems to have sought on the side of the father a powerful ally who would allow him to assume a certain distance with regard to the 'word-bearer' and give him some hope that an appeal to the desire of the father would not necessarily sink into a void or gulf of evil. This is *the stage of idealisation* of the paternal image, the stage of resistance towards the mother, but above all an attempt to project onto those two external supports, in this case particularly apt to play this role, the division and conflict that are tearing apart his own psychical space. If the 'good' and the 'bad' confront one another in the outside world, one may see oneself as a 'unity', allied to one of the 'halves' of the couple, fighting on his side, and think that one is experiencing 'one' feeling for one of them and 'another' feeling for the other, and that therefore, between feeling and conflict, equality is not a law of nature. This stage of idealisation of the paternal image is certainly induced by the fear of a return to a relation of fascination, shattering and shattered, with the representative of the Other, an experience that one has already had and which taught one that it could lead only to a renunciation of being. But a role is also played here by the attraction often exerted on the infantile I by the demonstration of strength, power, authority, demonstrations that are very close to one's own fantasy of omnipotence and to the forms that it will assume in play, in daydreaming and in the stories that one recounts. But this idealisation cannot do without a manoeuvre of seduction. One cannot 'desire with impunity': if one desires what one of the two desires, one defies and opposes the desire of the Other, an 'Other' that is still endowed with emblems of power; as for the ally chosen, he is not much more reassuring. It will be constantly necessary therefore to prove your fidelity, your submission, to offer yourself as the ally of his pleasure and not only of his right. That is why in these subjects the idealisation, on the one hand, preserves the aim that it always has – to keep the same object as a support of cathexis – but, on the other hand, maintains the libidinal element unchanged: there is no inhibition of the sexual aim, the idealised is also the eroticised, the ally him whom one hopes to seduce sexually. The homosexual temptation, always close to paranoiac experience, finds its source here; we now understand more clearly the intensity of the anxiety that it reactivates and the need for the fierce denial that the subject opposes to it.

In this first stage of infantile history one therefore meets:

1 The shaping of a 'primary delusional theory concerning origins' that gives to hate and conflict the role played elsewhere by desire and love.
2 The view of oneself as conflict, whenever one perceives oneself as desiring. Between self and world, self and the couple, the couple's two desires, the same relation is repeated. The eroticisation of the signs of conflict transforms them into equivalents of a primal scene and of a representation of origins, in which the desire of the procreator and the desire of the procreated are jointly '*desire to fight a desire*', and in which pleasure requires confrontation and violence.
3 The elaboration of a first defence, effective against the return of a schizo-phrenic position, but which, just as effectively, will forbid the I access to a structuring order, to a functioning that accords with the discourse of the group. The idealisation of the paternal imago, the alliance formed so that the intrapsychical conflict may be projected into the external world, and so that both halves of the couple may become the supports on which to project his tearing apart, his splitting or, as one of my analysands put it, 'breaking' (*cassure*) – these are the means used to consolidate a projected mechanism that would make it possible 'to see oneself' as a unified space, to posit a difference between desire and conflict, love and hate. It is an image that can be unified only in an *illusory* way: the various pieces of space and the image of the body offer a united front only as long as one can claim that they are fighting the same fight, in the name of the same cause. With defeat, one will see them break up and leave the field.

Now this third stage usually ends in bitter failure; to the eyes of the mature child, the father reveals how much of his force is unlawful, how much all his shouting shows about his shortcomings, the indisputable signs of a decline for which he is not forgiven, or a pathology that you find offensive. Violence and strength manifest what they conceal in terms of miserable, pitiful failure. The law-giver's rigidity reveals the abuses that he perpetrates in the name of a law that he betrays, the ideologies and big ideas are crudely disproved by the 'poor sod', who, for the benefit of others, presents himself as their defender. This disappointing image is intolerable, the observer is overcome by 'the horror of decline', which is the form in which the horror of castration is expressed here. With the loss of the support of his idealisation, and therefore of his ability to idealise one of the two images, to make himself its ally and to find in the familial space a place and a voice in which the truth and the law are present and verifiable, disappears the possibility of preserving on the external stage what he had projected onto it. What shatters into pieces on that stage may force the observer to realise that he is nothing but a locus of conflict and hate, a locus in which truth becomes undecidable. This usually results in a change of course: one will try to preserve the idealisation of the father, but as a 'negative'; he becomes once again what the mother's discourse made him out to be, the locus of a bad desire, who has nevertheless lost much of the brilliance that had been attributed to him, the desire against which one fights by making oneself the ally of the victim. This change of course will idealise the mother's 'suffering', the 'masterly woman' becoming the 'poor woman' whom he must protect. It is a shaky solution, since the alliance is formed to the benefit of the 'losers'; one accuses and fights against the 'brute', but one cannot completely forget that he was also the one who bore the signs of abuse and lies, the one sometimes accused by the law of the group.

It is a solution that usually turns out to be fragile; when it manages to maintain itself one is usually dealing with what is called the 'paranoiac character', a rather crude term that I am using for want of a better one. It denotes that set of features formed by a certain rigidity, a certain mistrust, a certain confidence in one's rights and one's knowledge, that is to say the 'front' that is rigid only in appearance and which allows one to glimpse, behind it, the gulf into which such subjects may fall with each step they take. When the wrong step is taken there will be formed a systematisation of primary delusional thinking; the world will become as paranoiac delusion reshapes it, so that the senselessness of the situation into which his birth projected him may recover some meaning.

Through that image of the world for which the organisation of familial reality encountered by the subject is responsible, delusion gives access once more to the field of meaning by reshaping what is heard and seen, according to a faultless logic that conforms to the postulate on origins created by delusional thinking.

7 The theses defended in the trial to the persecutor

I shall end these considerations of the paranoiac problematic by stressing the peculiarities of the relation to the persecutor, as it is manifested in that problematic; on the other hand, I shall leave to one side whatever features are always present in the relation. I shall say nothing therefore of the role played by idealisation, or of the erogenised link that binds persecuted and persecutor together; these are the invariants, present in every psychotic relation to the last, sole object that the subject has managed to preserve from the shipwreck in which he lost everything else.

What is striking in paranoia, as opposed to schizophrenia, is what I shall call the *need for communication*. In this case, the certainty, which all delusion offers, realises its full value only when put into the service of the specific rights and duties assumed by the subject: it has to be shared with and imposed on others. One has never agreed to lose this reality, which one 'reshapes', to use Freud's term: the 'retreat from cathexis' has never really been consummated. The world has continued to exist and it is because it must persist as a living world that it must be made to conform to an order, a law, a knowledge, which the group has forgotten or betrayed. The same goes for 'others': here, again, the fight that one puts up against them, like the exactions that they impose upon one are irrefutable proof of a mutual recognition between oneself and others. The logical system that sustains the persecutory relation takes over the postulate concerning origins, which it transforms into dogma: for there to be a living being and for there to be a world the conflict between them must never come to an end, it must remain in a constant state of activity, thanks to which the offer of hate and the offer of life coincide. Onto the stage of the world is projected the model of the primal scene: they confirm the truth of each other's message, and reveal to us what are the last bastions that the delusion is protecting: a knowledge, concerning the duality of the couple, which has replaced the category of difference with the category of the contradictory, which is another way of not falling into the chaos of the undifferentiated, and of offering the possibility of preserving the cathexis of something outside-self.

This closeness between the interpretation of the order of the world defended by the I and the representation of the parental couple by the activity of the primary, the irrefutable logic of the delusional system on the basis of its initial postulate, the certainty of the subject that he is speaking 'according to the law'; all these givens confront us once again with the question of the relation between the role imputed to the persecutor and the role that the paternal function ought to have given him.

Who, for the paranoiac, is the persecutor? One may, roughly speaking, distinguish between two cases:

- the one in which – and it is the more dangerous of the two in terms of the

actions that ensue – the persecutor is known, represented by a particular subject who is often a member of the family;
- the one that is represented by a 'class' – the Jews, the bosses, the freemasons, the judges, the dispossessed – an extrapolation that tries, with some success, to mediate a direct conflict that may always turn into a life and death struggle.

One fights the 'class'; one realises that one cannot destroy it in its totality: instead of murder one may satisfy one's just revenge in writings, demands, procedures. Another advantage: by projecting the persecutor into the order of the class, one also projects the persecuted into the order of a class, thus making it possible to find 'allies' on both sides. Thus is repeated the position originally assumed by the child.

Allies have a dual function and play an important role:

- As far as what affects the subject is concerned, it will enable him to deny that he is excluded by others, which, in fact, he is and to remain convinced that he is part of a 'group', a sort of 'silent majority' (and how silent it is!) fabricated by his imagination, a majority of which he makes himself the fiercest defender.
- As far as the persecutor is concerned, allies will play the role of intermediaries, thus making it possible to reduce still further the risk of a face-to-face combat between the subject and the enemy. These mediators act under the orders of a 'leader', absent or unknown, and are not therefore directly responsible for the misfortunes that come your way; they are often themselves victims of what they are forced to do and *always provide good reasons* to hate whoever exercises that evil, overwhelming power.

Everything is set in place to avoid a direct confrontation: the class makes it possible for a known, close object to be sheltered from hate; the allies make it possible for this substitute to remain at a distance, or unknowable, in any case 'unkillable', which makes it even less probable that the deception will be exposed. One realises the urgency and importance of this deception when one sees what may happen if it fails: the homicidal drive turned on self or on the representatives of the Other. This avoidance also preserves the possibility for the subject to keep a cathexis of the external stage, which he does not wish to abandon. Unlike the schizophrenic, the paranoiac does not take refuge in autism; he exists because, and in so far as, others exist, only he exists neither *for*, nor *by*, nor *with* others, but *against* them.

The reason for persecution

Here, too, one usually falls back into the similar. If one is angry with him, if one hates him, it is because of some privilege that he alone possesses. This privilege may relate to different spheres, but very often it concerns some 'knowledge', the source of a 'power', which one has the right to exercise because it is founded in the order of truth. One might add that in the register of knowledge, as is so often the case where this kind of discourse is concerned, this justification rests on a 'fragment' of truth: it denotes a quality that the subject actually possesses and which he merely idealises in a megalomaniacal way. In a number of cases, one is struck by the frequency with which this 'reason' participates in the social field and shares its ideologies: this being the case it also has the function of proving that, far from being excluded from this field, and far from excluding oneself from it, it is the object of your 'constant interest', just as you remain of 'constant interest' to the social field, social and subject referring back to one another.

But this appeal to the class, to allies, to a knowledge possessed concerning the law, order, justice, like the dogma that the subject derives from them, also seem to me to be the consequence of a specific character, which, more than any other, demonstrates the gap between this problematic and that of the schizophrenic: the position of heir defended by the paranoiac.

The legitimate heir

The paranoiac does not claim to be the founder of the truth of the knowledge that he lays claim to. Usually his discourse refers to a dogma, a religious sect, an ideology, a social discourse, a scientific truth, of which he has no wish to be the creator, but in relation to which he presents himself as *the sole faithful interpreter and sole legitimate heir*. It is as if in his relation to discourse, as a locus in which truth must be possible, and not arbitrary, the paranoiac manages to keep a place for a statement on foundations, guaranteed by another voice than his own. Once this third agency has been posited, all intermediaries that he might meet, and thanks to whom he ought to recognise the universality of the law and its applications, become for him 'others', to be demystified or opposed, because they have not understood, or have betrayed, the thought of the founder: for the fantasy of self-procreation is substituted a 'fantasy' of special filiation, since he plays on the exclusivity of the rights of inheritance. By means of this compromise he keeps, in a way, a place for the function that the subject has been unable to give the statement on foundations, a place that may alone be occupied by a particular referent that allows one to escape from the enclosure of an exclusive self-reference. But this compromise will require, by way of compensation, that the tables of the law be transmitted only to a single prophet, that all others are infidels who refuse to hear the true message.

This is one of the reasons why the *autodidact* is so often to be found among the paranoiacs: between 'knowledge' and his work of appropriation, between the text and himself, as sole legitimate heir whose rights are based on and proved by a law, the subject cannot accept that there should be either intermediary or sharing. In this way the paranoiac can still count up to three: himself, the referent, others. This trinomial takes up once again a triangulation present in the primal scene, thus avoiding a return to a dual relation, but reveals how badly constructed the first triangulation was and how fragile were its foundations.

From the point at which I now find myself, until I feel able to go further, the feature that seems to me to be the most decisive in the paranoiac problematic concerns his relation to the father. Of all that the paranoiac has to say the idea that stands out most is that there actually was a first phase, when a sort of coincidence was formed between the real father and the idealised father, in positive or in negative; a real father was endowed by the child with the attributes of omnipotence, an omnipotence that was confirmed by manifestations of real violence, whether explicit or whether, in a much more veiled way, it took the form of the imposition of an ideology. In that first phase, far from being absent, the father occupies centre stage and arouses a reaction of admiration and seduction in the child. It is the phase that follows the one in which the oral relation to the mother is played out, a relation that may be reconstructed only by putting one's trust in the maternal discourse.[6]

That stage of idealisation of the paternal imago seems to be followed by an experience that, for two apparently contradictory reasons, will make what is known as 'symbolic castration' impossible. The first is that the father's violence, if it goes beyond certain limits, will remove any distinction between the term 'castration' and the image of a real mutilation; as a result, the subject can no longer accept it as a trial undergone by every subject; it becomes a mutilation of the body that cannot be assumed and which one can only refuse and hope to turn back on him who is threatening you with it. The other reason, which I have often met, refers to what I have called the horror of decline, the unacceptable deception. What hitherto appeared as signs of power and strength turn out to be signs of psychopathy, decline or delinquence. It is now quite impossible to see that representative of others as the guarantor of a law and to preserve the identificatory markers necessary to the process of identification. It is during this phase that the subject will arrive at a first turning point, when he will try to place in the maternal locus what can no longer be situated in the field of the father. We have seen why this attempt has little chance of succeeding for very long. This brings us to the systematisation of primary delusional thinking: the first manoeuvre of the system will be to try to project the conflict into the social field by demonstrating that the notion of a 'class struggle' is well founded. Social categories, whether based on knowledge or age, are merely substitutes for those two adversaries whose struggle continues without let: the conflictual representatives of two desires, two sexes, two generations. This 'defensive' manoeuvre, carried out by the I in its own interests, can succeed only if the subject can find room in his system for the founding referent of a law, in relation to which he can see himself as exclusive heir.

What I have said about the function of this 'socialised' displacement of the conflict shows, on the contrary, how much more risky and less re-elaborated is the delusional system that is projected, without a mediator, onto the familial space: either the mediators had never been able to assume their roles, or their exit from the stage testifies to a breach in the system. This breach may be due to the exacerbation of the work of reshaping imposed on the I, the violence of the rejection that others show the subject, but also to certain therapeutic 'successes' involving chemotherapy or psychoanalysis.

In these cases, it is the place of the 'founder' that remains, or becomes again, vacant, with the danger that it will be occupied by the persecutor, now represented directly by the father, the mother, the child, the wife, or any other individual who is the object of a privileged cathexis on the part of the subject.

But recognising oneself as 'heir of the persecutor' will lead one to conclude that the only thing one is inheriting is the desire for murder that is being directed at you; there is a risk that one will respond by assuming the fate that has been bequeathed one and act it out on the persecutor or on oneself.

Son of conflict, effect of hate, creator of a delusional theory concerning origins, which protects him from a return to a more archaic position, but one that prevents him from cathecting a project that conforms to the functions and functioning of the I, the paranoiac shows us, in his discourse, the creative power of meanings possessed by delusion and the role played by a historical reality that has forced meaning to change course, to give up sharing the postulates of the group, which has been unable to provide the subject with the proofs of identity necessary if he is to have right of residence in a world and in a reality that must, 'structurally', seem to conform to the definition that the discourse of the group gives of them. This brings to an end my thoughts on the problematic of paranoiac delusion and on the reason for a 'theory' that brings together desire, hate and conflict.

'The space in which paranoia may come about': as in the case of schizophrenic potentiality, I have centred my analysis on the forces acting in that space outside the psyche that the infant encounters and with which he will from the outset and forever be in a state of interaction. It is a law from which no psyche and no 'world' can escape. This interaction seems to have been undervalued in psycho-analytic theory. Psychosis shows in a pure, often exemplary state the primordial role played in our way of life, whatever it may be. The maternal psyche proves, in turn, that although it has gone through the various stages from infancy to parenthood, it will interpret the first cry of the infant as a message whose power, structuring or disorganising, is the equal of that exercised, over the infant, by the message of the 'word-bearer'. The place that I had given to historical reality in no way entails a devaluation of the role played by the primal and by unconscious fantasy: everything that I have written is there as a reminder of it.

Confining my work on psychosis to these two chapters, I have left essential problems to one side. I have also said nothing about what my thinking owes to authors who have preceded me in the deciphering of a discourse that is more inclined to question, and to question us, than to reply.

In my preface I warned the reader against the risk of seeing in the hypotheses proposed a more complete construction than it in fact is. I have increased that risk by not resisting the temptation presented by any hypothesis, when it seems to make the obscure intelligible. Although I feel that most of those hypotheses are justified by the clinical experience on which they are based, I am aware that, in the case of others, this experience has remained inadequate.

I shall leave to the account of M. R . . . the task of ending these two chapters: more than any theoretician what he says has managed to make sense of what, in the absence of such theoretical discourse, would have remained for us all quite incomprehensible.

8 M. R . . . 's story[7]

M. R . . . is, as he tells me, a 'quadroon', but there is no visible trace of that quarter of French blood and he looks like a pure Malagasy type. Similarly, his tone of voice, his extreme gentleness, though without a trace of servility, his use of gesture when speaking suggest a culture that is not ours. I was able to have six meetings with him; I then lost track of him. I met him through a Dr D . . . , who dealt with his case at the community clinic after treating him as an inmate. His story, as he recounted it to me, might be divided into four chapters entitled:

1 *The past*:
    (a) the image of the father;
    (b) what was heard in the 'familial story of the fathers';
    (c) the conflict of the languages and the hate of the races;
    (d) the image of the mother.

2 *The decompensation*:
    (a) the first marriage and fatherhood;
    (b) involuntary confinement and the horror of the 'seen'.

3 *The turning point*:
    (a) mutilating reality;
    (b) deserved punishment;
    (c) masochistic pleasure.

4 *The present*:
    (a) the second marriage and the fallen object;
    (b) sado-masochistic fantasisation.

I hope that this story will arouse in the reader some of the sense of truth and disturbing strangeness that I felt when confronted by a discourse whose clarity, lucidity, thoughtfulness I could not but admire, but in which, suddenly and quite unpredictably, there erupted a fantasisation in the here and now so intensely charged with affect that I often feared that an unpredictable and uncontrollable acting out (but, actually, very acted 'in'!) was about to take place.

1   The past

(a)   The image of the father. (What follows is a word for word transcription of the beginning of our first meeting.):

For many years now I've been aware that I couldn't solve my problems on my own. I'd been thinking this for long time, when I read books and tried to think about it. At the moment I seem to be trying to become aware of my problems . . .

It seems to me that the important thing for me is education, how you live, a lot of things are still in contradiction, but thanks to the medicines I've been able to avoid what they call despair, otherwise I'd be going in that direction. For me, the main problem is this: I was brought up in a way I don't understand, my father was very severe. I remember very, very little about my father, just a bit here and there, all I remember is that he was very severe with me, he didn't try to understand, he used a cosh on me. For what I've been able to gather from my reading, I think he's paranoiac, a very big paranoiac. To me he has always seemed like an implacable, impassive judge, he said nothing, I only remember these few words: the father is the *dominus*, as in ancient times, he has the right of life and death over his children and employees . . .

At the age of sixteen or seventeen, I rebelled and left home. He used to hit me with a cosh that had nails on it, though that might not have been intended. My father also had a difficult upbringing. From what people have told me about him, I've learnt that he lived a very solitary life, he was very traumatised by his own existence. I remember very well how during Latin lessons my father would hit me, I couldn't understand anything at all . . .

My father worked in the magistrate's office, he didn't have a very important job, he worked in the juvenile court, his own father had had the same job, he wanted me to do the same . . .

When my father left Madagascar and came to Paris, I didn't see him for a long time, now I see him from time to time, he's become much calmer, I think he has learnt to control himself . . .

You know, there was a time when I admired my father a lot, even now sometimes, but especially when I was a kid, he frightened me, but I admired his strength and I'd say to myself, he managed to become something I've never

205

become, he knew how to control other people and to get his own way. It's a bit what I'd like to be able to do, that's why I admired him, but I soon realised I wouldn't be able to . . .

Yes, I admired my father at one time, when I was very small I admired him a lot. I began to judge him only when I was about fourteen, and then I thought he didn't love me, he was unfair to my mother and since then I've always taken my mother's side. From that time on we didn't get on together, I also told myself that was why he sent me away to school when I was little, because I was always at boarding school . . .

At bottom, I thought he was unjust, wicked, but I didn't realise he was ill. I was just angry with him because he was wicked, didn't love me, kept me away from my mother, *because he was afraid of me* [my italics to stress the emphasis that he put on these words]. He was afraid I'd side with my mother, he couldn't take it when I told my mother what her rights were, told her she shouldn't let her husband beat her, or things like that. I don't even understand why I felt like I did about my father, he was like someone you can't talk to because he wasn't listening, he never listened, he was always talking and showed his contempt for me even before I said anything, whenever I opened my mouth he said I was talking nonsense and would do better to keep quiet. When I was fourteen, when I went away on holiday, I felt he was a danger to me, I always felt that people could read into me, read my thoughts, and sometimes people called me a hypocrite because I was afraid that if I looked someone in the face he'd see to the very bottom of me, and I always felt that my father could guess what I was thinking, automatically, like that, continually . . . [8]

These extracts come from the first meeting that I had with M. R . . . : from the outset it was around the image of the father and the '*contradictory upbringing*' – a term that recurred in later meetings – that he situates the source of his 'despair' and about which he asks himself, and asks me, questions about his 'illness'. According to M. R . . . , this contradiction originated in a 'family story', which was repeated during the two generations before M. R . . . : this story possesses the characteristics of a delusional theory concerning origins and is comparable to a 'family romance'.

(b) *The 'familial story' of the fathers*. M. R . . . 's great-grandfather, a Frenchman living in France, married an aristocratic girl, a misalliance that the girl's family could not forgive. The couple were completely cut off from the family and, three or four years later, the young woman died after giving birth to a son.

As passed down to M. R . . . by his own father, legend has it that this son, M. R . . . 's grandfather, lived entirely alone, without a wife and surrounded by 'big black dogs'. After coming of age and dissipating the family fortune (deriving from the father or the mother?), he left France for Madagascar, where he got a job in the magistrate's office. He married a Malagasy woman and lived according to the customs of the country. M. R . . . came to know this grandfather. He remembers him as an extremely lonely, authoritarian man, who insisted that any vessel out of which he ate or drank should be used only by him. M. R . . . remembers an epic scene, at which he was present, when the grandfather suspected that someone had drunk tea out of the cup reserved for his use alone. From that marriage was born M. R . . . 's father, who in turn married a Malagasy woman and took as his official mistress his wife's half-sister. That marriage produced ten children, M. R . . . being the eldest of the sons.

(c) *The conflict of the languages and the hate of the races.* What strikes one as the characteristic feature of the situation, which is repeated in M. R . . . , three-quarters Malagasy, and in his father, a half-caste, as well as in the grandfather, who married a Malagasy woman, is a fundamental contempt and undisguised hate for the race to which the wives of these three men belonged, a contempt and hate that were to run deep enough for M. R . . . 's father to demand that his son should not speak and not know his mother's language and that he should express himself only in French. From early childhood, he was placed, despite the expense, in a strictly French-speaking boarding school. Now, it is important to note that M. R . . . 's mother hardly speaks French, a resistance to learning the language that her husband speaks and in which he addresses his son, which says a great deal about what, deep down, she must feel for the race to which her husband's father belonged. This prohibition meant that communication between M. R . . . and his mother was strangely limited:

> I couldn't as it were *speak* to my mother, I spoke Malagasy very badly, she hardly spoke French. It was only when, unknown to my father, I began to learn her language that I was able to talk to her and above all defend her against my father and explain to her that she shouldn't put up with him.

Nevertheless, throughout his childhood and adolescence M. R . . . was to hear his father speak with the greatest contempt of 'those natives', to which his own mother belonged. M. R . . . , himself, was to admit to me, with some embarrassment, that in fact for a long time he shared his father's views on the matter and that even now he cannot bear to be close to those who belong to her race.[9] But this extrapolation or extension of the conflict does not mean that it is not also manifested, and in the most acute way, in the personal relations between father and mother. For four years, the mother had to live with the fear that her husband might reject her at any time and that she would find herself alone with her children, with no means of subsistence. As soon as she was able to speak to her son she became aware of the injustice of her husband's treatment and of the demands that he imposed upon her; meanwhile the father, in just as overt a way, treated her as 'an illiterate', 'an inferior being' and, quite openly, sought more or less lasting adventures elsewhere with women of the same race, who were just as 'illiterate'.

(d) *The image of the mother.* M. R . . . says much less about his mother than about his father. Although he told me that, from the age of fourteen, he came to her defence, one has the impression that in fact he never had a very cathected relationship with her. With some feelings of guilt, he adopted his father's view of her: although he did come to her defence, although he was ready to defend the 'victim' against the 'brute', he could not help 'feeling ashamed' of a mother who spoke French so badly and who had retained her own cultural features. From what he told me, I have the impression that his mother married his father in order to escape her own authoritarian father, who insisted that she continue to work on the farm. He never observed the slightest sign of affectionate, tender, friendly feelings between his parents: the cultural features being what they were, he never witnessed open revolt on his mother's part, she being content, as soon as she could, to warn him against the risks that he was running if his father abandoned her and left the family home. M. R . . . remembered very little about his childhood and adolescent years: brought up, as I have said, in a boarding school, fully aware that he was cathected by an ambitious father, who hoped that he would have a glorious future in the French administration, the brief holidays spent in his family left him with feelings of utter loneliness, incomprehension and above all constant fear that his father would break out into a fit of rage. About the age of fourteen he began to face up to his father and up to the age of sixteen he was still being whipped by his father when punishment was called for. It was about this time that the family fled the country for political reasons and settled in France; from that time on, M. R . . . began to make his own way and had only distant contacts with members of his family.

2 *The decompensation*

M. R . . . recounted how his 'fears' began about the age of thirteen or fourteen: from then on he felt that 'people could read his thoughts and were angry with him'.

These 'feelings' were not to leave him; he was to go on living in an atmosphere of mistrust and withdrawal, interrupted from time to time by outbursts against injustice, or against the injustices of which he felt himself to be the victim. Nevertheless, during the eight years between his arrival in France and his first internment, he was able to find a stable position in a government office, where he was greatly valued and where his future prospects were not inconsiderable. In the 1960s, M. R . . . married a young Frenchwoman, who had a profession of her own. Was this an attempt to make up for the misalliance committed by his father and grandfather? A desire to rediscover a woman who was the imaginary descendant of his great grandfather's wife? I did not hear enough of M. R . . . 's story to answer such questions. Two children were born to the marriage. It seems that shortly after he married, he began to suffer symptoms of an active paranoiac delusion, which got worse after he became a father. The feelings of persecution were to be transformed into a conviction that he was a victim of the evil intentions of his colleagues and superiors; *after the birth* of his first child there appeared, in addition to the earlier delusion, a delusion of jealousy, accompanied by the conviction that his wife was being unfaithful while he was at work. During our last meeting, I learned that he felt violent, almost uncontrollable aggressive feelings towards his children. Faced with behaviour that was becoming increasingly pathological, his wife decided to leave home and take her children with her. Returning home unexpectedly early from the office, M. R . . . found packed suitcases standing in the hall; he went into a violent rage, broke everything he could lay his hands on, threatened to kill his wife, who managed to escape to a neighbour's and call the police: as a result, he went into involuntary confinement for the first time. It should be stressed that M. R . . . , during and after confinement, refused to acknowledge the slightest anomaly in his behaviour; he considered that his violence was justified by his wife's 'betrayals' and saw his confinement, despite the still very friendly attitude shown him by his departmental boss, as the work of enemies, in particular jealous colleagues and an evil wife.

M. R . . . remained hospitalised for a relatively short time, but from then on he embarked on a wandering, frankly pathological life. M. R . . . became incapable of keeping a job for longer than a few weeks or months; on each occasion, he had to leave either to escape his persecutors or following some outburst of aggressive behaviour towards his 'enemies'. Fairly short periods of hospitalisation followed. Up to the time when I spoke to him, M. R . . . remained convinced that he was in the right, that there really was a plot against him, that people hated him, and therefore that his aggressive reactions were justified and were being used as an excuse to confine him. It should be added that the signing of cheques that 'bounced' also resulted in his being brought to court and sent to prison. His love of gambling was not new, since M. R . . . had told me that it dated from when he was eighteen. However, it had become much worse, so much so that when he was paid he lost in twenty-four hours what he had earned in a month. There is an odd fact about this love of gambling: according to stories handed down from father to son, M. R . . . 's grandmother, and therefore the first Malagasy woman to enter the family, was an inveterate gambler, which led his grandfather to abandon her. According to M. R . . . , this 'shameful' matter was always hinted at, never actually stated. I would add that, in the family romance recounted to M. R . . . by the 'fathers', two female imagos stand out: on the one hand, the imago of the young French aristocratic girl, who died before any fault could be found in her and, on the other, the imago of the woman of *the other race*, who dissipated the family fortune, brought 'shame' on the family and so had to be condemned. M. R . . . said that his own father was always ashamed of that woman, his father's mother, and that it was because of this that he never talked about her, that it was a sort of 'stain' about which they all felt guilty, as if it were a matter of some 'shameful deed'. Apart from M. R . . . , nobody in the family, as far as I know, was a gambler: indeed I was struck in his account by how many 'features' M. R . . . had adopted from various members of his family, in an attempt, always unsuccessful, to find some unifying, structuring identificatory marker. In M. R . . . 's first sketch of the characters in his family drama, what struck me most was the repetition, through the male line, from grandfather, to father, to M. R . . . himself, of the same strange relation to women. It was as if father and grandfather had never forgiven their rejection by the family of the aristocratic Frenchwoman, the family that was to remain for them the *enemy clan*, and as if, on the other hand, they had always presented themselves as the sole legitimate heirs of a title to which, in fact, they had no right. M. R . . . told me how until very recently he had signed his name R . . . de . . . , adding to his own surname that of his great-grandmother. Father and grandfather had both married Malagasy women and lived out their lives 'ashamed': ashamed of the woman who gambled, ashamed of the illiterate woman, ashamed of the woman with the black skin. This sense of shame, linked with an imaginary filiation that effaced the real mother in favour of a legendary great-grandmother, is to be found unchanged in M. R . . . himself. In the admiration that he felt for his father an important role was played by the function that the paternal discourse assigned to the name of the grandmother: 'You are a de . . . , never forget it. You must show that you are worthy of the name.' That 'name', which no man in the family bore, and for very good reason, played the role of a right and a 'property', of which they had been dispossessed, an unjustified and unforgivable loss, which, by the same token, legitimated everything in the behaviour of the male line that might be open to criticism, and was criticised, by others. This 'name' also excluded the men from the racial group to which the last two belonged and, more importantly, established in the order of filiation a quite arbitrary system by which the last three generations of men descended directly from a 'first mother'[10] – the great-grandmother – and excluded the two 'real mothers', the women one was ashamed of. When M. R . . . married a young Frenchwoman, when he fathered children of mixed race in whom the two races were apparent, he seemed to be trying to repeat, in his own way, the choice of his great-grandfather. But in doing so, M. R . . . was faced with the fulfilment of a 'wish' that he found to be unsustainable. By reinserting a 'white mother' into the circuit, the woman who had taken the place of the first mother of family legend revealed to M. R . . . how contradictory and unassumable were his identificatory position and his relation to women:

- 'White', like the other one, she seemed to him to be endowed with the insignia that he had always desired for himself, but by that very fact she proved to him that it was not enough for him to have 'a white mother' for him to be no longer regarded as 'black' by others.
- 'A woman', like the mother and the grandmother, she belongs to the race of the rejected, objects that one is ashamed of; as a 'white' woman, the slightest

conflict arising between them makes her the ally of the enemy clan, of those who have rejected you.[11]

• Moreover, she would make him a father, the father of two half-caste children. M. R . . . told me that, when he looked at his sons, he felt that they were 'odd', that he was 'odd' himself. Indeed, how could he claim what was 'black' in them, a colour that he had always denied, and how could he not see what was 'white' in them as signs of the race to which those who rejected his great-grandmother and her descendants belonged? The various divisions that M. R . . . had set up between the great-grandmother, the good victim, and the family that hated and rejected her, between the father whom one admires and the mother who makes one feel ashamed, between the father one fights against and the mother one defends, are upset by this living example of 'inter-breeding' that appeared on the stage of the real, a product of his flesh and of that of his wife, who may force him to recognise that it was never a question of white on one side and black on the other, but a confused white–black existing in the same space, in the same body, in the same subject. M. R . . . could not face up to such a recognition: his response to being confronted by something that undermined the very ground on which he had constructed his defences was to systematise a delusional interpretation. He could now divide the world into 'white' and 'black': whatever was 'white' would go to the side of the persecutors, whatever was 'black' – which would include all those whom he considered, usually quite rightly, as the exploited, independently of their colour – would go to the side of the victims to be revenged.

3 The turning point

From then on, I knew I was ill. I knew I couldn't blame other people or society, that it was me. It was about that time I began to realise that something wasn't right inside me. I'll tell you what it was: it seemed to me that I was a sort of savage who couldn't digest, couldn't understand, couldn't assimilate certain problems, and I began to be afraid. It seemed to me that it all began with that fear, that anxiety that came over me. I tried to analyse that fear as if I was a savage afraid that the sun might fall on him. I'm depending on someone to help me to understand all this, to tell me what's normal and what isn't, because I can't do anything about that fear, those anxieties, I can't control them, when I have them I can't do anything else, I take medicines, they make me feel lighter, but it doesn't last. I daren't think about tomorrow, and by not thinking about tomorrow I try to escape the anxiety, I can't see ahead, that's what is terrible about me, if I think about tomorrow I get afraid that I'll think too far ahead and that's when the anxiety and fear come.

The *time* when M. R . . . 'knew' that he was ill and shouldn't 'blame other people or society' occurred in a very peculiar context: shortly after he left hospital for the second time, M. R . . . , in what seems to have been an anxiety fit, tried to commit suicide by throwing himself against a passing lorry on a road where he was hitching a lift. He didn't seem to be hurt and was able to continue on his way to Paris. He then began to suffer from acute headaches and dizziness. He asked to go into hospital and was taken to the neurological department of a general hospital:

> For seven days I had all kinds of examinations, lumbar puncture, radiology and they said: there's nothing wrong with you. I could always see objects moving on my right-hand side and I was in horrible pain. I may have been what they call a very bad patient, anyway that's what people told me, I was in pain, I yelled out, they didn't understand. They said there was nothing wrong with me and I was putting it on. One day I made so much noise that a professor came to see me, he said he would do an arteriography and operated on me that same day. I stayed in hospital for three months, I had big scars and was paralysed on my left side, but that got better later. I felt condemned and told myself that I wasn't even capable of killing myself. It seemed to me that the only people who existed were the unhappy, the sick, prisoners. I also told myself that I would always have something missing, be someone who didn't have his brain as it was before, who might stay paralysed and I thought of those three months when I had been in such pain, when people made fun of me, when people didn't believe me and said I was doing it on purpose in order to get compensation or because I liked to make everyone's life a misery. But after the operation, for the three months I was in hospital, I had no money at all and the doctors gave me good treatment, but didn't treat me kindly. When I asked them if I would have any after-effects from my accident, they didn't answer or just said: you'll see. It was then that I began to get used to the smell of dirt, of poverty, I, too, had become, how shall I put it, rotten, it made me sick to think about it, but I put up with it, I found it was natural, it was my lot. From then on, I knew I was ill . . . [There now followed the extract quoted above.]

So it was when M. R . . . actually underwent trepanation, when he turned out to be paralysed on one side, when he was surrounded, if not by hostility, at least by contemptuous indifference in a hospital where the staff at first regarded his very real pain as 'put on', that he suddenly became 'aware' that it was inside himself that something was wrong and that it wasn't the fault of other people and society. We shall see shortly how ambiguous is that 'critique' of delusional ideas. What I should like to point out here is the very peculiar response that M. R . . . made when, on the stage of the real, he actually came up against indifference, hostility and injustice. As reality approached, as far as such a thing was possible, the delusional interpretation that M. R . . . gave it 'before the event', when the surgeon's knife actually penetrated his cranial cavity and ran the risk of affecting his thinking, M. R . . . decided that up until then his thinking had been delusional – though it was not the term that he used – that people were not angry with him and that he was ill. Quite unexpectedly, and in a way that seemed to me to be quite specific to this case, he appropriated the discourse of the aggressor, as represented by the medical profession. He thus presented himself as an object to be examined, a 'mentally sick' (the term was his) object and renounced his past certainties. This change of direction was to be followed very shortly afterwards by intense *masochistic impulses*, alternating with aggressive impulses and equally violent sadistic fantasies. It was in this context that his second marriage took place. Once again and in a caricatural way, this marriage repeated not the choice made by his great-grandfather but that of his grandfather and father: he married a very backward young woman, who could neither read nor write. She was the daughter of an alcoholic father who had tried to push her into prostitution and who, in a fight, wounded one of her eyes, which had to be removed. So, at the age of twenty, she found herself one-eyed, with a scar on one cheek and interned in a psychiatric hospital: it was there that M. R . . . met her and decided to marry her. So the first wife, whom he had regarded as a copy of his great-grandmother, was followed by 'the rejected object', a woman whom society made you feel ashamed of, a woman 'who had black in her brain', an expression by which he describes the moments of absent-mindedness or unmotivated panic that often overcame his wife. Nevertheless, that second marriage had had a rather beneficial effect on M. R . . . : he told me how it was thanks to his wife that, for two years, he had been able to find a job and, for the first time for many years, a stable home. His relations with her were reminiscent to some degree of his father's relations with his own wife: on the one hand, he claimed to be her protector, which in a sense he was, he who had the knowledge, thanks to which she could live outside a psychiatric hospital. On the other hand, he often treated that 'object to be protected' as an object, in the most literal sense of the term. He was quite capable of flying off into unreasonable fits of anger when she proved incapable of doing the simplest addition and could even be violent with her, though he was filled with remorse soon afterwards.

For the two or three years following his marriage, which coincided with his new 'awareness', M. R . . . managed to preserve the precarious balance that rested on the relationships that he had with his wife and with his doctor: the first seems to have had the function of assuring him of his superiority, of his knowledge, of the validity of his role as protector of the weak; the second, which was just as positively cathected, seems to have acted as a screen against 'persecutors', by enabling him to valorise his 'awareness', and therefore his 'knowledge', of his mental states and thus, to some extent, to control an aggressiveness that was likely at any time to find expression in acts.

4 The present

When I met M. R . . . that period of relative calm was certainly in danger. Though still married to his wife, he had for several months been unemployed, living more or less on the edge of society and showing signs of profound distress. Throughout our six meetings, I was struck by the various elements of the family history, as I have described them, but three facts stand out:

1   The patent contradiction between a critique of the 'delusional ideas' that M. R . . . 'exhibited' more or less constantly, together with an evident desire to convince me as much as to convince himself of their truth, and the constant activity of those same ideas from which, in fact, he could not in any way distance himself.
2   The sudden, unpredictable shift in the course of a single meeting from moments during which, with the greatest calm and the greatest lucidity, he recounted his story, tried to understand and to find in what way the behaviour of members of his family may have disturbed him, and moments during which M. R . . . was clearly in the grip of a fantasisation, there and then, moments when he would stand up, move from the past to the present tense and relive in front of me, with the same intensity, an episode that he had just been telling me about and which had taken place a few hours or a few days before.
3   A continuous alternation, in his conscious fantasy life, between a masochistic position, in which he experienced obvious pleasure in imagining himself reduced to excrement, buried in the earth, trodden on, and a sadistic scenario, in which he acted out, with equally intense pleasure, the tortures to which he might subject one or other of his 'persecutors' or indeed any passer-by unfortunate enough to jostle him. It was a constant movement between the two, the sadistic daydream immediately leading on to the masochistic daydream, before in turn reverting to the first scenario, a movement that could only end, as he told me, no doubt quite rightly, with his death: 'The only thing I could do was to kill myself, really go back under the ground, disappear.' The fear of suicide or homicide was always present in M. R . . .'s mind, a source of anxiety at every moment: he could defend himself against the fantasies that invaded his psychical space only by going, in each case, to the extreme limit of each scene, stop at the very edge and suddenly go into reverse. Through the masochistic fantasisation, he punished himself 'for thinking such things'; through the sadistic fantasisation, he tried to avoid his own destruction.

I've been thinking about what I told you last time, how for years, after my confinement, I saw everything about psychiatry as something arbitrary, something I was very afraid of, I'm not afraid of it now, I know I'm ill, I recognise that and try to understand. I think about my upbringing, my father, and things get clearer. When I say I'm ill, I mean there's something blocked somewhere in the way I think about things, I mean, I didn't seem to be able to think in a logical way, a consecutive way. I think someone who is ill is someone who is confused, that's why I really like coming and talking to you because when I do, when I'm here, all those ideas, those aggressive fantasies, those fantasies of dirt and death go away. But I don't understand it, yesterday, for instance, this chap [at this point M. R . . . , without being aware of it, shifted his position on the chair, sat on the very edge of it, as if about to rush off, his gaze left mine and was fixed on a point of the wall directly opposite him, where some scene seemed to be taking place that had him rooted to the spot and to which he reacted] yesterday, for instance, that chap in the métro, pushed me, well I was going to get hold of him and get my revenge on him, I was going to mutilate him, I thought how I would do it, probably his eyes, mutilation after mutilation, I then realised that this was being crazy and was terrified: why do such ideas come into my head? When I'm here, I feel I'm a monster and want to kill myself . . . That's the only way I could escape all these fantasies that frighten me so much, I imagine those things, those ideas that come into my head, and I'm afraid of that: and when I'm just sitting there, like this, at moments like this, I'm afraid, for instance, I got angry with someone when I lost a seat, I went home and began to kick my dog, then I broke something, then I broke everything else, then I said to myself: but what's the matter? The main problem is I have a brake on me most of the time, then suddenly I can't stand it any more and afterwards, you know, I feel worried when I realise what I've done . . . then I think about killing myself, I also think about shit, I had to clean the w.c.s in prison, and all that filth, all those disgusting things almost give me pleasure, I'd like to take . . . make a hole in the ground, get into it, get into very dirty things, it's all very disgusting, I think of decay, I think of human excrement, it's terrible . . . Then there are the others, I always feel they're angry with me, then I tell myself it isn't true, it's because I'm ill, but I can't help thinking what I'd like to do to them . . . [and here begins once again the fantasisation of a sadistic scene, the victim of which might be one of his former colleagues, his wife, or someone seen in the street].

By the end of the sixth meeting, I was convinced that M. R . . . would go on seeing me: however, confounding my predictions, he telephoned me and, apologising very politely, said that he would not be able to come to our next meeting, and asked me to arrange an appointment at a later date. I never heard from him again. So everything that I know about M. R . . . derives from our six meetings: it does not amount to a great deal. That is why I have decided to conclude this book with his story: to recount the case of one of my own analysands would have taken me well beyond the limits set for this book. But my choice was dictated above all by two other reasons:

1 M. R . . . 's story seemed to me to offer an enlargement of a 'family photo-graph' that I had already encountered in other cases, even if in a less vivid way, one more yellowed with time.

2 The question posed by what I have called the 'turning point', the time when he became 'aware' – and the extracts quoted above show how ambiguous that awareness was – of his illness and so weakened what was left of his defence system. The 'delusional ideas' and the impulses that flowed from them lost nothing of their virulence; M. R . . . suffered them as forces that were destroying him and against which, when he could, he defended himself by appealing to the language of the doctors who treated him. It should be added that, in my opinion, one can absolutely not rule out a return to a frankly delusional episode that will leave M. R . . . 's interpretative system intact.

The short duration of our meeting would preclude any exhaustive theorisation of his history: to believe that in the space of a few meetings one could know the psyche of another person, whether that of M. R . . . or anyone else, is an illusion and an abuse of knowledge, and therefore false knowledge. Nevertheless, this fragment of a story seems to me to confirm what may happen when the subject, discovering the stage outside himself, is confronted by a spectacle in which reign the sound and fury of conflict and hate. M. R . . . 's first sight of the stage of the world showed him a space in which two colours, two races, two languages, two classes confront one another: the couple of which he is the issue is offered as the exemplary, evident embodiment of that confrontation. It might be added that the parental conflict is, in this case, reduplicated by an 'environmental' conflict: the outside-self and the social field brought M. R . . . a similar confirmation of the universality and 'naturalness' of the state of conflict.

The voice of the 'word-bearer' speaks a language that the child must unlearn when he has to acquire language: at the father's insistence, maids have to speak to him in French. The pleasure of listening and the pleasure of understanding would have to be split apart: one can listen to the mother's voice, but one cannot understand it without incurring the father's wrath. As for the father's voice, it transmits to you and imposes upon you a 'kinship system' created by his own 'delusional' theory about filiation: father and grandfather exclude the real couple in favour of a founding couple formed by the Frenchman whose name they bear and the aristocratic girl whose patronymic they claim.

'Legitimate heirs' to a title, of which they claim to have been dispossessed, but to which in fact they had no right, M. R . . . 's father and grandfather, like M. R . . . himself, turn that 'inheritance' into armour with which they can fight those 'not like themselves', whether this refers to those of their own race with whom they claim to have nothing in common, or to those who belong to the great-grandmother's family, and therefore to a clan that has always excluded them. M. R . . . inherited a kinship system rearranged in an arbitrary way by the father's desire and by his own weaknesses. It was a system that he appropriated, so much so that for years he was to include in his signature a name that did not belong to him and tried to pass himself off as the direct descendant of that 'first mother', while knowing perfectly well that the colour of his skin exposed the folly of such a system. I did not hear enough of M. R . . . 's story to be able to define his particular contribution to the construction of the 'primary delusional ideas', but it was certainly present: I believe that in his case it was fixated on an 'idea' handed down by the paternal line, which, for two generations, had autocratically created for itself its own system of filiation. The character of the mother remained too much in the shadows for me to be able to propose anything at all about her own problematic. I shall now, in turn, put a final touch to my reflections on this story by asking a question to which I do not know the answer: what happened when M. R . . . was subjected to his cranial trauma, to trepanation, paralysis of one side, the contemptuous, hostile attitude of the hospital staff, the state of real misery, economic and moral, in which he found himself . . . , at the moment when, on the stage of the real, a surgeon's knife 'mutilated' his brain and the voice of the doctors actually treated M. R . . . like a piece of rubbish, a 'minus', as he put it, that is treated out of pity and to whom one recognises no rights? This similarity between a fantasy representation of a persecuting world and the reality of what appeared on that stage ought, if my hypotheses are correct, to have encouraged the risks of acting out and strengthened the delusional system: and it is true that, shortly afterwards, M. R . . . tried to kill himself with barbiturates, followed, shortly afterwards, by the choice of his second wife. Nevertheless, if M. R . . . is to be believed, that turning point brought him above all what he calls his 'awareness'. Was this an identification with the language of an aggressor to whom, in one sense, one owed one's life? However brutal the knife and the surgeon's hand that held it may have been, the operation did enable M. R . . . to survive the sequelae of his accident. What seems to me to be more enigmatic is the relation between that awareness and the eruption of the masochistic fantasisation that, according to M. R . . . , did not exist before. Personally, I see that eruption as the effect of a weakening of the system of delusional defences built up by M. R . . . As long as the paranoiac is able to designate the persecuting object, the enemy to be fought, on the stage of the real, he is able to gather together *the fragments of his body and give them a sort of imaginary, but operant unity*, using them in a common struggle, a fight in which all the parts play a role. But if, for one reason or another, this designation is no longer possible, if the persecutor disappears from view, the subject finds himself dispossessed of that external surface onto which he could project his own splitting, his own tearing apart, his own contradictions, and can now only 'see himself' as the space in which conflict and hate reign. At this point two solutions, and only two, seem to be possible:

• to act out that conflict and that hate in oneself and on oneself, and this will be the suicide attempt – M. R . . . experienced this three times;

• to succeed in eroticising the desire for hate of which one is both object and subject, the masochistic pleasure being in this case the last defence that Eros can put up against the attacks of Thanatos.

During the years prior to the surgical operation, M. R . . . had regarded psychiatrists as highly active persecutors for whom he had feelings of intense hate: why, then, did the surgeon not take over the same role? Would not the reality of the surgical aggression have made the hate uncontrollable and led to a real murder? Did the fact that the surgical act had given him back some kind of life bring the image of the surgeon too close to that of a father who would thus have recovered all his idealisation, which would have meant that he would have had to abandon any right to hate him? Or, a more likely hypothesis, was that moment accompanied by other events, of which I know nothing, that were the real cause of a certain shift in M.R . . .'s relations with his persecutors? These are questions that cannot but be left open.

However, they do enable us to see more clearly the ambiguity of the 'sudden awareness' that M. R . . . claimed and how what he said about it might seem, on a superficial hearing, to correspond to what psychiatry calls 'the critique of delusion'. In fact there was neither awareness, nor, in the true sense, critique: M. R . . . appropriated a 'knowledge' that remained at the service of his representations, masochistic and sadistic.

It was quite clear to me, as I listened to him, that when M. R . . . spoke of himself as 'sick', a 'minus', he enjoyed identifying himself with those literally rejected objects that he had observed in the psychiatric hospitals and prisons in which he had stayed. For a long time that 'knowledge of others', and more especially that 'knowledge of Whites', served as a property that he claimed to possess and which he saw as the reason for the envy and hate that he aroused around him: that 'knowledge' was also what his father had possessed and still more what his father had imposed on him as a property to be conquered *against* his mother and those like her. It was the same 'knowledge-object' that M. R . . . found in medical language, the same 'knowledge' that he appropriated, but this time placing it in the service of a masochistic pleasure that gave him the terms that he owed to that language and allowed him to designate himself as a 'minus', an object to be rejected and destroyed. But that 'knowledge' was also what kept the obtaining of pleasure in the service of the sadistic drive.

By claiming that it was not he who 'hated', but another 'sick' person that he carried inside himself, M. R . . . , while enjoying his representation of the mutilation imposed on the other, was assured of a 'knowledge' concerning the reason for the hate, the cause of which he implicitly designates in his 'contradictory upbringing' and in the contradiction between his 'educators'. His 'illness' was the fault of others, and in this he was not wrong, which is why he could tell himself that he was 'not responsible' for the 'hate' directed at him, which he blamed on his 'educators'.[12]

As I have said, I believe that this was a temporary phase in M. R . . . 's pathological experience; it was during that phase that I met him, so I can only speak of that phase.

Beyond M. R . . . 's actual case, the phase described shows us what the paranoiac risks encountering if the delusional system is put into question, the function of protective screen performed by the sadistic drive, the last defence that the subject can put up against a representation of himself that would send back to him the image of a space that was actually torn to pieces by others' hate, of an 'object' that the couple treated as the stake in a game that they were playing out between themselves. The danger of finding oneself once again the object of one's own hate is all the stronger in that it revives as an echo and takes as an ally a primal position that the earliest encounters with the outside-self strengthened in a particularly dangerous way: that is why there is always a risk of suicide. By appealing to a persecutor who can redirect onto himself a desire for death, of which one remains, in fact, oneself the privileged object, the paranoiac manages, more successfully than the schizophrenic, to protect himself against that danger.

To create a reasonable interpretation of the violence endured: that is the task that the I assumes when it becomes 'delusional'. The paranoiac problematic shows how the psyche, by coinciding desire and hate, manages to make sense of a scene played out by a couple to whom the subject owed his existence, but to whom he must also owe having encountered a senseless discourse in the outside-self, senseless because it actually lacks what alone may ensure its logic and its functioning: a statement concerning foundations, which speaks of desire and of the legitimacy of the pleasure that one has a right to expect from it.

7

By way of conclusion: the three ordeals that delusional thinking reshapes[1]

Psychotic discourse, I wrote in my introduction, confronts others with the non-evidence of the evident: it is rarely forgiven for doing so. It also confronts the category of power: the power of discourse, the power of reality, the power of the psyche, the power of violence in the social field.

The power of discourse is manifested in the abuse that often accompanies it, an abuse that, while claiming to be in the service of a *superior* knowledge, manages to dispossess those against whom it is directed of any possibility of recognising the violence to which they have been subjected and to transform their most legitimate right of defence into feelings of guilt.

The power of a reality in which the I continues to seek the verification par excellence of its statements and of which it can never know more than the discourse in which it is couched. A reality that it thinks it can objectify, place before it, make it a neutral object of one's reflection, whereas what comes back from it is a representation of one's own relation to the object, and to the objects in the world, a presentation of itself that will force it to reverify *its own* identificatory markers and impose on it a quest that can have no end.

Finally, the power of the psyche to defend itself against a desire for death that it carries within it and against a desire for death present in others and from which they protect themselves by offering one of their number as object.

Of these three powers psychosis offers us the most extreme form – and the most extreme struggle that they are capable of waging. In this second part, I have paid special attention to the analysis of what relates to the work of the I, to its creation and to its mode of response. I shall conclude by showing that the psychotic response and the delusion by which the I defends its ability to exist are the culmination of *three conditions* that become operant only because of their repetition during the three encounters that initiate the three forms by which the psychical processes represent their relation to the world.

1 The encounter between the primal and the organisation of the outside-self

The first condition entails that the primal and its pictograms encounter an external reality that does not lend itself – or does so very badly – to reflecting the state of fusion, totalisation, joining together. It is possible, but undecidable in theory, that the 'constitution' of the psyche may present 'by its very nature' a greater or lesser sensitivity to the absence of the object, to inevitable frustration, to waiting. It is more important to stress that, when the age of the child or the mother's discourse allow a relatively detailed historical reconstruction of the first year (I am speaking, of course, of children or subjects presenting psychotic manifestations), one hears in the majority of cases two types of account: (a) *empty history* – what is put forward is a silence, the non-history of a bodily machine that seems, in effect, to function as a perfect, but uninhabited machine; (b) *somatic history* – illnesses, eating disorders, insomnia, toxicoses, convulsions, etc. I believe that, in such cases, both the void of the expressive manifestations and the plenitude of the language of the body testify to a break in the alternation of the pictographic representations and of the precedence assumed by the pictogram of rejection and by the desire for self-destruction that is coextensive with it.

The first stage of life, the first experience, the first effect of the encounter with external reality: they are not enough to constitute the schizophrenic or paranoiac kernel, but they play an inductive role if later encounters with external reality cannot dress that first wound. It is evident that no subject can remember those 'primal' experiences, which cannot be inscribed in the psyche by using a word-presentation; they can be discussed only through the theoretical reconstruction that the analyst makes of them, whatever concepts he may employ in doing so. What is played out in the primal cannot, as such, have a place on the stage of the primary and cannot therefore be remembered, but, on the other hand, what will be constructed on that stage will bear its mark. The primary is that by which the psyche represents an outside-self, the space in which it will project the cause of the affects that invade its field, thus making it possible to discuss them in a *secondary* manner.

The more such affects are under the sway of Thanatos, the more the primary will metabolise for its representations the materials that, in the external world, are offered as signs of aggression, hate, rejection. This observation throws some light on what occurs in the second stage of the establishment of psychotic potentiality.

2 The encounter between the primary and the signs of reality

The condition and also the cause of the primary is the recognition by the psyche of the existence of an outside-self: as I have said, except in the case of early death, no subject escapes that recognition. During the first stage, that outside-self will have no other psychical existence but the fantasy representation that the psyche makes of it. That representation, however autocratic it may be, presupposes the introjection of those elements of information that come from the outside world and are the source of a *combined* perception of the 'perceived' and of the 'space' of the world occupied by that perceived. Fantasy may reject the reality principle, but it has a much more ambiguous relation with the principle of existence: from the outset its aim, and the hallucination of the breast exemplifies this, is to recreate a fragment of the external world, as it would be if it conformed to the wish of the primary. Fantasy does not deny the existence of the outside-self; it denies the existence of an outside-desire; its dream is not that the world should be abolished but that it should be identical with the image that fantasy makes of it. The dream of the primary is to be in the place of a wish-god who would create a world in his own image – *a dreamed world*, no doubt, *but still a world*. That relation between the primary and the world justifies the importance that I give to the events and experiences that this world may impose on the 'presenter' of the representation. The role of what Freud called *ananke* will be to get everybody to accept that there can be no identity between the world and its representation, that is to say its fantasy construction; that is the verdict imposed by 'harsh reality'. But that verdict is just as true, it has to be said, for representations that are coextensive with the anxiety of rejection, the fear of hate, the desire for death: there too a denial is necessary and ought to be encountered 'normally'. I would add that this lack of conformity between the representation and the world does not mean that there cannot be moments of coincidence between the legend of the scene, the source of pleasure and the perceptions imposed by reality: what is necessary, for the development of the psyche, what must become capable of being assumed, may be subsumed under the concept of the *different*. The difference between states and moments of pleasure and unpleasure, the difference between hallucination and real satisfaction, the difference between the dream of a continuous pleasure and a time that follows the rhythm of different successive experiences. In other words, what the psyche rightly expects of the experiences imposed on it by reality and of the effects that result from it for the psyche is that there *may be* moments of concordance between the pleasure that the scene represents and the pleasure that reality offers it. It is *this concordance* that will allow a separation between the pleasure offered by the object and the pleasure due to hallucination, the desire that the representative of the Other is actually offering and the desire that one imputes to it by means of projection, the presence of a sign that conforms to the intention of the agent and the presence of a sign that one creates in order to compensate for too long or too definitive an absence. In the cases that I have dealt with, the reality of maternal desire is *actually* manifested by the absence or rarity of those moments of concordance between the representation, the source of pleasure, and the pleasure that one expects from its presence and from what it has to offer. Historical reality, encountered when the primary begins to function, lacks signs of a positive, non-conflictual desire; this is shown by:

- firstly, whatever concerns upbringing, learning, what, in reference to ethology, should be called training;
- secondly, what may be called the 'ambient atmosphere', whether it is the locus of 'scenes', of silence or mourning;
- thirdly, what concerns the outside-the-family, whether the family nucleus remains closed in upon itself, refuses to recognise the existence and function of the group's discourse, or whether that discourse, which periodically will require that one obeys its rules, and not its law, is simply an occasion for tension, aggression, deception.

As such, this context forms part of what I call the historical reality encountered by the child's psyche; I hope that it is clear that it does not come solely under the heading of unconscious desire (the mother's, the father's, the subject's). This reality reveals of this desire what is manifest (in the sense that theory gives to this term, in opposition to that of latent, in the case of discourse) and is manifested there by signs, acted out and spoken. In the mother's behaviour (as well as that of the milieu), in her way of offering and demanding, in what she gives and what she demands, the child recognises, *rightly*, the signs of non-desire and conflict. Whether he projects his fantasy onto them, or whether he tries to deny them by a contrary fantasy, it is not enough to foreclose from his psychical space what will end up being imposed as a correct perception of the *real* absence, not of what one desires, but of what one expects, something that is, for the psyche, a right and a necessity. Those experiences of weaning, potty training, absence, possible illness or possible mourning, which are shared by everyone, now take on forms that transform them into the traumatic experiences of a history. They are traumatic, not because of the subject's projection but because of the meaning that they actually assume in the mother's discourse and for the mother's psyche. The examples cited above may seem exceptions or extreme cases, but this is not so. Whether the mother splashes water on the child's face, or gives him her breast while showing signs of haste, brutally snatching the nipple away, it amounts exactly to the same thing. In each case the signs of her unpleasure are manifest; reality *confirms* the representation of rejection and *undermines* the representation of a state of pleasure that the child represented, and represented to himself, as a response to what he judged to be maternal desire. The work of the primary process is this metabolisation that transforms the perceptions offered by the external world and imposes as signs intentions from the outside-self with regard to the perceiver: for the subject who may become psychotic 'the representations and judgements', to use Freud's phrase, expected from reality repeatedly reveal the forces at work in the outside-psyche: non-desire, conflict, anxiety, secrecy, lack. Weaning was *actually* shown to be, *for the mother*, a decision that exemplified, after the event, a prohibition, posited from the outset, on all pleasure that might have been recognised as such by the child, but which could not be reduced to need or received passively, as a pleasure that was in her gift alone. The apprenticeship of cleanliness is not imposed in the name of a shared ethic: 'to do it on oneself' and 'to do everything on one's own' is intolerable for her, because any manifestation of autonomous pleasure arouses an echo that she cannot hear. Those 'representations and judgements' are perceived; the 'presenter' of the representation may transform them, try not to hear them, but unfortunately *they find their major ally in the primary itself*: the meaning and manifestation of the mother's actions will confirm the legend of a fantasy that, in any case, would have had a place, *but side by side with another, with the opposite meaning*, in which weaning equals mutilation of an oral pleasure, cleanliness equals a refusal to receive the excremental gift, mourning equals retaliation, absence equals desire not to see the subject, to deny his existence.

We now come to the third condition necessary for a psychosis to become established, which shows the resistance with which the psyche defends itself against that risk.

3 The encounter between the I and the identifying discourse

I do not recall which sage in Antiquity tells how, when invited by the gods to make a wish, he replied: 'Let me never undergo everything that a man is capable of enduring.'

The psychotic destiny confronts us with all the anxiety, fear, pain that a subject is capable of enduring. That it should be capable of living with others in a world in which persecution reigns, in which mutilation lies in wait for you, in which the word of the Other is usually a threatening message and in which your words are denied any sense, has never ceased to astonish me, whenever I have listened to and observed the 'mad'. But equally astonishing is the resistance that the psyche puts up to that destiny. The encounter between the primal and a world that conforms to the pictogram of nothingness, the encounter between the representation of the primary and a world in which the signs of desire, which one has a right to expect, are lacking, are not enough to create the psychotic split. A third condition must be added to them: the encounter with the reality of discourse, what should be called *the historical reality of the heard*. This heard concerns the meaning that the 'word-bearer's' discourse claims to impose on the cause of the affects experienced. These affects could lose something of their dramatic intensity only if the psyche could see 'sensible' signs offered to which it could relate them, which would make it possible to relativise their effect, by recognising that, if the desire for pleasure is not omnipotent, the same goes for the desire for death. It is not enough to desire the breast to reappear, but it is not enough either to represent to oneself that it is for ever lost for it not to reappear and offer, once again, pleasure and love. It is only if this second statement is demonstrated by the reality test that the first will be accepted, without risk that the mourning that results from it exceeds the I's ability to respond. The third condition is constituted during the encounter with an 'ability to hear' and the statements of the 'word-bearer'; this ability to hear and to appropriate part of the messages lies at the foundation for the process by which the I is established. This third period confirms what Freud said about the development of the libidinal phases: the one before paves the way for the next one, which will bear the mark of what was played out there, of the victory or defeat that brought it to an end. Similarly, the primal precedes the primary in the work of which it traces the way and in the destiny that it shares. But, as we have seen, the secondary process and the I have a relationship of reciprocal creation with discourse; the I is established thanks to that part of discourse, which, heard and cathected, returns onto the psychical stage in order to offer the I its identificatory statements. These statements cannot be self-created by the agency to which they owe their birth; that first stage is not substitutable; it involves the appropriation by the psyche of statements imposed and formulated by discourse, whose representative must be the mediator. These statements, which contradict the representation, must also confirm the right to recognise oneself in a narcissising and valorising image. In the cases analysed here, what the child hears is confronted with an attempt to make sense of his body, his functions, his experiences and a world that denies the primary, which imposes a series of painful mournings, without any compensation. The identificatory image, which the statements impose, offers neither an image of the unified, unifying body, nor an image of the 'thinking' that valorises, as 'something of one's own', that new function that one has to carry out, nor an image of the world in which desire and pleasure have right of residence, without legal proceedings and without having to be naturalised and adopting a foreign language. The I coming to birth finds itself confronted by a triple negation and a triple violence:

- It is denied any right to recognise itself as agent of an autonomous, thinking function, to experience pleasure in having 'thoughts' that it might claim as its own production and cathect narcissistically.
- It is denied any right to claim that the feelings that it expresses are true, to say that it is sad when told that it should be happy, or the reverse.
- A historical account is imposed on it that lacks any foundation, in the sense that I have given to the foundation of statements, and which hides this lack by substituting for it a false statement. This substitution reveals, in its *manifest formulation*, the maternal desire that forbids the subject to find his original meaning in the couple's desire. In order to be respected, this prohibition will impose on the subject a postulate concerning the foundations, including the foundations of discourse, that is senseless and contradictory with the set of statements that it is asked to repeat, as well as with the statements of the group.

When Mme B . . . 's mother obliterated the name of her own father, when, on the other hand, she became extremely prolix on the subject of the 'mother', a quack endowed with 'supernatural' gifts, and when she was content, without further explanation, to tell her older daughter, in the presence of the younger one,

225

that 'you don't kiss your father', it actually confronted the child with a paradoxical discourse. Why did that name of 'mother', so often mentioned, have no counterpart in that of 'father'? Why mustn't you kiss him when, at the same time, you are taught to love your parents?

When she told her little girl, home from hospital, that what she had swallowed was not dangerous, that she *and the doctors* were exaggerating, and denied her the right to have the truth about the pain that she was feeling recognised, just as she was later to forbid her to 'remember' that experience and to try to convince her that in fact 'almost nothing happened', she was forcing her to deny a truth of which the child was perfectly well aware.

Whatever peculiarities there may be in the histories of these children, we always find the dramatic effect of an encounter in which the appropriation of knowledge – concerning language, himself, the world – was apparently imposed on the I, yet whenever it shows the result of that acquisition, it comes up against a prohibition, a negation of the value of that result, a counter-truth that denies the meaning that it had glimpsed and constructed. '*It is forbidden to think, it is obligatory to think "what others think"*.' What we have here is an unsustainable and impossible order, just as impossible as an order that would require that one should block up one's ears and hear, or that one should open one's mouth wide and speak. To think 'what others think' has, as its condition and precondition, that one should be able to think, yet this is what the mother fears more than anything else.

This third stage reduplicates, amplifies the experience imposed by the first two:

- The pictograms have encountered a world that resisted reflecting one of them.
- In its turn, the primary has sought in vain in the outside-self for signs that might allow it to find in the locus of the Other the cause of a state of pleasure that one may link to one's desire and, what is more, signs that would deny one's fantasies of rejection, which would help one to recognise that the world and the other's body are also loci in which pleasure is possible, in which desire may be fulfilled.
- Last but not least, the I encounters in the space in which it must come about, in the statements that must establish it and which will constitute it, *the order of having to be*, whereas *whenever it becomes*, in each image of itself that it tends to cathect, it comes up against the prohibition of being that form, that image, that moment, as soon as they are presented as *its* choice.

The field of the secondary or the space of the I is mined; with each step taken, the I is blown up, either on leaving the ground or on touching it when landing. One moves forward, by a series of random jumps, along a path reduced to a few poor fragments, a path in which the surface ahead consists of holes and where the surface behind is always likely to become the same. It is a space that is little more than a puzzle made up of bits and pieces, which cannot claim to provide any route and, still less, to indicate what one would find there once one got to the end of it.

The I soon realised that it could not inhabit that space unless it changed something in it; just as quickly it realised that it was better to pretend that one did not see the holes, if one did not wish to be stopped in one's tracks by the surrounding dangers, and also that it was forbidden to hope to find in that place anything that one might offer the libido, so that the libido might give up its privileged representations in favour of the productions of the 'sense-making' faculty. In order not to be forced to abandon the route and to prevent the reproduction of that primal-world specularisation that marks its moments of annihilation, the I will set up three operations (a term to be understood in the sense of strategic operation, a surgical operation, a mathematical operation):

- to create 'primary delusional thinking' – that is, to invent *one's own* statement concerning foundations;
- to try, by means of this, to make the secondary receptive to the primary;
- to use part of one's energy in the work of *self-exclusion*, by disavowing what it has acknowledged, misconstruing what it knew, denying what it 'knows' to be the case and its knowledge of its own being.

At the beginning of this book, I said that there would be no psychosis if there were no I and if that agency did not find its precursor, its 'raw material' in the 'ambient' discourse. It is indeed between the ego and the external world, as Freud says, that the conflict in psychosis breaks out – not because of the excessive power of the id's influence but because of a powerlessness in the discourse of the Other and an excessive power in its desire to appropriate what it 'lacks' by taking over the child's psychical space and the child's work of thinking. The I is confronted by a historical reality in which, in a repetitive way, it encounters a series of statements, concerning it, that contradict the perceptions that reality has imposed upon it and to which it is neither blind nor deaf. It is a discourse in which the basic language lacks a meaning, which would have been necessary to set up the kinship system; the result of this would be to forbid one, in the register proper to 'the naming of feelings', to name '*correctly*' any experience whose cause might refer to the missing meaning.

Confronted by this demand, imposed by a discourse actually spoken and heard, the I will respond by creating a meaning, where there was none, by means of its construction of primary delusional thinking; it will interpret the contradictions, the counter-truths, the omissions of discourse as the manifest form of a latent meaning of its own creation. It is a meaning that is substituted for what can be said about its own origin and, therefore, about origins in general. Although the delusion of filiation is an illuminating example of this, 'delusional thinking' about filiation is to be found again in psychosis and lies at its very centre. On the basis of that 'thinking', what is said and what is contradicted, coming either from the mother or the father, will remake meaning since one will convince oneself that if there is contradiction, omission, negation, it is because what is said must be referred, not to the postulate on which the logic of others' discourse is based, but on the postulate that can be known only by oneself and one other.

The I cannot inhabit a space whose organisation would make one's own desire for life unintelligible: that is why it will reshape that of which *it can deny neither the existence nor the consequences*, in order to make what is seen, which would make it senseless to inhabit such a space, conform to a logic borrowed from the primary.

The I *sees* the holes in the ground, *hears* the mine explode, *feels* the wounds caused by falling shrapnel, but denies any relation of causality between what takes place on the stage of the real and the *non-desire* and *lack* present in the mother. It will now declare that *a desire that concerns it* is still a cause of what it experiences: the desire of the persecutor, the desire of God or his own desire to blow up, to be blown up, to suffer. This being the case, the I can still keep its cathexis for the mother, believe in the postulates of her discourse and protect *itself* from the danger of no longer having a place in which it can exist, a place in which speech is possible.

'The case begins all over again, but again it is possible, just as before, to secure an ostensible acquittal. One must again apply all one's energies to the case and never give in.'[2]

The psychotic, more disillusioned than Kafka's J. K., would not find such a statement 'incredible': he has long known that, in the trial that he is being subjected to by the discourse of the Other and in the trial to which his delusion is subjecting the discourse of others, any acquittal, when it arrives, is only *apparent*. He may also discover that the rags in which the representatives of the law dress themselves are often no more than 'fragile appearances': that is perhaps one of the reasons that make him refuse to hand himself over and declare the trial closed.

Notes

Preface to this edition

1 P. Aulagnier, *Un Interprète en quête de sens*, Paris, Ramsay, p. 22.
2 Ibid.

Preface

1 Under the term 'neurotic' I also include the psychical functioning of the analyst.
2 I explain what I mean by 'postulate' in Chapter 1.
3 This involves the appearance on the scene of the secondary process.

Chapter 1

1 From this point of view the terms 'conscious' and 'sayable' are synonymous.
2 A term to be understood as synonymous with knowledge.
3 Freud, *An Outline of Psycho-Analysis*, S.E., XXIII, p. 196.
4 It should be said at once that the logic of the primary is based on this paradox.
5 Cf. P. Castoriadis-Aulagnier, 'Demande et identification', *L'Inconscient*, no. 7, juillet–septembre 1968, Paris, P.U.F.
6 It is the frequency of a relation involving opposition between subject and others that explains why madness, like discourse that responds to the violence of those others, is in turn to be understood as an interpretation of violence (see Part II of this work).
7 By the term 'feeling' I mean the conscious affect; that is, an affective experience of which the I is aware and about which it can formulate a statement.

Chapter 2

1 Freud, 'Instincts and their Vicissitudes', S.E., XIV, p. 122.

2 This bonus of pleasure does not imply that the existence of the breast as an object separate from one's own body is already recognised, even if it foreshadows it. On the other hand, it presupposes that the object represented as self-engendered is also represented as an object experiencing pleasure.

3 One may well wonder whether Freud's 'philosophical' considerations on the death drive, or my hypothesis of a movement towards pre-desire or of a desire for non-desire are merely fantasies. But where might these fantasies, made intelligible for and by the I, find their source if not in the existence of a force *x* that the subject can make intelligible only by calling it the death drive? That the I cannot accept the existence of a desire for death, which runs counter to the feeling of scandal that it experiences when confronted by it, is quite natural.

But when that same I accepts the risk of wanting to know what is not it, it is forced to see the unacceptable and to recognise the impact of a desire that is heterogeneous to it, which it will tame by transforming it into a theoretical concept. What remains to it as a bonus is the ability to tell itself that, even if it does not know it, it will die because that it is what it wants to do: is this a final illusory victory of the I? Perhaps, but one has the impression that this victory is certainly experienced as such in another space. And where could that 'impression', so foreign to the I, and one that, as we know from history, existed long before Freud, come from if not from deep down in a psyche that expects and hopes no longer to have any reason to pursue its work of quest? If the 'death drive' is one of Freud's 'fantasies', it is, like any fantasy, the fulfilment of an unconscious desire of which he is trying to make sense in order to give it access to the field of the I.

4 On the subject of the primary process, we shall see why this inability to foreclose information derived from hearing will give the voice a particular status.

5 In fact, one ought to speak of a ruse concerning what Freud began by calling preservation drives.

6 Freud, 'Instincts and their Vicissitudes', S.E., XIV, p. 120.

7 When I speak of 'self' I mean nothing more than *the representing agency*.

8 I remain faithful to a notion that I adopted long ago; namely, that death anxiety precedes castration anxiety, which is a re-elaboration of it.

9 Freud, 'Instincts and their Vicissitudes', S.E., XIV, pp. 138–9.

10 By the same token, this lack refers to the objects necessary to the needs of the body and to the 'needs' of the psyche, objects that the outside-self must be able to provide.

11 Or more specifically to acting out, as I shall describe it.

Chapter 3

1 For reasons that, re-reading this text, seemed to me to be open to criticism, I have preferred to give a more detailed analysis of the fantasy organisation and of its successive representations in my last chapter, which concerns paranoia and its fantasisation of the primal scene. I would ask the reader to refer to it.

2 When the difference between these two desires disappears or becomes too small,

instinctual play becomes impossible: there is then a risk that this third pole, which is the gaze, will disappear from the fantasy scene. In becoming one, observer and observed fixate the desirer in an unchangeable position, with the result that the capacity to recognise the gap between the fantasy stage and the stage of reality is dangerously reduced. The reduction of that gap is at the centre of the psychotic phenomenon; its most serious consequence will be that the stage of reality may be presented in such a way as to allow the pictogram to become once again primal specularisation. If that occurs, we shall see what I have described above as the 're-acting' responsible for acting out.

3 The early appearance of the 'desire of the father' shows the error of many theories concerning psychosis, and more particularly schizophrenia, in which the only place left to that desire is its 'foreclosure' by the mother or its absence. Clinical experience constantly denies this. The desire of the father plays a very important role in the subject's psychical destiny: by abusively privileging the 'desire or non-desire' of the mother for the father, while ignoring the consequences of *the father's desire for the child*, the forms and the aim that he pursues, theoreticians have become, without knowing it, accomplices of an effect that they take for a cause. The frequency of paranoiac features in the father of the 'schizophrenic', and the frequency of a para-nursing attitude, is worthy of reflection. The same goes for cases in which the father exercises a power that will make any form of power identical with an abuse of power, which will brook no challenge. I shall return to this problem when dealing with the subject of paranoia.

4 The analysis of this transmission of a 'wish for a child' and its role on to repression will be taken up and developed in Chapter 4, section 5.

5 What I am saying about the gaze is obviously valid for any other erogenous zone-function.

6 Freud, *The Ego and the Id*, S.E., XIX, p. 20.

7 A consequence that the psychoanalysis of psychosis never lets us forget.

8 To see, to hear, to think what one hears: as soon as word-presentation becomes raw material that can be metabolised by the primary process, any hierarchisation becomes impossible.

9 This analysis of the relation to the persecutor shows that at the basis of its infrastructure is the other side of any phenomenon of persecution; namely, the phenomenon of idealisation. The persecuting object is always an object whose power is idealised (and how!). But this second phenomenon is also the work of the primary. Persecution–idealisation: this binomial denotes the two psychical actions, complementary and contradictory, that the cathected object may undergo in the register of the primary. This same binomial is found again whenever one analyses the psychotic's relation to his body, to others, to the world.

10 This protection may fail: its success implies in effect that the Other – the mother – may also accept this game of substitution. If, on the other hand, the activity and the oral functioning of the child retain for her a privileged value, for which there can be no substitute, the child can only maintain the exclusive cathexis of that function or give up asking for anything.

11 The I certainly continues, throughout its existence, to give credence to beliefs that accord with the aims of the primary, but it is also necessary, outside psychopathology,

that these beliefs should remain non-contradictory with the I's identificatory project.

Chapter 4

1 The author's term, '*porte-parole*', is usually translated as 'spokesman'. This would have been singularly inappropriate in so far as Piera Aulagnier has the mother in mind. 'Spokeswoman' would not have conveyed the play that she makes on the *literal* meaning of the French term as bearer of words. Given the author's large number of neologisms, often placed in inverted commas, I felt free to add another. (*Translator's note.*) The author's note continues: In my introduction, I emphasised the pendulum movement necessitated in any psychoanalytical research by having to analyse in succession what takes place in two psychical spaces at the same time, during the same encounter, during the same initial discovery. This pendulum movement cannot avoid certain repetitions whenever the analyst encounters the same phenomenon. Once the angle of vision has shifted, we also discover the heterogeneity of the shaping of experience, which the similarity of certain effects and above all the continuous interaction that is therefore at work for both partners present. The inevitable repetition of certain themes confirms the pitfalls encountered by theoretical reflection in this field. While exposing the fiction of separation, we are confronted by the impossibility of conceiving of psychical space, whatever the stage chosen, other than as a locus of communication, of continuous osmosis with the space-outside that surrounds it.

2 The wish that he or she should become a father or mother implicitly entails the future right of choice of another subject, who will make the fulfilment of the wish possible. It is that temporal distance that makes the mother forget what that wish involves: the end of her role as privileged object, the end of a relation in which she appears to the child as sole dispenser of pleasure, the depository of whatever could possibly be demanded. This forgetting traces its way in so far as she will have to know and accept the future autonomy of the child in her regard, his inevitable moving away and, implicitly, her own death.

3 It might also be said that the mother occupies the place of a giver of desire, an essential gift to the psychical structure, but refuses to be the giver of the object, a refusal that is just as necessary.

4 In the section dealing with psychosis it will be seen that it is this abuse of power that is the primary cause of the constitution of a delusion.

5 On this subject, see the annex at the end of this chapter.

6 Cf. Daniel Paul Schreber, *Memoirs of my Nervous Illness*, trans. Ida Macalpine, London, Wm. Dawson & Sons Ltd, 1955, p. 50.

7 In a sense it might be said that any delusion, whatever form it takes, has as its aim to provide this proof that one indicates or hallucinates in the space of the outside-self. Delusional certainty is the price the subject pays for the impossibility of finding in others' discourse those points of certainty that allow doubt to find the necessary limits if discourse is to carry out its function.

8 Freud, *An Outline of Psycho-Analysis*, S.E., XXIII, p. 197.

9 These images projected back by the utterance of the feeling expressed form the basis

of the identificatory process: the deferred action of the naming of the affect is the identifying operation that establishes the I.

10 In fact it would be truer to speak of the relation between the linguistic sign and its referent, not only in this passage but in the whole of my work. But there are habits of thinking that one finds difficult to throw off!

11 It is perfectly possible to imagine a system in which this representative is not the father. But whoever he may be (uncle, ancestor, priest, class or caste, as well as the class of Mothers), his role is none the less necessary. The mother's discourse, therefore, will have to find that point of reference and then accept being the voice that declares the existence of that reference to the infant. The maternal function requires that the mother finds support on a model and that the child is referred to this model as reason, law, the reasonableness of her action. The support that, according to different cultures, sustains that role of representative of others' discourse is not without its effect on the subject's psychical destiny, just as there are differences as to the greater or lesser valorisation of the model by the group. That is why there are cultures and periods in cultures that aggravate or reduce the risk of psychosis.

12 This is prefigured in the paradox of *jouissance*: a bodily experience that nevertheless excludes quite radically anything that might be in the nature of biological rationality.

13 This complicity plays an important role in the problematic of the pervert, cf. Piera Aulagnier, 'La structure perverse', in *L'Inconscient*, no. 2, 1967.

14 By this I mean the father as object of a hate that may, thanks to him, designate its cause in the outside-psyche.

15 In such cases one often sees the father making claims for the 'naturalness' of what has happened, without realising that by sleeping with his daughter it is to his own mother that he has shown his victory. In the clinical cases that I have been able to follow there has always been a complicity on the part of the wife, rather as if, in these cases, her daughter continued to be part of her own objects that she wishes to lend to another, certain that this can only increase her power over the father (assisted in this by the disapproval of society and possible legal sanctions).

16 As far as the difficult relation between the psyche and the social, and the problems posed by its analysis are concerned, cf. Cornelius Castoriadis, *L'institution imaginaire de la société* (in particular chapter VI), Paris, Seuil, 1975.

17 In Chapter 6, we shall see why these statements concerning foundations are necessary to the handling of language by the subject, for whom any response concerning origins – of the world, of language, of the law – is understood as a response concerning his own origin.

18 In this register scientific ambition does not fall short of the ambition of the sacred: they share the same excess.

19 A group of voices or written texts whose role as referent is necessary for the child if he is to free himself from his dependence on that first referent embodied by the mother's voice.

20 Which coincides with the register of the imaginary, cf. Annex.

21 On this subject I cannot do better than summarise a text written some years back and to which I can add little: cf. P. Castoriadis-Aulagnier, 'Demande et identification', *L'Inconscient*, no. 8.

22 A characteristic proper to that question means that one can say nothing about 'who'

I is without reference to what I thinks it will become. Without that projection into the future, the I could say nothing about the present, which as such is beyond reach. It should be added that reference to the past is also indispensable.

23 I am indebted to Ernst Cassirer for his discussion of the term 'symbolic', though it does not reduce the gap between the mode of positing and resolving a problem in philosophical reflection and the mode and the parameters required by psychoanalytical reflection. Cf. Ernst Cassirer, *The Philosophy of Symbolic Forms*, especially vol. 3: *The Phenomenonology of Knowledge*, chapter 1, New Haven, Yale University Press; London, Oxford University Press, 1957.

24 And more generally when I use it in the psychoanalytical field.

Chapter 5

1 Readers will find at the end of Chapter 6 the detailed account that M. R . . . gave me of his history.

2 Here again the term 'psychotic potentiality' denotes what ought more correctly to be called, depending on the cases, schizophrenic potentiality or paranoiac potentiality.

3 *Moments* of a silence, 'deadly' for the I, that may occur as much in the experience of psychotic potentiality as in its manifest forms.

4 An expression that is also to be found as such in simply neurotic structures; but in this case it assumes a very different meaning, which relates it to an Oedipal problematic.

5 We shall see how a father's 'wish for a child' may present the same anomalies and for similar reasons. I believe that it is no accident that they appear in one or the other, or in both. The function of the mother and the anticipatory effect of her discourse act during an earlier stage of psychical life; her role in satisfying bodily and libidinal needs endows her with the attributes of an absolute power that is in fact that first representative of the Other, which is also the first representative of the world. It follows that the consequences of what, in her behaviour, is an obstacle to the structuring of the infant's psyche will be earlier and more difficult to rectify. That is why a certain type of maternal pathology heightens the risk of a schizophrenic response, another type of maternal pathology those of a paranoiac response: it is obvious that this is in no sense a rule, still less a law. I shall return to the consequences of this difference in my analysis of the representation of the primal scene for the schizophrenic and the paranoiac.

6 This 'desire for motherhood' is the negation of a 'desire to procreate', in the sense of the power to give birth to a life and to a new being; what is desired concerns the register of the return and the same. It might also be said that, in this case, a 'duty of identity' in the successive representatives of that function is substituted for identity and the transmission of a symbolic function.

7 From what I have said about the function of the kinship system, it is obvious that it can function only if *all* the terms are present.

8 When this girl was fifteen, she was in some 'mysterious' hospital for six months, where no one had been to see her except her mother, who 'cried a lot'. It seems to me that it must have been a psychiatric hospital, which would explain the guilt that the mother seems to have felt towards her first daughter.

9 I have placed between inverted commas a few short quotations from Freud's article 'Family Romances', S.E., IX, p. 239.

10 I would strongly recommend a highly instructive book on this subject, the conclusions of which seem to me to be irrefutable: A. B. Hollingshead and F. C. Redlich, *Social Class and Mental Illness*, New York, John Wiley, 1958.

11 In these cases, little purpose would be served by believing that one has understood everything once one has declared that there has been 'non-access to the symbolic' or 'a foreclosure of the Name-of-the-Father' or that the events 'cannot be symbolised': such formulas become very unconvincing when transformed into theoretical all-purpose clichés.

12 On this matter, I would refer the reader to Gitta Sereny, *The Case of Mary Bell*, London, Eyre Methuen, 1972 (2nd edition: London, Arrow Books, 1974).

13 Cf. Freud, 'Neurosis and Psychosis', S.E., XIX, pp. 150–1.

14 Ibid., p.151.

15 Ibid., pp. 184–5.

16 Morton Schatzman, *Soul Murder: Persecution in the Family*, London, Penguin Press, 1973, pp. 17, 19–21.

17 It will be noticed that I often use the terms 'real' and 'reality' interchangeably, though I tend to prefer the second. If I had to state the difference between them, I would say that reality is the 'humanised' real, the only one of which specialist and non-specialist alike can speak, and that the 'real' is that 'raw material', utterly unknowable, that is subjected to the metabolisation of the three processes. That which resists, to use Lacan's word, that metabolisation, its residue, is what allows the psyche to encounter the world in the form of the *living*; that is to say, what has endlessly to be re-presented, re-represented, re-interpreted.

18 The question posited by the presence of spontaneous respites in schizophrenic experience, alternating with delusional episodes, would be worthy of re-examination, in view of what has been said concerning the role played in 'potential' schizophrenia by the presence on the stage of the real of an Other embodying a non-internalised agency. This role proves the dependence that results from it for the I and the price that it pays for not going over to a manifest psychosis, but it also demonstrates the ability shown by that same I to answer anyone who demands that it take up the role again, or at least to 'pretend' to do so in order that the recognition of which he is still capable may not be imposed upon him: to acknowledge that a misdeal has taken place, that there is no identity between the postulates of these two discourses, that the dialogue is between two parties both equally deaf to what is essential.

Chapter 6

1 Cf. what I have said about the persecuting object (pp. 60–2).

2 Guy Rosalato's 'Scène primitive et paranoïa' (in *Essais sur le symbolique*, Paris, Gallimard, 1969) has lost none of its relevance and originality. On the same subject, cf. also Micheline Enriquez's article in the review *Topique*, no. 14, May 1974.

3 The concept of 'white psychosis', which we owe to Jean-Luc Donnet and André Green, defines a psychical organisation some of whose characteristics are to be found

in what I have described as schizophrenic potentiality. Their approach and conclusions differ from mine. The importance that they give to the 'thought' and to the thinking function, to Bion's contribution, to the word-by-word analysis of the texture of discourse, lead to different, but very valuable conceptualisations of the psychotic problematic. Cf. Jean-Luc Donnet and André Green, *L' enfant de Ça*, Paris, Editions de Minuit, 1973.

4 Jacques Lacan, *Ecrits*, Paris, Seuil, 1966, p. 579, and *Ecrits: A Selection*, trans. Alan Sheridan, London and New York, Routledge, 1977, pp. 218–19.

5 Freud, 'The Economic Problem of Masochism', S.E., XIX, p. 163.

6 I analysed this discourse above: we saw how it can only forbid the child any autonomy in the register of desire; from the outset and from the entrance of the I onto the stage, the child is ordered to reject and to struggle against a desire. This verdict concerning what he 'must not desire' has as its counterpart an unacceptable identificatory verdict concerning 'what he must not be': indeed in order to make it his own he would have to refuse to hear what, at the same time, is designated to him as a desire that played a part in his origin. The 'bad' paternal desire is nevertheless a desire that the mother recognises as having been present. One understands the child's attempt to see the father as he who might give back to his desire a right to speak: it is true that in doing so it is the desire of the 'word-bearer' that he must reject. It is also true that if the child cannot escape this trap, it is because both parental discourses have imposed upon him the same single necessity: to valorise a state of conflict in order to make sense of their discourse.

7 This account is not a case history: I played no analytical role and was content simply to listen to M. R . . . The almost word-for-word reproduction, from the first interview, of part of that discourse will allow the reader to reflect with a knowledge that is hardly less than my own as to what this account shows, concerning the hypotheses that it gives rise to and to whether it confirms or undermines what I wrote in the preceding pages.

8 During all my meetings with M. R . . . , he moved continually between the imperfect and the present tenses.

9 The word 'race' is mine: M. R . . . himself spoke of 'those who aren't French', and I had the impression that he regarded himself as French, in terms of race if not nationality. Indeed I have no idea whether or not he opted for French nationality.

10 It seems to me that M. R . . . inherited a 'delusional theory concerning origins' from his father, a theory that he took over and altered.

11 It is interesting to note that, although there was a 'shame' of 'black skin' in the family, there was also a hate for 'white skin', a feature that becomes the metonymic representative of the noble family that dispossessed them of some imaginary right and which, in fact, always refused to accept the great-grandfather.

12 Even though the treatment undergone by M. R . . . , involving chemotherapy, was relatively light, I did ask myself the question, not about the disappearance of the actual experience of persecution – which, as is very clear, has never disappeared – but about a sort of 'fluidification' of the persecutor. As I listened to him, it often seemed to me as if it was precisely because there was no longer any privileged support embodying this role that M. R . . . found himself dispossessed of the pivot that could sustain the interpretative system, which he paid for by the feeling of distress that

overcame him periodically. Hence, in my opinion, the suicidal risk that accompanies the dismantling of the paranoiac system if one does not first try to offer the subject other identificatory supports.

Chapter 7

1 These conclusions stress the reshaping that one owes schizophrenic potentiality: if I give it precedence it is because it seems to me, on the stage of our present world, more frequent than is usually thought.
2 Franz Kafka, *The Trial*, trans. Willa and Edwin Muir, London, Penguin, 1953, p. 178.

Index

listening: primary sign and linguistic sign 64–5, *see also* discourse; hearing; reduplication; word-bearer
love: and hate 8, 28, 37; and hate in primal process 20; and hate in primary process 42; meaning of 96–7

material reality *see* historical reality
meaning: deprivation of and schizophrenia 174; discourse of others 63–9; origin and delusional thinking 140; system of primary meanings 53–7, *see also* knowledge; reality
mentally deficient child 169
metabolisation 3–4; mutual cathexis or rejection in the primal 29–32; pictographic representation 17–18; sense-making 9
minimum pleasure 18–19
mirror stage 123–4
mother: appropriation of child's thinking 149–53; desire for child 76, 78; desire for motherhood 141–2, 146–8; discourse addressing spoken-shadow 75–7; failure of repression in discourse 145–8; feeding xxi; forbidden knowledge concerning origin 154–5; interpretation and response to thinking 85–9; maternal unconscious and psychosis xviii; 'normal' mother and pathology 76; 'perfect' mother in conflict with father 189–92; transmission of repression 78–9; as word-bearer xxi–xxii, 72–5, *see also* kinship; Oedipus complex; word-bearer
mouth: mouth-breast encounter, ambivalence 21; as representative of all zones in primal process 26
mutilation: prototype of castration 50–3, *see also* castration; destruction

naming 66; affect and representation 23; deferred action of 92–8; and swallowing 73
narcissistic contract 106–13, 169, *see also* primary narcissism

necessary condition 132–3
need: and drive 23; representation 24; search for non-desire in primal process 16–17
Nirvana principle, and death drive 20
non-desire 7; desire of in primal process 20; non-desire of a desire 141–5

object, and zone, complementarity of 25, 27
Oedipus complex: decline of 12; encounter with the father 101–6; inversion of Oedipal wish 79; kinship and parental desire 80–5; 'Oedipal' fantasy 178; prototype of 48–50
omnipotence: desire for unity in primary process 40–1; mother's desire 183; of Other xx, xxi, 6; primary meanings 54; self-procreation in primal process 16–18, 20
original process *see* primal process
origins: delusional theory concerning 154–5, 194–8; delusional theory concerning: case study 155–68; mother's desire for motherhood 141–2, 146–8; schizophrenia 141–5; word-bearer's discourse and delusional thinking 136–40, 147
Other: desire for 45–6; intention of and projection in the primary 43–5; omnipotence of xx, xxi, 6, 44; powerlessness in the discourse 227–8

pain: and hallucination in primal process 16–17, *see also* unpleasure
paranoia: case studies 187–9, 204–19; conflict, family portrait of 189–94; conflict and delusional theory concerning origins 194–8; hate 133–4, 186–7; persecutor 199–204
parental attribute 49
parental couple: conflict, failed idealisation 189–94; conflict and the delusional theory concerning origins 194–8; desire for child 49; desire and origin of life 138; and the paranoiac

186–7; pleasure, quality of demonstrated to child 181
particular, and universal: symbolic function 121–2
passion 13
pathology, and the 'normal' mother 76
Pcs., and *Ucs.* 53–4
persecuting object, voice as 60–2
persecutor, paranoia 199–204
Philosophy of Symbolic Forms (Cassirer) 54–5
pictograms 4; borrowing made from sensory model 21–4; conjunction and rejection xx; delusional thinking 140; erogenous pleasure 26–9; experience xxx; and I 33; metabolisation of experience, and undifferentiation 29–32; primal process xix–xxi; rejection and primary delusional thinking xxiii; representability of encounter 17–21; self-procreation 16–18; sounds 57; specularisation 24–6; and thinking 32–4, *see also* primal process
pleasure: act of representation 7; child-couple relation 139; and displeasure, mental representations by infant xx; integrating effect of 51; necessary for representation in primal process 18–21; primal process 25; renunciation of 50; suckling 25
pleasure principle, difference eliminated 67
power, mother-infant relationship 146
presentation 3
primal process 4, 34–9; borrowing from sensory model 21–4; creation repeating itself 23; encounter with external reality 221; erogenous pleasure 26–9; first representation 9; and hearing 55; ignores persecutor 61; metabolisation of experience, and undifferentiation 29–32; and pictogram xix–xxi; pictogram and specularisation 24–6; regression to xx; representability of encounter 18–21;

and self-procreation 16–18, *see also* original process; pictograms
primal scene 142, 194–5; fantasy of 178–81, 183–5; primary construction of 42, *see also* couple
primary delusional thinking xxiii–xxiv, 134–7, 145–6, 152; origins: case study 155–68, *see also* delusion; hallucination
primary masochism 43
primary meanings 145; system of 53–7; and word-presentations 59
primary narcissism 26, *see also* narcissistic contract
primary process xx–xxi, 4; desire to understand 58–60; encounter with external reality 221–4; pleasure of hearing 57–8; primary meanings 53–7; recognition of extra-territoriality 9; signs 62–3; thing-presentation and body fantasisation 40–53; word-presentation 53–70, *see also* fantasy representation
primary signifier 62
primary violence, and secondary violence 11–15
primary-secondary process 68
projection: desire in the primary 43–5; and introjection 47
prosthesis, role of 69, 72–5
psyche: and information 6–8; relationship with body xxx
psychic representation, metabolic processes xix
psychical life 12
psychosis: function of I in 134–6; psychic construction of I xvii–xviii; rediscovery of primary state of undifferentiation 31–2; and regression to primal process xx; representative background 38; symbolic function 122–3; use of concept 131; voice as persecuting object 61
psychotic potentiality 135, 163–8
puerperal psychosis 147

theory, danger of 132

thing-presentation: and body fantasisation 40–53; as prerequisite for word-presentation 53

thinking: activity of part-function zone 32–4, 37; and autonomy 87–9; contradictory orders 226; mother's appropriation of child's 149–53; threshold of autonomy required 13

Ucs., and *Pcs.* 53–4

unconscious, fantasy representation 42–3

unconscious I, identificatory project 119

understand, desire to 58–60

undifferentiation, re-production of the same in the primal 29–32

universal, and particular: symbolic function 121–2

unpleasure xx; and desire 7–8; desire for 47; fantasy of mutilation 51–2; and origin of subject 139; and Other's desire 138–9; primary masochism 43; reign of in psyche-world relation 174; submission to Thanatos in primal process 19–20; voice as source of 55–6; wish to destroy object and zone in the primal 27–8, *see also* pain

violence: mother–infant relationship xxi–xxii; primary and secondary 8–15

voice: as persecuting object 60–2; source of unpleasure 55–6

weaning 223

Winnicott, Donald W., feeding by mother xxi

word-bearer xxi–xxii; discourse of and schizophrenia 141–5; mother as 10–11; and origin of history 138; and primary delusional thinking 134–5; psychosis and mother's non-desire of a desire 141–5; role of prosthesis 72–5, *see also* hearing; language; mother; reduplication

word-presentation 53–69; thing-presentation as prerequisite for 53

zone, and object, complementarity of 25, 27